MW00834206

Plays

VLADIMIR NABOKOV

Plays

Lolita: A Screenplay
The Tragedy of Mister Morn

PENGUIN
CLASSICS

PENGUIN CLASSICS

Published by the Penguin Group
Penguin Books Ltd, 80 Strand, London WC2R ORL, England
Penguin Group (USA) Inc., 375 Hudson Street, New York, New York 10014, USA
Penguin Group (Canada), 90 Eglinton Avenue East, Suite 700, Toronto, Ontario,
Canada M4P 2Y3 (a division of Pearson Penguin Canada Inc.)
Penguin Ireland, 25 St Stephen's Green, Dublin 2, Ireland (a division of Penguin Books Ltd)
Penguin Group (Australia), 250 Camberwell Road, Camberwell, Victoria 3124, Australia
(a division of Pearson Australia Group Pty Ltd)
Penguin Books India Pvt Ltd, 11 Community Centre,
Panchsheel Park, New Delhi – 110 017, India
Penguin Group (NZ), 67 Apollo Drive, Rosedale, Auckland 0632, New Zealand
(a division of Pearson New Zealand Ltd)
Penguin Books (South Africa) (Pty) Ltd, Block D, Rosebank Office Park,
181 Jan Smuts Avenue, Parktown North, Gauteng 2193, South Africa

Penguin Books Ltd, Registered Offices: 80 Strand, London WC2R ORL, England

www.penguin.com

Lolita: A Screenplay first published in the United States of America
in this form by Vintage International 1997
This translation of The Tragedy of Mister Morn first published in Penguin Classics 2012
This edition published in Penguin Classics 2012

001

Lolita: A Screenplay copyright © Metro-Goldwyn-Mayer, Inc., 1961
Foreword for Lolita: A Screenplay copyright © McGraw-Hill International, Inc., 1974
Excerpts from the novel Lolita copyright © Vladimir Nabokov, 1955
The Tragedy of Mister Morn copyright © the estate of Vladimir Nabokov, 2012
Translation of The Tragedy of Mister Morn copyright © Anastasia Tolstoy and Thomas Karshan, 2012
Introduction for The Tragedy of Mister Morn copyright © Thomas Karshan, 2012

Set in 10.5/15pt Joanna MT Pro
Typeset by Jouve (UK), Milton Keynes
Text design by Claire Mason
Printed in Great Britain by Clays Ltd, St Ives plc

A CIP catalogue record for this book is available from the British Library

ISBN: 978-0-141-19721-0

www.greenpenguin.co.uk

MIX
Paper from
responsible sources
FSC
www.fsc.org
FSC™ C018179

Penguin Books is committed to a sustainable
future for our business, our readers and our planet.
This book is made from Forest Stewardship
Council™ certified paper.

ALWAYS LEARNING   **PEARSON**

Contents

Lolita: A Screenplay

To VÉRA

This is the purely Nabokov version of the screenplay and not the same version which was produced as the motion picture *Lolita*, distributed by Metro-Goldwyn-Mayer, Inc.

Foreword

Sometime at the end of July 1959 (my pocket diary does not give the exact date), in Arizona, where my wife and I were hunting butterflies, with headquarters at Forest Houses (between Flagstaff and Sedona), I received through Irving Lazar who was representing me a message from Messrs Harris & Kubrick. They had acquired the film rights of Lolita in 1958, and were now asking me to come over to Holly-wood and write the script. The honorarium they offered was considerable, but the idea of tampering with my own novel caused me only revulsion. A certain lull in the activity of the local lepidoptera suggested, however, that we might just as well drive on to the West Coast. After a meeting in Beverly Hills (at which I was told that in order to appease the censor a later scene should contain some pudic hint to the effect that Humbert had been secretly married to Lolita all along), followed by a week of sterile meditation on the shores of Lake Tahoe (where a calamitous growth of manzanita precluded the presence of good butterflies), I decided not to undertake the job and left for Europe.

We sojourned in Paris, London, Rome, Taormina, Genoa, and Lugano, where we arrived for a week's stay on December 9 (Grand Hotel, rooms 317–318, says my 1959 agenda, which now grows more talkative). I had long ceased to bother about the film, when suddenly I experienced a small nocturnal illumination, of diabolical origin, perhaps, but unusually compelling in sheer bright force, and clearly perceived an attractive line of approach to a screen version of *Lolita*. I regretted having had to decline the offer and was aimlessly revolving bits of dream dialogue in my mind when magically a telegram came from Hollywood urging me to revise my earlier decision and promising me a freer hand.

We spent the rest of the winter in Milan, San-Remo, and Mentone and on Thursday, February 18, 1960, left for Paris (2 singles Mentone-Paris, beds 6 and 8, car 9, leaving 7:15 P.M., arriving 8:55 A.M., these and other informative items from my diary are mentioned not only for mnemonic comfort but because I have not the heart to leave them ignored and unused). The first lap of the long journey to Los Angeles began with a rather ominous gag: the damned sleeping car stopped before reaching the platform, amid the mimosas and cypresses in the aquarelle elegance of a Riviera evening, and my wife and I, and the almost demented porter, had to swarm up from ground level to board the train.

By next evening we were at Le Havre, on the *United States*. We had booked an upper-deck cabin (61) but were transferred at no extra cost, with a bonus of fruit and whiskey, to a charming suite (65) by courtesy of the charming management – one of the many treats an American writer is granted. On Saturday, February 27, after four busy days in New York, we left for Chicago (10 P.M., car 551, bedrooms en suite E–F, enjoyable jottings, naive trivia of yore!) and next evening boarded the Super Chief on which the next installment of our bedrooms welcomed us with a twin burst of music, whereupon we scrambled frantically to stop, kill, stamp out, annihilate the heinous gadget and, not finding the switch, had to call for help (of course, the situation is incomparably worse on Soviet trains where you are strictly forbidden to turn off the muzakovitch).

On March 1, Kubrick and I, at his Universal City studio, debated in an amiable battle of suggestion and countersuggestion how to cinemize the novel. He accepted all my vital points, I accepted some of his less significant ones. Next morning, sitting on a bench under a lovely bright yellowgreen *Pyrospodia* tree in a public park not far from the Beverly Hills Hotel (one of whose cottages Mr Lazar had taken for us) I was already attending with all my wits to the speech and pantomime in my head. On March 9, Kubrick had us meet Tuesday Weld (a graceful ingénue but not my idea of Lolita). On March 10 we rented, from the late John Francis Fay, a pleasant villa (2088 Mandeville Canyon Road). On March 11, Kubrick sent me by messenger a rough outline of the scenes he and I had agreed upon: they covered Part One of the novel. By then his attitude had convinced me that he was willing to heed my whims more closely than those of the censor.

During the next months we met rather seldom – every fortnight or so, at his place or mine; outlines ceased altogether, criticism and advice got briefer and briefer, and by midsummer I did not feel quite sure whether Kubrick was serenely accepting whatever I did or silently rejecting everything.

I worked with zest, composing mentally every morning from eight to noon while butterfly hunting in the hot hills, which, except for some remarkably skittish individuals of a little-known Wood Nymph, produced nothing noteworthy, but *per contra* teemed with rattlers whose hysterical perform-ance in the undergrowth or in the middle of the trail was more comical than alarming. After a leisurely lunch, pre-pared by the German cook who came with the house, I would spend another four-hour span in a lawn chair, among the roses and mockingbirds, using lined index cards and a Blackwing pencil, for copying and recopying, rubbing out and writing anew, the scenes I had imagined in the morning.

By nature I am no dramatist; I am not even a hack scenar-ist; but if I had given as much of myself to the stage or the screen as I have to the kind of writing which serves a tri-umphant life sentence between the covers of a book, I would

have advocated and applied a system of total tyranny, direct-
ing the play or the picture myself, choosing settings and
costumes, terrorizing the actors, mingling with them in the
bit part of guest, or ghost, prompting them, and, in a word,
pervading the entire show with the will and art of one
individual – for there is nothing in the world that I loathe
more than group activity, that communal bath where the
hairy and slippery mix in a multiplication of mediocrity. All
I could do in the present case was to grant words primacy
over action, thus limiting as much as possible the intrusion
of management and cast. I persevered in the task until I could
tolerate the rhythm of the dialogue and properly control the
flow of the film from motel to motel, mirage to mirage,
nightmare to nightmare. Long before, in Lugano, I had
adumbrated the sequence at the Enchanted Hunters Hotel,
but its exact mechanism now proved tremendously difficult
to adjust so as to render by the transparent interplay of
sound effects and trick shots both a humdrum morning and
a crucial moment in the lives of a desperate pervert and a
wretched child. A small number of scenes (for example,
McCoo's phantom house, the three poolside nymphs, or
Diana Fowler starting to repeat the fatal cycle through which
Charlotte Haze had passed) are based on unused material
that I had kept after destroying the MS. of my novel, an act
which I regret less than my having discarded those passages.

By the end of June, after having used up over a thousand

cards, I had the thing typed, sent to Kubrick the four hundred pages it made, and, needing a rest, was driven by my wife in a rented Impala to Inyo Country for a short stay at Glacier Lodge on Big Pine Creek, where we collected the Inyo Blue and other nice bugs in the surrounding mountains. Upon our returning to Mandeville Canyon, Kubrick visited us to say that my screenplay was much too unwieldly, contained too many unnecessary episodes, and would take about seven hours to run. He wanted several deletions and other changes, and some of these I did make, besides devising new sequences and situations, when preparing a shorter script which he got in September and said was fine. That last stretch was the toughest, but also the most exhilarating part of the six-month task. Ten years later, though, I reread my play and restored a few scenes.

My final meeting with Kubrick must have taken place on September 25, 1960, at his house in Beverly Hills: he showed me that day photographs of Sue Lyon, a demure nymphet of fourteen or so, who, said Kubrick, could be easily made to look younger and grubbier for the part of Lolita for which he already had signed her up. On the whole I felt rather pleased with the way things had worked out, when on October 12, at P.M., my wife and I took the Super Chief (bdr. E + F, car 181) for Chicago, changing there to the Twentieth-Century (bdr J–K, car 261) and reaching New York, at 8:30 A.M. on October 15. In the course of that splendid journey – and

the following note can stir only the dedicated extra-sensor-
ialist – I had a dream (October 13) in which I saw written:
'They say on the radio that she is as natural as Sarah Footer.'
I have never known anybody of that name.

Complacency is a state of mind that exists only in retro-
spective: it has to be shattered before being ascertained.
Mine was to endure for a year and a half. As early as October
28 (New York, Hampshire House, room 503) I find the
following plan penciled in my little book: 'a novel, a life, a
love – which is only the elaborate commentary to a gradually
evolved short poem.' The 'short poem' started to become a
rather long one soon after the *Queen Elizabeth* ('Buy dental
floss, new pince-nez, Bonamine, check with baggage-master
big black trunk on pier before embarcation, Deck A, Cabin 71')
deposited us at Cherbourg on November 7. Four days later,
at the Principe e Savoia in Milan and then throughout the
winter in Nice, in a rented flat (57 Promenade des Anglais)
and after that in Tessin, Valais, and Vaud ('Oct. 1, 1961, moved
to Montreux-Palace') I was absorbed in *Pale Fire*, which I finished on December 4, 1961. Lepidopterology, work on the
galleys of my *Eugene Onegin* mammoth, and the revising of a
difficult translation (*The Gift*) took care of the spring of 1962,
spent mostly in Montreux, so that (apart from the fact that
nobody insisted on my coming to Elstree) the shooting of
the *Lolita* film in England was begun and concluded far
beyond the veil of my vanities.

On May 31, 1962 (almost exactly twenty-two years after we emigrated from St-Nazaire aboard the *Champlain*), the *Queen Elizabeth* took us to New York for the opening of *Lolita*. Our cabin (main deck, cabin 95) was quite as comfortable as the one we had on the *Champlain* in 1940 and, moreover, at a cocktail party given by the purser (or surgeon, my scribble is illegible), he turned to me and said: Now you, as an American businessman, will enjoy the following story (story not recorded). On June 6 I revisited my old haunts, the entomological department at the American Museum of Natural History, where I deposited the specimens of Chapman's Hairstreak I had taken the previous April between Nice and Grasse, under strawberry trees. The première took place on June 13 (Loew's State, BW at 45, E2 + 4 orchestra, 'horrible seats' says my outspoken agenda). Crowds were awaiting the limousines that drew up one by one, and there I, too, rode, as eager and innocent as the fans who peered into my car hoping to glimpse James Mason but finding only the placid profile of a stand-in for Hitchcock. A few days before, at a private screening, I had discovered that Kubrick was a great director, that his *Lolita* was a first-rate film with magnificent actors, and that only ragged odds and ends of my script had been used. The modifications, the garbling of my best little finds, the omission of entire scenes, the addition of new ones, and all sorts of other changes may not

have been sufficient to erase my name from the credit titles
but they certainly made the picture as unfaithful to the original script as an American poet's translation from Rimbaud
or Pasternak.

I hasten to add that my present comments should definitely not be construed as reflecting any belated grudge, any
high-pitched deprecation of Kubrick's creative approach.
When adapting Lolita to the speaking screen he saw my novel
in one way, I saw it in another – that's all, nor can one deny
that infinite fidelity may be an author's ideal but can prove
a producer's ruin.

My first reaction to the picture was a mixture of aggravation, regret, and reluctant pleasure. Quite a few of the
extraneous inventions (such as the macabre ping-pong
scene or that rapturous swig of Scotch in the bathtub) struck
me as appropriate and delightful. Others (such as the col-
lapsing cot or the frills of Miss Lyon's elaborate nightgown)
were painful. Most of the sequences were not really better
than those I had so carefully composed for Kubrick, and I
keenly regretted the waste of my time while admiring
Kubrick's fortitude in enduring for six months the evolution
and infliction of a useless product.

But I was wrong. Aggravation and regret soon subsided as
I recollected the inspiration in the hills, the lawn chair under
the jacaranda, the inner drive, the glow, without which my

task could not have been accomplished. I told myself that nothing had been wasted after all, that my scenario remained intact in its folder, and that one day I might publish it – not in pettish refutation of a munificent film but purely as a vivacious variant of an old novel.

VLADIMIR NABOKOV

Montreux

December, 1973

Prologue

SOUND TRACK:

A feminine voice (Lolita's, or rather Dolly Schiller's) repeats exactly a fragment of speech from her last conversation with Humbert at the end of Act Three:

> . . . Oh, what does it matter. Up in Parkington, I guess. He's got a house there, a regular old castle (*rustle of rummaging*). There was a picture of it somewhere. (*flip-flip*) Yes, here it is.

Pavor Manor, an Elaborate, Antiquated Wooden Mansion at the Top of a Winding Forest Road
This is Clare Quilty's lair, not far from Parkington, Ramsdale Country. The sun is rising above the gnarled old trees. After a brief still, the CAMERA glides around an ornate turret and dips into an upper-story casement. A prone sleeper (Quilty) is glimpsed in dorsal view. The CAMERA also locates the drug addict's implementa on a bedside chair, and with a shudder withdraws. It slides down the gutter pipe, returns to the porch

and meets a car which stops in the driveway. Humbert Humbert, hatless, raincoated, emerges. Lurching a little (he is drunk), he makes for the front door. He rings the doorbell. He uses the knocker. There is no response. He rings and knocks again. Still no response. With a petulant snarl, he pushes the door – and it swings open as in a medieval fairy tale.

CUT TO:

A Spacious and Ugly Hall with a Long Mirror and a Huge Boar's Head on the Wall
Humbert enters. With a drunkard's fussy care he closes the door behind him. He looks around. He produces a pistol.

CUT TO:

The Central Staircase
down which slowly comes a large man (Clare Quilty) in a silk dressing gown, the sash of which he is tying as he goes. The host sees the visitor. They face each other. Now begins a silent shadowy sequence which should not last more than one minute. As Humbert levels his weapon, Quilty retreats and majestically walks upstairs. Humbert fires. Once more. We see him missing: the impact of a bullet sets a rocking chair performing on the landing. Then he hits a picture (photograph of Duk-Duk ranch which Lolita had visited). Next a large ugly

vase is starred and smashed. Finally, on his fourth fire, he stops a grandfather clock in its clacking stride. The fifth bullet wounds Quilty, and the last one fells him on the upper landing.

CUT TO:

Dr John Ray
a psychiatrist, perusing a manuscript on his desk. He swings around toward us in his swivel chair.

DR RAY   I'm Dr John Ray. Pleased to meet you. This here is a bundle of notes, a rough autobiography, poorly typed, which Mr Humbert Humbert wrote after his arrest, in prison, where he was held without bail on a charge of murder, and in the psychopathic ward where he was committed for observation. Without this document his crime would have remained unexplained. Naturally, in my capacity of psychotherapist, I would have preferred obtaining the information revealed here not from the typewriter but from the couch.

The murder Humbert perpetrated is only a side product of his case. His memoir is mainly an account of his fatal infatuation with a certain type of very young girl and of the torments he underwent in his vortex of libido and guilt. I have no intention to glorify Humbert. He is horrible, he is abject. He is a shining example of moral leprosy. But there are in his story depths of passion and suffering, patterns of tenderness and distress, that cannot be dismissed by his judges. As a case history, his autobiography will no doubt become a classic in psychiatric circles. But more important to us is the ethical impact it should have on a serious audience. For here lurks a general lesson: the wayward child, the egotistic mother, the panting maniac – these are not only vivid characters in a unique story. They warn us of dangerous trends. They point out potent evils. They should make all of us – parents, social workers, educators – apply ourselves with still greater vigilance and vision to the task of bringing up a better generation in a safer world. Thank you.

CUT TO:

Humbert's Cell in The Tombs
He is writing at a table. Conspicuous among the reference books at his elbow are some tattered travel guides and maps. Presently his voice surfaces as he rereads the first sentences of his story.

HUMBERT'S VOICE   I was born in Paris forty dark years ago. My father was a gentle easy-going person, a Swiss citizen of mixed French and Austrian descent with a dash of the blue Danube in his veins. He owned a luxurious hotel on the Riviera. In a minute I am going to pass around some lovely picture postcards. My mother was an Englishwoman. Her death preceded that of my father by two decades: she was killed by a bolt of lightning during a picnic on my fourth birthday, high in the Maritime Alps.

CUT TO:

A Mountain Meadow — A thunderhead advancing above sharp cliffs
Several people scramble for shelter, and the first big drops of rain strike the zinc of a lunchbox. As the poor lady in white runs toward the pavilion of a lookout, a blast of livid light fells her. Her graceful specter floats up above the black cliffs holding a parasol and blowing kisses to her husband and child who stand below, looking up, hand in hand.

CUT TO:

HUMBERT'S VOICE   Aunt Sybil, my mother's eldest sister, a severe spinster, helped my father to bring me up. My childhood was spent in the bright world of the Hotel Mirana, at St-Topaz.

CUT TO:

A Picture Postcard of the Mirana Palace flying its flag in a cloudless sky
There are palm trees in front of it, and a system of stone
steps winding down from terrace to terrace, among rhodo-
dendrons and roses. Back to the memoirist's murmur:

HUMBERT'S VOICE   I remember a certain summer. My
    father was away in Naples attending to the affairs of an
    Italian lady he was courting at the time. In the east wing
    of our hotel an English family occupied a first-floor suite.

CUT TO:

Picture Postcard of Hotel
A clumsy cross is scrawled over one window.

HUMBERT'S VOICE   This was Annabel's room. How strange
    to recollect today, in the light of another love, those past
    pangs! I was fourteen and she was twelve, in that king-
    dom by the sea. Young as we were, we fell in love. My
    Aunt Sybil and Annabel's parents apparently realized that
    if she and I filched somehow five mad minutes of privacy,
    God knows what would come of it. Therefore, they saw
    to our not obtaining that privacy. In fact, *any* meeting
    between us was allowed only on condition we kept in the

public domain. Good Lord, how I envy today's youngsters and their progressive Freudian freedom. Poor Humbert, poor Annabel. I would now like a shot of two hands.

CUT TO:

Two Young Hands — right boy's, left girl's — both slender, long-fingered, tanned, hers with the modest star of a topaz ring, his with fine glistening hair on the back of the wrist, and a wristwatch (11:55), creeping toward each other — belonging to Humbert and Annabel (who are prone on the beach, sunning their backs in symmetrical similar adjacent positions), now through shifting sifted sand, now under sand, now in the shimmer of midday — and now they meet like two wary sensitive insects — and suddenly separate, a pretty scene for the subtle camera as the shore-fortress gun booms noon.

CUT TO:

HUMBERT'S VOICE   I loved her more tenderly than Tristan adored Isolde, more hotly than Petrarca desired his Laura, more romantically than Poe loved little Virginia. Once, on a rosy rock in the purple sea, I made her promise me an old-fashioned assignation at night in the palmy hotel garden.

CUT TO:

Rocky Promontory
Annabel supine, Humbert murmuring passionate plaints.
Two Englishmen, robust freckled swimmers, interrupt these throbbings.

CUT TO:

The Garden of the Mirana Palace at Night
On a lower lighted balcony Annabel's parents, Humbert's Aunt Sybil, and a Mr Cooper are playing cards (poker, European fashion). Aunt Sybil narrowly fondles three kings. Annabel in pale pajamas slithers through the honeysuckle from a first-floor window into the dark garden where she is joined by young Humbert near the balustrade under the oleanders. She sits on a stone shelf, he worships her from below, his arms embracing her haunches, and the light of an ornamental lamp imprints on a stone wall the emblematic silhouettes of long leaves. He is groping his way to a secret fount when her mother claps down her cards and loudly calls her daughter's name.

HUMBERT'S VOICE   And then summer was over. Aunt
    Sybil, after a torrential rain, broke her leg on a slippery
    terrace, and I was supposed that evening to sit at her bed-
    side and read to her *South Wind*, her favorite novel; instead

22

of which I escaped to the little railway station where the great European expresses so grandly stopped. I just made it – and saw Annabel off.

CUT TO:

A Côte d'Azur Station – luminous evening – black cypresses and a young moon
The *train bleu* is pulling out. We follow a youth trotting alongside the sleeping car *Nice-Paris* from the window of which the young girl he is seeing off leans out in an ecstasy of blown kisses and streaming tears.

HUMBERT'S VOICE   We parted. Never again did I see her alive. A few months after she left the Riviera I was sent to school in England. That same year she died of pneumonia in a seaside town. I learned of her illness at the last moment and barely managed to arrive in time for the funeral. This is her tomb at the end of that vista.

CUT TO:

That Vista
We see her highborn kinsmen, in a romantic Poe-esque arrangement, bearing her away down an alley of tall cypresses. Our young mourner watches, cloaked in his grief. A related nympher places a wreath on the tomb.

HUMBERT'S VOICE   I am writing this in prison, and the physical seclusion I am condemned to here strangely helps to encompass and concentrate the remote, diffuse, personal past I'm evoking. If I am given enough time before my trial I hope to proceed onward from that first young love and relate in all possible detail of circumstance and emotion the story of my later life in Europe and America. And if I manage to finish my difficult task, I shall place these pages in the capable hands of my adviser and physician, Dr John Ray.

CUT TO:

Dr Ray in His Study as Before, holding the typescript

DR RAY   And here they are, those precious pages. From them we learn that Humbert could never forget graceful Annabel, and her shape and shadow haunted him in every alley of his love life. He finished college in England and continued his graduate studies – in the field of comparative literature – in Switzerland, where his nationality and temperament kept him away from the tumult of World War Two. He then moved to Paris, where he engaged in various literary pursuits and taught English at a boys' school. But we are not concerned with his intellectual life. We are interested in his emotional tribulations. Everywhere: In public parks—

CUT TO:

A Nymphet Readjusts the Straps of Her Roller Skate
She has placed her armored foot on the edge of Humbert's
bench, and her shining curls tumble over her sun-dappled
bare leg.

DR RAY'S VOICE — at bus stops—

CUT TO:

Chattering, Jostling Schoolgirls crowd into a bus and push against Humbert
One nymphet glances at him, nudges another lass, and
both giggle.

DR RAY'S VOICE — on street corners—

CUT TO:

Two Nymphets play at marbles under a sidewalk maple

DR RAY'S VOICE — in the garden of an orphanage—

CUT TO:

Pale, Black-stockinged Girls performing tame calisthenics directed by a nun

DR RAY'S VOICE — and in many other haunts, Humbert

wrestled with strange wretched urges and kept searching for the child of his shameful obsession, for some incarnation of his boyhood sweetheart. At thirty, he decided to marry. His choice fell on the daughter of a Polish-born doctor in Paris who was treating him for a heart condition.

CUT TO:

Humbert and the Doctor – playing chess
The doctor's daughter Valeria flirts with Humbert. She is in her late twenties and rather shopworn and pudgy, but imitates in attitudes and attire a little girl. 'She looked fluffy and frolicsome, dressed *à la gamine* . . . and pouted, and dimpled, and romped, and dirndled, in the cutest and tritest fashion imaginable.'*

DR RAY'S VOICE He married Valeria, but reality soon asserted itself, and presently unsatisfied Humbert had on his hands not a nymphet but a large, puffy, dull, adult woman.

CUT TO:

A Bourgeois Evening in a Tiny Parisian Flat
Humbert reads the evening paper. Plump-shouldered, in a rumpled slip, scratching her rump, Valeria looks after the *pot-au-feu*.

* Passages in quotation marks denote excerpts from the novel *Lolita*.

DR RAY'S VOICE   The marriage dragged on for several years. In the meantime, Humbert went on with his literary and educational studies. A handbook of French translations from English poetry enjoyed some success, and an Institute of Comparative Literature in an American city invited him to come over for a series of lectures.

CUT TO:

The Prefecture in Paris. Humbert and Valeria come out.
He is checking a batch of documents, she looks perturbed.

HUMBERT   We have all our papers now.

DR RAY'S VOICE   They have all their papers now. They are all set to go. Good-bye, gray Paree!

HUMBERT   Good-bye, gray Paree. Now, my dear, don't lose your passport. (*Gives it to her.*)

They follow the sidewalk. A taxi starts creeping along the curb as if inviting them to take it. Valeria is silent, and keeps shaking her poodle head.

DR RAY'S VOICE   Watch that cab.

HUMBERT   Why are you shaking your head? Something in it? A pebble?

She shakes it.

HUMBERT   I can assure you it is quite empty.

VALERIA   No-no-no-no-no—

HUMBERT   That will do.

VALERIA   — I cannot go on with it. You will sail alone.

HUMBERT   What? What's that, you fool?

VALERIA   We must separate.

HUMBERT   I refuse to discuss this in the street. Taxi!

The cab that had been quietly escorting them glides up.

HUMBERT   *Quarante-deux, rue Baudelaire.*

DR RAY'S VOICE   Forty-two Baudelaire Street.

They get into the taxi.

HUMBERT   May I inquire *why* you want us to separate?

VALERIA   Because life with you is sad and horrible. Because you've got impossible eyes. Because I cannot imagine your thoughts. Because I'm afraid of you and hate you.

DR RAY'S VOICE   She had never been so voluble.

HUMBERT   You've never been so voluble before. All right. Let's get this straight—

DR RAY'S VOICE   My patient is flabbergasted. As Professor Gast used to say: 'Woe to him who gets stuck in his own guilt complex like an angry fly.' Mr Humbert cannot react rationally, he splutters. That's the famous *Place de l'Etoile*, Place of the Star. Need good brakes. Oops. See what I mean?

The taxi driver is strangely erratic.

VALERIA   It's all finished now. I'm going to be free. There's another man in my life and I'm leaving you.

HUMBERT   What man? What are you talking about? How dare you?

DR RAY'S VOICE   Dare indeed. A very curious situation. Humbert is accustomed to making the decisions. Now the fate of his marriage is no longer in his hands. I think the cab driver ought to have turned left here. Oh, well, he can take the next cross street.

VALERIA   He's a human being, not a monster. He's a White Russian. He was a colonel in the Russian army. His father was a Councilor of the Tsar.

HUMBERT   I don't know whom you are speaking of. I'll — I don't know what I'll do to you if you go on like that.

DR RAY'S VOICE   Look out! Close shave. When you analyze those jaywalkers you find they hesitate between the womb and the tomb.

VALERIA   Oh, you can't do anything to me now — because I love him.

HUMBERT   But damn you — who the devil is he?

VALERIA   Him, of course (*Points at the thick back-head of the driver who turns briefly revealing a Russian profile, potato nose, and bristly mustache.*)

The taxi pulls up at the curb.

CUT TO:

Sidewalk in Front of 42, rue Baudelaire.
The driver and both passengers get out of the cab.

DRIVER   I am Colonel Maximovich, allow me to present myself. I have seen you often in the cinema of the corner, and she was sitting between us. (*Smiles fondly at Valeria.*) Let us discuss.

HUMBERT   We have nothing to discuss.

MAXIMOVICH   Perhaps we can move her and her things immediately in my auto. (*turning to Valeria*) You want? You are prepared?

HUMBERT   I will not have anything to do with either of you. This is ridiculous.

MAXIMOVICH   She is quite pale today, the poor. You must permit me to help with her baggage.

VALERIA   The percolator!

MAXIMOVICH   Yes, all the presents of marriage. Also, the

white dress, the black dress, library books which she must return, her furry coat, and her diet.

HUMBERT   I beg your pardon? What was that last fascinating item?

VALERIA   My diet. He means the printed list father gave me.

HUMBERT   Oh yes. Oh, of course. Anything else?

MAXIMOVICH   One will see. Let us mount upstairs.

DR RAY'S VOICE   Divorce was inevitable. Valeria had found herself another, more suitable mate, and lone Humbert set out for America.

CUT TO:

Humbert Dramatically Standing on a Liner's Deck
The towers of New York loom in the autumnal mist.

DR RAY'S VOICE   For the following year Humbert had been promised a lectureship at Beardsley College in Idaho. Meanwhile in New York he spent all his time in libraries preparing his course, a series of lectures under the general title of 'Romanticists and Rebels.'

CUT TO:

Library

In the vicinity of Humbert's carrel a brood of bored schoolgirls are shown by their teacher The Place Where Books Live.

DR RAY'S VOICE   He also accepted lecture engagements out of town. A nervous breakdown in result of his solitary exertions and repressed dreams interrupted one such engagement at a Women's Club.

CUT TO:

A Women's Club

A full-blown matron, Mrs Nancy Whitman (her name pinned to her breast), rises above a carafe to introduce the speaker.

MRS WHITMAN   Before introducing the distinguished visitor on tonight's program, you will be glad to learn that next Friday the well-known psychiatrist, Dr John Ray, will talk to us on the sexual symbolism of golf.

(applause)

We have here tonight Dr Humbert, who has spent many years in *very* continental surroundings, and who will talk to us right now on romantic poetry. Please, Dr Humbert.

CUT TO:

Feminine Eyes Watching the Speaker – changing expressions come and go on various elastic faces
some plump, but changing to eights and snapping in a distorted mirror; others, lean and long, developing abysmal décolletés; others again blending with the flesh of rolling bare arms, or turning into wax fruit in arty bowls.

HUMBERT'S FALTERING VOICE   Let me illustrate my point by reading to you Edgar's poem about . . . about . . .

CUT TO:

The Lecturer is now shown clearly except for a ripple or two of optical interference

He fumbles feverishly through a volume to find a quotation he needs.

HUMBERT   I put a marker in, but it dropped out, evidently. Somebody ought to collect all the markers we shed. I'm sure, though, it was in this volume. Oh God, oh God . . .

He fumbles feverishly through a volume to find a quotation he needs.

HUMBERT   (*in a pearly sweat*) It is supposed to be a very complete anthology. There should be an index. Here it is, here it is. Oh, I must find that poem. It is sure to be here. It began with an 'N': n, y, m. N, y, m . . . n. y. m . . . Oh, I'm sure it began with an 'N' as in 'Annabel.'

HELPFUL VOICE   Title or first line?

HUMBERT   Don't ask me. This is atrocious. The term I wish to illustrate is 'nymphet.'

MURMURS IN AUDIENCE   What? What? What did he say?

HUMBERT   After all, I don't really need this stupid book. Stupid book, go!
>   (*Tosses it away.*)
So the term is nymphet. I intend to introduce the following idea: Between the age limits of nine and fourteen there are certain maidens: they bewitch the traveler who is twice their age and reveal to him their true nature, which is not human but nymphid – in other words, demoniac – and these chosen creatures I propose to designate as nymphets.

He is speaking very loud, almost screaming, and there is a rising rumble in the audience.

HUMBERT   Let me finish, ladies. Now the question is: between these age limits are *all* girl-children nymphets? 'Course, not. Otherwise the lone traveler would have long gone insane. Neither are good looks any criterion. I am speaking of a certain fey grace, of the elusive, shifty, soul-shattering, insidious charm that separates the pre-teen demon from the ordinary sweet round-faced child with a tummy and pigtails. You have to be an artist and a madman, a creature of infinite melancholy. – Silence!

His audience is coming out of its stunned stupefaction.

HUMBERT   Yes, only a madman can really distinguish at once – oh, at once – by ineffable signs – the feline outline of a cheekbone, the slenderness of a downy limb, and other indices which despair and shame and tears of tenderness forbid me to tab – tab – tabulate—

CUT TO:

Distorted Matronly Faces
and a good deal of rubbery, enveloping, adult flesh is now crowding Humbert out of the picture

HUMBERT   We cringe and hide, yes, but our dreams contain enchantments which normal men never know. What indeed could Edgar Poe see in Mother Clemm, the mother of his pubescent bride? Oh, how horrible full-grown women are to the nymphet-lover! Don't come near me! Hands off! I'm not well – I—

He faints.

CUT TO:

The Office of the Psychotherapeutic Home
Humbert, in a vicuña coat, applies for admission.

HUMBERT   I have come because I need help.

BUXOM RECEPTIONIST   And I'm sure you will get it. Have you filled that other form too? Okay.

HUMBERT   I want to say that I am perfectly aware of the real nature of my problems. All I need is some mental rest. Not a solution but solitude.

RECEPTIONIST   Dr Ray will easily establish a working relationship with you.

HUMBERT   The point is I don't need a cure, because I'm incurable—

RECEPTIONIST   Oh, come. Everything and everybody can be cured. Sure.

HUMBERT   Well, anyway I'm not interested in being cured. What I need, what I badly need, is some kind of diversion, some peace of mind.

RECEPTIONIST   Our occupational therapy provides many fascinating contacts and outlets.

HUMBERT   I mean I have the feeling that something in my mind is poisoning everything else. I know this thing cannot be eliminated but perhaps it could be reduced to reasonable dimensions, watered down, so to speak.

RECEPTIONIST   Well, I'm sure Dr Ray will fix all that. He'll assign you to a delightful group of patients we have here, mainly European immigrants. See these shoes?
(*Proffers her foot.*)
A wonderful Hungarian patient made them for me. Aren't they something!

HUMBERT   Please tell Dr Ray that I want a private room. And then I must have silence and peace all the time.

RECEPTIONIST   Oh, I must disagree with you there. I think silence is terrible. Let me try again. Dr Ray's office.

CUT TO:

DR RAY'S VOICE   So it happened that in the nursing home where Humbert spent three weeks I met him and talked with him. The patient refused to reveal the reasons for his breakdown, but it was plain he needed relaxation. Tranquilizers and a regular mental regime brought considerable improvement to his condition. An acquaintance of his, whose cousin had an attractive house in Ramsdale on the beautiful lake of that name, suggested that Humbert come to lodge there during the summer, before traveling west to the university where he had been invited to teach.

Act One

Ramsdale, a pretty, sedate town with opulent shade trees. The time is around noon in early summer.

The words LAST DAY OF SCHOOL are gradually scrawled across the blackboard.

CUT TO:

Three Girls Near Bay Window:
Virginia McCoo (polio cripple, sharp features, strident voice); Phyllis Chatfield (chubby, sturdy); and a third girl (head turned away, tying her shoe).

VIRGINIA   (*to Phyllis*) Well, Phyllis, what are your plans for the summer? Camp?

PHYLLIS   Yes, camp. My folks are going to Europe.

VIRGINIA   Getting rid of you, huh?

PHYLLIS   Oh well, I don't mind. I like camp.

VIRGINIA   Same place – Lake Climax?

PHYLLIS   Same old place. And what about you, Ginny?

VIRGINIA   I'm going to have a wonderful time. I'm going to have French lessons with our new paying guest.

PHYLLIS   Oh – has he come?

VIRGINIA   Coming tomorrow. My mother saw him in New York and she says he's a real man of the world and awfully handsome. I guess it will be fun.

PHYLLIS   (to the third girl) And you, Lolita?

Lolita turns toward them. A smile, a shrug.

CUT TO:

A Car Drives up to the School. Charlotte Haze Emerges.

LOLITA   There's my dear mother.

CUT TO:

A Teacher Coming out meets Charlotte Coming in.

TEACHER   How are you, Mrs Haze?

CHARLOTTE   Fine. And you, Miss Horton – glad to be rid of them until the fall?

TEACHER   I should say so. Now it's Mama's turn to take over. Is Lolita going to the Lake Climax camp?

CHARLOTTE   I don't know. I sort of never got around to planning our summer yet.

CUT TO:

Charlotte Drives Lolita Homeward.
Heavy traffic. Red light.

LOLITA   Our luck as per usual. (*Pause.*)

Light changes

With our luck it is sure to be some ugly old hag.

CHARLOTTE   What are you talking about?

LOLITA   About the lodger you are trying to find.

42

CHARLOTTE   Oh, *that*. Well, I'm sure she will be a lovely person. When the time comes. The agency tells me it is going to be quite a season here this summer. What with the new casino.

LOLITA   Ginny McCoo was telling me about the roomer they are getting. He's a professor of French poetry. And her uncle's firm is going to publish a book he has written.

CHARLOTTE   We don't want any French poets. *Please*, stop rummaging in that glove compartment.

LOLITA   I had some candy there.

CHARLOTTE   You are wrecking your teeth on those mints. By the way, you have not forgotten you have Dr Quilty at three and – oh, darn that dog!

CUT TO:

Mr Jung's Dog, a Large Collie,
waits at the corner of Lawn Street, then races the car barking lustily and nearly gets run over.

CHARLOTTE   Really, I am fed up with that beast.

CUT TO:

She Draws up at the Curb
where old Mr Jung is inspecting the contents of his mailbox.
Over his spectacles he peers at Mrs Haze.

CHARLOTTE   (*leaning out*) Mr Jung, something must be done
about that dog of yours.

Mr Jung, beaming and a little gaga, walks around the car to
her window.

CUT TO:

Lolita, leaning out of her side of the car,
fondly stroking the pleased hound and speaking confidentially—

LOLITA   And I think he is a good, good dog – yes, a *good* dog.

CUT TO:

Mr Jung, who is a little deaf
and seems to listen with his mouth, comes closer to the
driver's window.

CHARLOTTE   I am talking about your dog. Something must
be done about him.

44

MR JUNG   Why? What's he been up to?

CHARLOTTE   He's a nuisance. He chases every car. He has taught two other dogs to do it.

MR JUNG   He's gentle intelligent beast. Never hurt anybody. Most alert and intelligent.

CHARLOTTE   I'm not interested in his I.Q. All I know he's a nuisance. And it will be your fault if he gets hurt.

MR JUNG   He won't hurt nobody. Come here, boy! You just don't mind him, Mrs Haze. Come, boy!

LOLITA   Mother, I'm hungry. Let's be moving.

WIPE TO:

Dinner Time.
Quick view of Ramsdale. White church with clock against an inky sky. Lolita dines from a plate watching TV.

DISSOLVE TO:

A Ragged Sunset.
The plashing lake. A thunderhead looming.

Details of approaching electric storm: an empty milk bottle overturned by a gust.

The wind brutally turns the pages of the mangled magazine forgotten on the folding chair. It is suddenly whisked away in rotating mad flight.

Nightfall. Lolita barefooted hastens to close a bedroom window. Lightning. Charlotte folds and drags in the garden chair. The thunder claps and rolls. Another flash.

CUT TO:

LOLITA   (undressed, on landing, to her mother downstairs) I'm going to bed. I'm scared!

Big Thunderclap

CUT TO:

Charlotte in the Living Room.
The storm never stops. Far away the fire engine is heard. Nearer. Far again. Charlotte looks out of the window. Details of nocturnal storm: gesticulating black trees, rain drumming on roof, thunder, lightning printing reflections on wall, Lolita sits up in bed. More sounds of firefighting.

CUT TO:

A Car,

shedding its moving beam on 342 Lawn Street, and then on 345 Lawn Street, turns in to the driveway next door. The Farlows, John and Jean. The storm is abating.

JEAN   John, while you are parking the car I'll dash over to Charlotte and tell her—

JOHN   Oh, but she must be fast asleep.

JEAN   No, she's in the living room. The lights are on.

CUT TO:

Charlotte, Who has noticed their return, opens the front door. A cat's eyes in the dripping-dark. Sheet lightning.

JEAN   Oh, what's that cat doing there? Have you heard about the fire, Charlotte?

CHARLOTTE   I heard the engines.

JEAN   Well, it was at the McCoos'.

CHARLOTTE   No!

JEAN   Yes. Their house got struck by lightning. We were at John's club and could see the blaze five blocks away.

CHARLOTTE   My goodness! Are they safe?

JEAN   Oh yes, they're okay. They even saved the TV. But the house is practically a burnt-out shell.

CHARLOTTE   But how *dreadful!*

JEAN   Naturally they were insured and all that – and they have that apartment in Parkington. Well, see you tomorrow. Bye-bye.

CUT TO:

Early Morning Next Day.
Robin pulling out worm on damp lawn. One new dandelion. Milkman collects empty bottles. Tinkle. Telephone takes over, rings.

Lolita in pajamas, barefoot, leaning over banisters, half a story above Charlotte, who attends to the telephone in the hallway. The conversation is nearing its end. We hear only her side.

CHARLOTTE   I certainly could, Mr McCoo. Oh, I just keep thinking and thinking of you and that dreadful fire—

(*Listens.*)

No trouble at all. In fact it's just the kind of lodger—

(*Listens.*)

Yes, I see. Yes, of course.

(*Listens.*)

Well, I'm glad he's old-fashioned enough to prefer lakes to oceans. That means a quiet lodger.

(*Laughs demurely.*)
(*Listens.*)

Oh, I could fetch him if you'd like.

(*Listens.*)

I see.

(*Listens.*)

Look, why don't you meet him at the station, explain things to him, put him into Joe's taxi, and send him over here.

(*Listens.*)

Aha. Naturally. I understand that.

(*Listens.*)

Okay then. I'll be expecting him around noon.

(*Listens.*)

Not at all, not at all (*melodious laugh*). Everything in the world happens at short notice.

(*Listens.*)

Yes, do that. You know, I could not sleep all night thinking of that dreadful fire and your poor wife. You're so right to have sent her and Ginny to Parkington. Well, please do tell your wife that if there's anything I can do—

(*Hangs up.*)

LOLITA   Mother, is that man going to stay with us?

CHARLOTTE   He is. Oh dear, Louise is not coming until after tomorrow. You had better get dressed and pick up all those books and things you brought back from school. The hall is a mess.

CUT TO:

Humbert's Arrival

FADE IN

Ramsdale (a thriving resort, somewhere between Minnesota and Maine) as seen by a traveler arriving by plane. We are served the dish of the large, pine-fringed, scintillating Ramsdale Lake, with, at one end, a recreation park and a stucco pleasure dome. A small cloud of dark smoke is hanging over part of the suburban development. Beyond this is the cheerful, neat-looking town in the sunshine of a serene May morning. The airport spreads out beneath us, flying its flags and gently gyrating as the plane's shadow sweeps over it.

CUT TO:

Alfalfa Fields, Asphalted Spaces, Parked Cars: Ramsdale Airport Humbert carrying briefcase lands and enters the office. His bags follow. He looks around.

HUMBERT   Somebody was supposed to meet me . . .

He consults a little black diary.

DESK CLERK   Can I help you, sir?

HUMBERT   May I use this phone?

He attempts to dial McCoo's number. Consults his diary
again. Redials. There is no answer.

HUMBERT   Funny. (*to the clerk*) Where can I find a taxi?

CLERK   (*pointing with pencil*) Down there. He'll take your bags.

CUT TO:

Humbert in Taxi
They cross the town and turn in to Lake Avenue. Sounds of
fire engines. Firefighters going back to their station.

TAXI DRIVER   We sure had a big storm last night. Lightning struck a house in Lake Avenue, and oh boy, did it
burn!
(*does a double take*)
Say, mister, what number you said you were going?

HUMBERT   Nine hundred. Nine oh oh.

TAXI DRIVER   (*chuckling*) Well, 'oh-oh' is about all that's left of it.

CUT TO:

The Black, Hosewater-drenched, Still Smoking Remains of a Burned-Down House Policemen are still keeping away a thinning crowd of spectators, most of whom have come by car or bicycle. The charred ruins are those of the McCoo villa in a pine-treed, sparsely populated part of Lake Avenue. Humbert's taxi stops at a roped-off puddle.

TAXI DRIVER   (*continuously indulging in raw, ready humor*) Here you are, sir.

HUMBERT   My goodness! You mean this is the McCoo residence?

TAXI DRIVER   Residence? Oh, brother!

Humbert, automatically carrying raincoat and briefcase, climbs out of the car. Faint cheers from the crowd.

PATROLMAN   You can't come any closer.

HUMBERT   I'm supposed to live here.

PATROLMAN   Why don't you speak to the owner? That's
    Mr McCoo down there.

(In the following scene the grotesque humor turns upon
McCoo's conducting a kind of guided tour through a nonexistent house. He makes the belated honors of the home
Humbert would have shared.) McCoo, a small fat man,
emerges from the ruins of the patio. He staggers along with
a big barbecue roaster in his arms. He is dirty and wet, and
utterly bewildered. He stops and stares at Humbert.

HUMBERT   How do you do. I am your lodger. Or rather I
    was to be your lodger.

MCCOO   (setting down his burden) What do you know! Mr
    Humbert, I must apologize. I thought my wife would
    leave you a message at the airport. I know she found
    other lodgings for you. Look at this dreadful disaster.

He gestures toward architectural ghosts in the aura of the
vanished villa.

MCCOO   Follow me. Look, sir, look. Your room was right
    here. A beautiful, sunny, quiet studio. That was your bed –

with a brand-new mattress. Here you had a writing desk — you see, that's where the wall ran — where that hose lies now.

Humbert blankly considers a heap of water-soaked volumes.

MCCOO   Ginny's encyclopedia. (*Glances up at a nonexistent upper story.*) Must have dropped through the floor of my daughter's room. Good illustrations. Cathedrals. Cocoa Industry. It's a wonder that bolt did not kill Mrs McCoo and me in the master bedroom. Our little daughter was quite hysterical. Oh, it was such a lovely home. A regular showpiece. People came all the way from Parkington to see it.

Humbert stumbles over a board.

MCCOO   Careful. I know there is not much left but I'd like you to see the patio. Here was the barbecue table. Well, that's all out now. I had planned to have you give lessons in French to my little Ginny, the poor pet. I've bundled them off to Parkington. And of course I'm fully insured. But still it's a terrible shock. Now, about that other place for you—

McCoo, wiping a dirty face with a dirty hand, walks back to the street with carefully high-stepping Humbert. The camera escorts them.

MCCOO   We thought that other place would be the best arrangement, under these sad circumstances. We all have to rough it now. She's a widow, a delightful personality with a lot of culture. But it's not as grand as here, though much nearer to town. The address is 342 Lawn Street. Let me direct your taxi. Hullo, Joe.

CUT TO:

Hysterical Bark of a car-chasing *Collie* on Lawn Street, down which Humbert's taxi arrives to stop at No. 342, an unattractive white clapboard suburban house, with a smooth philistine lawn where only one dandelion has survived the leveling power mower. Humbert emerges, watched by Charlotte from an upper window. The driver is about to help with the suitcases.

HUMBERT   No, leave those bags. I want you to wait a few minutes.

DRIVER   Sure.

HUMBERT   I doubt very much that I'll stay here. (*in vocal brackets*) What a horrible house.

The door is ajar. Humbert enters. The hallway is graced with Mexican knicknacks and the banal favorites of arty middle-class (such as a Van Gogh reproduction). An old tennis racket with a broken string lies on an oak chest. There is a telephone on a small table near the living-room door, which is ajar.

From the upper landing comes the voice of Mrs Haze, who leans over the banisters inquiring melodiously: 'Is that Monsieur Humbert?'

A bit of cigarette ash drops from above as Humbert looks up. Presently the lady herself – sandals, slacks, silk blouse, Marlenesque face (in that order) – comes down the steps, her index finger still tapping upon the cigarette.

Shake hands.

HUMBERT   How do you do. Allow me to explain the situation.

CHARLOTTE   Yes – I know everything. Come on in.

CUT TO:

Humbert and Charlotte enter the parlor
She makes Javanese-like gestures: inviting him to choose a seat. (N.B.: these gestures will be repeated by Dolly Schiller in last scene of play). They sit down.

CHARLOTTE   Let's get acquainted and then I'll show you your room. I have only Dromes.

HUMBERT   Thanks, I don't smoke.

CHARLOTTE   Oh well, one vice the less. I'm a tissue of little vices. *C'est la vie.* (*Lights up.*) You're sure you're comfortable in that old chair?

He removes from under his thigh an old tennis ball.

HUMBERT   Oh, perfectly.

CHARLOTTE   (*relieving him of the ball*) I think, Mr Humbert, I have exactly what you are looking for. I understand you wanted to stay at Ramsdale all summer?

HUMBERT   I'm not sure. No, I really could not say. The point is I have been very ill, and a friend suggested Ramsdale. I imagined a spacious house on the shore of a lake.

The CAMERA meanwhile examines ironically various crannies of the room.

CHARLOTTE   Well, the lake is only two miles from my spacious house.

HUMBERT   Oh, I know. But I envisaged a villa, white dunes, the accessible ripples, a system of morning dips.

CHARLOTTE   Frankly, between you and I, the McCoo residence, though perhaps a bit more modern than mine, is not at all on the lake front, not at all. You have to walk two blocks to see it.

HUMBERT   Oh, I'm sure there would have been some flaw, some disappointment. What I mean is that I was pursuing a particular dream, not *any* house but *that* house.

CHARLOTTE   I'm sorry for the McCoos – but they should not have promised too much. Well, I can offer you congenial surroundings in a very select neighborhood. If you like golf, as I am sure you do, we are practically at walking distance from the country club. And we are very intellectual, yes sir. You are a professor of poetry, aren't you?

HUMBERT   Alas. I shall be teaching at Beardsley College next year.

CHARLOTTE   Then you will certainly want to address our club, of which I am a proud member. Last time we had Professor Amy King, a very stimulating teacher type, talk to us on Dr Schweitzer and Dr Zhivago. Now let us take a peek at that room. I'm positive you're going to love it.

CUT TO:

Charlotte and Humbert reach the upper landing

CHARLOTTE   It's what you might call a semi-studio — or *almost* a semi-studio.

She closes quickly the door to Lolita's room, which is ajar, and opens a door opposite.

CHARLOTTE   Well here we are. Isn't that a cute bookshelf? Look at those colonial book ends. Now, in that corner (*meditative pause, with elbow in palm*) I shall put our spare radio set.

HUMBERT   No, no. Please, no radio.

He winces as he glances at a picture: a reproduction of René Prinet's 'Kreutzer Sonata' — the unappetizing one in which a disheveled violinist passionately embraces his fair accompanist as she rises from her piano stool with clammy young hands still touching the keys.

CHARLOTTE   Now, that's a rug Mr Haze and I bought in Mexico. We went there on our honeymoon, which was – let me see – thirteen years ago.

HUMBERT   Which was about the time I got married.

CHARLOTTE   Oh, you are married?

HUMBERT   Divorced, madam, happily divorced.

CHARLOTTE   Where was that? In Europe?

HUMBERT   In Paris.

CHARLOTTE   Paris must be wonderful at this time of the year. As a matter of fact, we were planning a trip to Europe just before Mr Haze died, after three years of great happiness. He was a lovely person, a man of complete integrity. I know you would have enjoyed talking to him and he to you. Now, here we have—

Humbert opens a closet. A painted screen of the folding type topples into his arms. Pictured on it is a nymphet in three repeated designs: (1) gazing over a black gauze fan, (2) in a black half-mask, (3) in bikini and harlequin glasses. There is a rent in the fabric.

CHARLOTTE   Oops! I *am* sorry. We bought it at the store here to match our Mexican stuff but it did not wear well. I'll have Lolita remove it to her room. She loves it.

HUMBERT   You have a maid living in the house?

CHARLOTTE   Oh no, what do you think? Ramsdale is not Paris. There's a colored girl who comes three times a week and we think we're lucky to have her. I see this bedlamp does not work. I'll have it fixed.

HUMBERT   But I thought you said—

Carefully and rather wistfully, Charlotte closes the door of the unsuccessful room. She opens another door next to it.

CHARLOTTE   This is the bathroom. I'm sure that as a European intellectual you hate our luxurious modern monstrosities – tiled tubs and goldern faucets. This here is a good old-fashioned type with the kind of quaint plumbing that should appeal to an Englishman. I must apologize for this dirty sock. Now, if we walk down again I'll show you the dining room – and, of course, my beautiful garden.

HUMBERT   I understood there would be a private bath.

CHARLOTTE   Sorry.

HUMBERT   I don't want to take so much of your time. It must be a frightful bother—

CHARLOTTE   No bother at all.

Humbert and Charlotte walk via the parlor into the dining room, the camera trucking with them.

CHARLOTTE   Here we have our meals. Down there is the sun porch. Well, that's about all, *cher Monsieur*.
                              (*sigh*)
I'm afraid you are not too favorably impressed.

HUMBERT   I must think it over. I have a taxi waiting out there. Let me take down your telephone number.

CHARLOTTE   Ramsdale 1776. So easy to remember. I won't charge you much, you know. Two hundred per month, all meals included.

HUMBERT   I see. Didn't I have a raincoat?

CHARLOTTE   I saw you leave it in the car.

HUMBERT   So I did. Well—

He bows.

CHARLOTTE   Oh, but you *must* visit my garden!

Humbert follows her.

CHARLOTTE   That's the kitchen there. You might like to know I'm a very good cook. My pastries win prizes round here.

Humbert follows Charlotte to the veranda. Now comes the shock of dazzling enchantment and recognition. 'From a mat in a pool of sun, half-naked, kneeling turning about on her knees, my Riviera love was peering at me over dark glasses.'

It might be a good idea at this point to film the extended metaphor of the next paragraph: 'As if I were the fairy-tale nurse of some little princess – lost, kidnapped, discovered in Gypsy rags through which her nakedness smiled at the king and his hounds, I recognized the tiny dark-brown mole on her side.' Humbert, much disturbed, follows Charlotte down into the garden.

CHARLOTTE   That was my daughter, and these are my lilies.

HUMBERT   (*mumbling*) Beautiful, beautiful. . . .

CHARLOTTE   (*with winsome abandon*) Well, this is all I can offer you — a comfortable home, a sunny garden, my lilies, my Lolita, my cherry pies.

HUMBERT   Yes, yes. I'm very grateful. You said fifty per week, including meals?

CHARLOTTE   So you *are* going to stay with us?

HUMBERT   Why — yes. I'd like to move in right now.

CHARLOTTE   You dear man. That's wonderful. Was my garden the decisive factor?

CUT TO:

Veranda where Lolita, in briefs and bra, is sunning herself on the mat
Charlotte and Humbert returning to the house mount the steps from the garden.

CHARLOTTE   I'll pay your taxi and have the luggage put in your room. Do you have many things?

HUMBERT   There's a briefcase and a typewriter, and a tape recorder, and a raincoat. And two suitcases. May I—

CHARLOTTE   No, it's okay. I know from Mrs McCoo that you are not supposed to carry things.

HUMBERT   Oh yes, and there's also a box of chocolates I intended to bring the McCoos.

Charlotte smiles and exits.

LOLITA   Yum-yum.

HUMBERT   So you are Lolita.

LOLITA   Yes, that's me.

Turns from sea-star supine to seal prone. There is a pause.

HUMBERT   It's a beautiful day.

LOLITA   Very.

HUMBERT   (*sitting down on the steps*) Nice here. Oh, the floor is hot.

LOLITA   (*Pushes a cushion toward him.*) Make yourself comfortable.

She is now in a half-sitting position.

LOLITA   Did you see the fire?

HUMBERT   No, it was all over when I came. Poor Mr McCoo looked badly shaken.

LOLITA   You look badly shaken yourself.

HUMBERT   Why, no. I'm all right. I suppose I should change into lighter clothes. There's a ladybird on your leg.

LOLITA   It's a ladybug, not a ladybird.

She transfers it to her finger and attempts to coax it into flight.

HUMBERT   You should blow. Like this. There she goes.

LOLITA   Ginny McCoo – she's in my class, you know. And she said you were going to be her tutor.

HUMBERT   Oh, that's greatly exaggerated. The idea was I might help her with her French.

LOLITA   She's grim, Ginny.

HUMBERT   Is she — well, attractive?

LOLITA   She's a fright. And mean. And lame.

HUMBERT   Really? That's curious. Lame?

LOLITA   Yah. She had polio or something. Are you going to help me with my homework?

HUMBERT   *Mais oui*, Lolita. *Aujourd'hui?*

Charlotte comes in.

CHARLOTTE   That's where you are.

LOLITA   He's going to help me with my homework.

CHARLOTTE   Fine. Mr Humbert, I paid your taxi and had the man take your things upstairs. You owe me four dollars thirty-five. Later, later. Dolores, I think Mr Humbert would like to rest.

HUMBERT   Oh no, I'll help her with pleasure.

Charlotte leaves.

LOLITA   Well, there's not much today. Gee, school will be over in three weeks.

A pause.

HUMBERT   May I – I want to pluck some tissue paper out of that box. No, you're lying on it. There – let me – thanks.

LOLITA   Hold on. This bit has my lipstick on it.

HUMBERT   Does your mother allow lipstick?

LOLITA   She does not. I hide it here.

She indraws her pretty abdomen and produces the lipstick from under the band of her shorts.

HUMBERT   You're a very amusing little girl. Do you often go to the lake shore? I shaw – I mean, I saw that beautiful lake from the plane.

LOLITA   (*lying back with a sigh*) Almost never. It's quite a way.

And my mummy's too lazy to go there with me. Besides, we kids prefer the town pool.

HUMBERT   Who is your favorite recording star?

LOLITA   Oh, I dunno.

HUMBERT   What grade are you in?

LOLITA   This a quiz?

HUMBERT   I only want to know more about you. I know that you like to solarize your solar plexus. But what else do you like?

LOLITA   You shouldn't use such words, you know.

HUMBERT   Should I say 'what you dig'?

LOLITA   That's old hat.

Pause. Lolita turns over on her tummy. Humbert, awkwardly squatting, tense, twitching, mutely moaning, devours her with sad eyes; Lolita, a restless sunbather, sits up again.

HUMBERT   Is there anything special you'd like to be when
  you grow up?

LOLITA   What?

HUMBERT   I said—

Lolita, eyes shuttling, listens to the telephone ringing in the
remote hallway and to her mother attending to it.

LOLITA   (*yelling*) Mother, is it for me?

HUMBERT   I said what would you like to be?

Charlotte enters from dining room. Humbert, interrupted
in his furtive lust, scrambles up guiltily.

CHARLOTTE   It's Kenny. I suspect he wants to escort you to
  the big dance next month.

Lolita, groping, skipping on one foot, half-shod, shedding
beach slipper, whirling, taking off, bumping into humid
Humbert, laughing, exits barefoot.

CHARLOTTE   I'll be driving downtown in a few minutes.
  Like me to take you somewhere? Like to see Ramsdale?

HUMBERT   First I'd like to change. I never thought it would be so warm in Ramsdale.

CUT TO:

Humbert's Room. A few days have elapsed.

Humbert jots down last night's dream: A somewhat ripply shot reveals: a knight in full armor riding a black horse along a forest road. Three nymphets, one lame, are playing in a sun-shot glade. Nymphet Lolita runs toward Humbert, the Dark Knight, and promptly seats herself behind. His visor closes again. At a walking pace they ride deeper into the Enchanted Forest.

DISSOLVE TO NEXT ENTRY:

We are on the piazza. Humbert takes up a strategic position in rocker, with voluminous Sunday paper, in the vicinity of two parallel mats. He rocks and feigns to read. Exaggerate the volume of the paper.

Mother and daughter, both in two-piece bathing suits, come to sun themselves.

CUT TO:

Charlotte transposes jar of skin cream from farther mat (mat 2) to nearer mat (mat 1) and sits down on mat 1. Lolita yanks the comics section, and the family section, and the magazine section out of Humbert's paper and makes herself comfortable on mat 2.

There is an area of shade beyond her. Into this area Humbert, the furtive writer, gently rocking arrives in his ambling chair. He is now near Lolita.

Mother, far, supine, on mat 1 (now the farthest) lavishly anointed, exhibits herself to the sun; daughter, near, prone, on mat 2, showing Humbert her narrow nates and the seaside of her thighs, is immersed in the funnies.

Tenderly, the rocker rocks.
A mourning dove coos.

Charlotte gropes for her cigarettes but they are on mat 2, nearer to Humbert. She half rises and transfers herself to a new position, between him and her daughter, whom she shoves onto mat 1.

Charlotte, now on mat 2, near Humbert, fusses with lighter and casts a look at what he is grimly perusing: book review, a full-page ad:

WHEN THE LILACS LAST
most controversial novel of the year, 300,000 copies in print.

CHARLOTTE   Have you read that? *When the Lilacs Last*.

Humbert (*Clears his throat negatively.*)

CHARLOTTE   Oh, you should. It was given a rave review by
Adam Scott. It's about a man from the North and a girl
from the South who build up a beautiful relationship –
he is her father image and she is his mother image, but
later she discovers that as a child she had rejected her
father, and of course then he begins to identify her with
his possessive mother. You see, it works out this way: he
symbolizes the industrial North, and she symbolizes the
old-fashioned South, and—

LOLITA   (*casually*) and it's all silly nonsense.

CHARLOTTE   Dolores Haze, will you go up to your room
at once.

THREE WEEKS LATER, THE DAY OF THE SCHOOL DANCE.

FADE IN:

Kitchen – the Cat and the Morning Milk are let in
Charlotte, dainty-aproned, prepares breakfast for Humbert.
He enters, wearing a silk jacket with frogs.

HUMBERT   Good morning.

He sits down at the breakfast-niche table. Puts his elbows on it and meditates.

CHARLOTTE   Your bacon is ready.

Humbert considers the calendar on the wall and reaches into his back pocket for his wallet.

HUMBERT   My fourth week starts today.

CHARLOTTE   The time certainly flies. Monsieur is served.

HUMBERT   Fifty, and the eight twenty I owe you for the wine.

CHARLOTTE   No, it's sixty-two thirty-five: I paid for the *Glance* subscription, remember?

HUMBERT   Oh, I thought I had settled that.

He settles.

CHARLOTTE   Well, today is the big party. I bet she'll be pestering me all morning with her dance dress.

HUMBERT   Isn't that rather normal?

CHARLOTTE   Oh, yes. Definitely. I am all for these formal affairs. It may suggest to the hoyden she is some elements of gracious living.

(*Sits down at the table.*)

On the other hand – this is the end of that blessed era, school year. After which we'll be in for a period of slouching, disorganized boredom, vehement griping, feigned gagging, and all the rest of it.

HUMBERT   Hm. Aren't you exaggerating a bit?

CHARLOTTE   Oh, I leave that to her. Exaggerating is all hers. How I hate that diffused clowning – what they call 'goofing off.' In my day, which after all was only a couple of short decades ago, I never indulged in that sprawling, droopy, dopy-eyed style.

Lolita's voice is heard calling from the stairs.

CHARLOTTE   (*making a grimace of resignation*) See what I mean?

(*to Lolita*)

Yes? What is it?

LOLITA   (*carrying a slip*) You promised to fix this.

CHARLOTTE   Okay. Later.

LOLITA   (*to Humbert*) Well: coming to our hop?

CHARLOTTE   My daughter means: Do you intend to attend her school dance.

HUMBERT   I understood. Yes, thank you.

CHARLOTTE   We parents are not supposed to dance, of course.

LOLITA   What do you mean 'we'?

CHARLOTTE   (*flustered*) Oh, I mean adults. Parents and their friends.

Lolita exits singing.

HUMBERT   When does it start?

CHARLOTTE   Around four. I have some nice cold chicken for you afterwards.
                               (*seeing him rise*)
    Back to Baudelaire?

HUMBERT   Yes. I wanted to write in the garden but our neighbor's gardener has again set loose his motor mower or whatever you call it. It's deafening and sickening.

CHARLOTTE   I always think of it as an exhilarating, cheerful kind of sound. It brings back heaps of green summers and that kind of thing.

HUMBERT   You Americans are immune to noise.

CHARLOTTE   Anyway, Lesley stops work at noon, and you'll have lots of time before the party.

CUT TO:

The Garden

Humbert in the leafy shade, writes in his little black book. Mourning doves moan, cicadas whirr, a jet beyond sight and sound leaves its twin wakelines of silvery chalk in the cloudless sky. A mother's voice is heard calling somewhere up the street: 'Rosy! Ro-sy!' It is a very pleasant afternoon. Humbert consults his watch and glances up at the house. He gets up and strolls around, quietly trying to locate Lolita, whose voice is heard now in one room, now in another, while radio music comes from a third. Presently the bath water is heard performing, filling the tub, and then emptying into the drain. Humbert assembles his papers and walks to the house.

CUT TO:

The Living Room

Humbert feigning to read a magazine. Lolita swishes into the room wearing a pale billowy-skirted dance dress and pale satin pumps. She gracefully gyrates in front of Humbert.

LOLITA   Well? Do you like me?

HUMBERT   *(a phony judge)* Very much.

LOLITA   Adoration? Beauty in the mist? Too dreamy for words?

HUMBERT   I am often amazed at your verbal felicity, Lolita.

LOLITA   Check my back zipper, will you?

HUMBERT   There's some talc on your shoulder blades. May I remove it?

LOLITA   It depends.

HUMBERT   There.

LOLITA   Silly boy.

HUMBERT   I am three times your age.

LOLITA   Tell it to Mom.

HUMBERT   Why?

LOLITA   Oh, I guess you tell her everything.

HUMBERT   Wait a minute, Lolita. Don't waltz. A great poet
said: Stop, moment——. You are beautiful.

LOLITA   (feigning to call) Mother!

HUMBERT   Even when you play the fool.

LOLITA   That's not English.

HUMBERT   It's English enough for me.

LOLITA   D'you think this dress will make Kenny gulp?

HUMBERT   Who's Kenny?

LOLITA   He's my date for tonight. Jealous?

HUMBERT   In fact, yes.

LOLITA   Delirious? Dolly-mad?

HUMBERT   Yes, yes. Oh, wait!

LOLITA   And she flew away.

She flies away.

CUT TO:

The Landing
Humbert in a flannel suit and Charlotte in a glamorous gown (from Rosenthal, The Rose of Ramsdale, 50 South Main Street).

HUMBERT   Are we supposed to pick up her young man?

CHARLOTTE   No. He said he'd call for her. He lives two blocks from here. I'll bet she'll be prettying herself up to the last moment.

CUT TO:

The Driveway, Facing the Garage
Kenny helps Lolita to get into the back of the Haze two-door sedan. On the other side Humbert opens the driver's door for Charlotte. Daughter and Mother settle down with the

same preenings, the same rhythm of rustle and rerustle. Humbert starts walking around the car. Charlotte turns to Kenny, who is about to join Lolita.

CHARLOTTE   It's the new building, isn't it?

KENNY   Yes, ma'am.

CHARLOTTE   And Chestnut Street is closed for repairs?

KENNY   Yes. You have to turn after the church.

CHARLOTTE   Church? I thought it was the other way. Let me see—

LOLITA   Look, Kenny, why don't you get in beside Mother and direct her?

CHARLOTTE   Don't bother. I'll find it.

LOLITA   No, you won't. Please, Ken. And you come here.

Pats the seat next to her for Hum. Humbert, not without hitting his head against the lintel, climbs in and arranges his long limbs beside Lolita's bouffant skirt. The backrest of the passenger seat is pushed into place by Kenny who briskly seats himself next to Charlotte. She gives vent to her irritation by getting into reverse gear so abruptly that Lolita's purse leaps off her lap. Lolita and Humbert fumble for it.

LOLITA   (*laughing*) Easy, Mother.

CHARLOTTE   (*controlling herself*) No backseat driving, children.

And that is how Humbert obtains a few minutes of secret alliance with the nymphet. Deliberately, Lolita lets her hand rest on his, lets it slip into his, be enveloped by his.

CUT TO:

The New Hall
School punch and cookies are served in the gallery where teachers, parents, and their friends stand around in more or less garrulous groups. Music comes from the adjacent room, where the children are dancing. Charlotte introduces Humbert to the Chatfields.

CHARLOTTE   Ann, I want you to meet Professor Humbert, who is staying with us. Mrs Chatfield, Mr Chatfield.

How do you do's are exchanged.

MRS CHATFIELD (*to Charlotte*) Your Lolita looks perfectly enchanting in that cloud of pink. And the way she moves . . . Oh, my!

CHARLOTTE Thank you. And I was about to compliment you on your Phyllis. She's a darling. I understand you are sending her to the Climax Lake camp next week?

MRS CHATFIELD Yes. It's the healthiest place in the world. Run by a remarkable woman who believes in natural education. Which, of course, is progressive education combined with nature.

CHARLOTTE Say, who is that gentleman in the fancy waistcoat whom those women are mobbing? He looks familiar to me.

MRS CHATFIELD Oh, Charlotte! That's Clare Quilty, the playwright.

CHARLOTTE Of course. I quite forgot that our good old dentist had such a distinguished nephew. Didn't you adore his play which they had on the TV, *The Nymphet?*

CUT TO:

Another Part of the Gallery

84

In the meantime, after some dreary small talk with Mr Chatfield (Chatfield: I hear, Professor, you're going to teach at Beardsley College. I believe the wife of our president – I work for the Lakewood corporation – majored there in Home Economics.), Humbert drifts away. He wanders toward the dance floor and watches Lolita. The second or third slow dance has terminated and now a more boisterous strain hits the eardrum. Kenny and Lolita go through an energetic rock 'n' roll. Humbert leans his shoulder against a pillar. The camera picks out his Adam's apple.

CUT TO:

The Refreshments Table Near Which Charlotte Stands
She casts a questing look around. She has lost Humbert. Two gigglers in full skirts rustle past rapidly, heading for the ballroom.

FIRST GIRL   (*to second*) D'you know who that was? Clare Quilty! Oh, gosh, I got a real bang out of seeing him.

Charlotte's roving eye meets the gaze of the English teacher, Miss Adams, in the Quilty group. Miss Adams beckons to her. Charlotte floats thither. Introductions. Quilty is a tremendously successful phony, fortyish, roguish, baldish, with an obscene little mustache and a breezy manner which some find insulting and others just love.

CHARLOTTE   Oh, but I have met Mr Quilty before.
                    (*Elegantly appropriates him.*)
  Mr Quilty, I'm a great fan of yours.

QUILTY   Ah yes – ah yes—

CHARLOTTE   We met two years ago—

QUILTY   (*ironically purring*) An eternity—

CHARLOTTE   We had that luncheon in your honor at the
  club—

QUILTY   I can imagine it better than I recall it—

CHARLOTTE   And afterwards I showed you my garden and
  drove you to the airport—

QUILTY   Ah yes – magnificent airport.

He attempts to leave her orbit.

CHARLOTTE   Are you here for some time?

QUILTY   Oh, very briefly. Came to borrow a little cash from

Uncle Ivor. Excuse me, I think I must go now. They are putting on a play of mine in Parkington.

CHARLOTTE   Recently we had the pleasure of enjoying your *Nymphet* on Channel 5.

QUILTY   Great fun those channels. Well, it was a joy chatting about the past.

He moves away sidling into the crowd but stops suddenly and turns.

QUILTY   Say, didn't you have a little girl? Let me see. With a lovely name. A lovely lilting lyrical name—

CHARLOTTE   Lolita. Diminutive of Dolores.

QUILTY   Ah, of course: Dolores. The tears and the roses.

CHARLOTTE   She's dancing down there. And tomorrow she'll be having a cavity filled by your uncle.

QUILTY   I know; he's a wicked old man.

MISS ADAMS   Mr Quilty, I'm afraid I must tear you away. There's somebody come from Parkington to fetch you.

QUILTY   They can wait. I want to watch Dolores dance.

CUT TO:

Gallery Near Refreshments
Humbert appears.

CHARLOTTE   Where have you been all this time?

HUMBERT   Just strolling around.

CHARLOTTE   You look bored stiff, you poor man. Oh, hullo, Emily.

MRS GRAY   Good evening, Charlotte.

CHARLOTTE   Emily, this is Professor Humbert, who is staying with us. Mrs Gray.

Handshakes

MRS GRAY   Isn't it a lovely party?

CHARLOTTE   Is your darling Rose having a good time?

MRS GRAY   Oh, yes. You know, that child is insatiable. She got some new records for her birthday, so she plans to dance to them with Jack Beale and a couple of other kids after the party. She'd like to ask Lolita and Kenny. Could Lolita go with us from here? I'll give her supper.

CHARLOTTE   By all means. That's a delightful arrangement.

MRS GRAY   Wonderful. I'll bring her back. Around ten?

CHARLOTTE   Make it eleven. Thank you very much, Emily.

Mrs Gray joins another group.

CHARLOTTE   (taking Humbert's arm) And we can go home and have a nice cozy supper. Is that all right with you, cher monsieur?

CUT TO:

The Haze Living Room
Charlotte and Humbert have finished their cold chicken and salad and are now sipping liqueurs in the parlor.

CHARLOTTE   I consider crème de menthe to be the supremely divine nectar. This was given me by the Farlows. Cost them a small fortune, I suspect.

Humbert eyes casually a diminutive circular sticker with the price '$2.50.' They clink and drink.

CHARLOTTE   Well – *votre santé*. Now let's have some good music.

Humbert looks at his wristwatch, and then at the clock.

CHARLOTTE   Bartók or Bardinski?

HUMBERT   Doesn't matter – Bardinski, rather. I am not at all sure that those parties are properly chaperoned.

CHARLOTTE   What parties? What are you talking about?

HUMBERT   Parties at the homes of mothers. Record-playing sessions in the basement with the lights out.

CHARLOTTE   Oh, that! Really, Mr Humbert, I have more exciting things to think about than the manners of modern children. Look, let's change the subject. I mean, after all . . . can't we forget my tedious daughter? Here's a proposal: why don't I teach you some of the new dance steps? What say you?

HUMBERT   I don't even know the old ones. I'm an awkward tripper and have no sense of rhythm.

CHARLOTTE   Oh, come on. Come on, Humbert. May I call you Humbert? Especially as nobody can tell which it is of your two names? Or do you think the surname is pronounced a little different? In a deeper voice? No? Humbert . . . Which is it now, first or second?

HUMBERT   (*getting more and more uneasy*) I wouldn't know.

CHARLOTTE   (*going to the phonograph*) I'll teach you the cha-cha-cha.
       (*returning to her armrest perch and coyly questioning*)
Cha-cha-cha?

He rises from his low armchair, not because he wants to be taught but because the ripe lady might roll into his lap if he remains seated. The record clacks and croons. Charlotte demonstrates her ankles. Bored, helpless, Humbert, hands clasped on his fly, stands looking at her moving feet.

CHARLOTTE   It's as simple as that.
              (*Darts to the phonograph to restart*)

Now come here, Humbert.

(smiling)

That was not the surname.

Humbert surrenders. She leads him this way and that in a tactile drill. Releases him for a moment.

CHARLOTTE   Now do like this with your hands. More life. Fine. Now clasp me.

CUT TO:

Lawn Street in Front of No. 342

A station wagon with Mrs Gray at the wheel, two or three boys and Lolita, stops at the lawn curb. Rigmarole of resonant good-byes. Car drives off. Lolita runs up the porch steps.

CUT TO:

Living Room

Charlotte pulsates and palpates Humbert's (stuffed) shoulder.

CHARLOTTE   In certain lights, when you frown like that, you remind me of somebody. A college boy I once danced with, a young blue-blooded Bostonian, my first glamor date.

The Door Chimes go into action.

CHARLOTTE   (*shutting off the record player*) Oh, darn it!

Humbert lets in Lolita.

LOLITA   (*casually*) Hullo, sweetheart.

She saunters into the living room.

CHARLOTTE   Well, you came earlier than I hoped – I mean, I did not hope you would be back so early.

LOLITA   You two seem to have been living it up here?

CHARLOTTE   How was your party?

LOLITA   Lousy.

CHARLOTTE   I thought Kenny looked cute.

LOLITA   I'm calling him Shorty from now on. I never realized he was so short. And dumb.

CHARLOTTE   Well, you've had your fling – and now to bed, my dear.

During this exchange, Humbert in abject adoration, gloats over the limp nymphet who has now filled a low chair with her foamy skirt and thin arms.

HUMBERT   You remind me of a sleepy flamingo.

LOLITA   Cut it out, Hum.

CHARLOTTE   Do you permit, Mr Humbert, this rude child—

LOLITA   Oh, Mother, give us a break. May I take these cookies upstairs?

CHARLOTTE   Well, if you want to pamper your pimples—

LOLITA   I don't have pimples!

CHARLOTTE   Take anything you want but go.

LOLITA   All in good time.
                    (*Stretches.*)
    Did you talk to the famous author?

CHARLOTTE   Yes. Please go.

LOLITA   Rose is crazy about him. Okay, I go. Bye-bye.

Indolently she moves out of the room. At the bottom of the stairs – as seen from the parlor – she stops, lingers, with her fair arm stretched out on the rail and her cheek on her arm. Meditates in this posture.

HUMBERT   What author did she mean?

CHARLOTTE   The author of *The Nymphet*. He's the nephew – will you *please* go upstairs, Lolita?

Lolita sighs, grimaces, and slowly comes into lazy motion.

HUMBERT   Thanks for this charming evening, Mrs Haze.

CHARLOTTE   Thank *you*, Mr Humbert. Oh, sit down. Let's have a nightcap.

HUMBERT   No, I think not. I think I'll go up to bed.

CHARLOTTE   It's quite early yet, you know.

HUMBERT   I know. But my neuralgia is about to strike . . . With heartburn, an old ally.

CUT TO:

Stairs and Upper Landing
The nymphet is still there, now sliding up dreamily, half-reclining on the banisters. Humbert and she reach the upper landing together.

HUMBERT   Good night, Lolita.

LOLITA   Huh?

HUMBERT   I said 'good night, Lolita.'

LOLITA   Night.

She totters to her room.

CUT TO:

Humbert's Study, a Couple of Days Later
Humbert in his room is tape-recording his lecture, 'Baudelaire and Poe.' He plays back the last sentences:

HUMBERT'S VOICE   Before discussing Baudelaire's methods of translating Poe, let me turn for a moment to the romantic lines, let me turn to the romantic lines in which the great American neurotic commemorates his marriage to a thirteen-year-old girl, his beautiful Annabel Lee.

(*The machine clicks and stops.*)

Now Lolita is heard bouncing a tennis ball. Humbert softly opens his door and listens. She is in the hallway. Humming to herself, Lolita walks upstairs plucking at the banisters and quietly clowning. Bluejeans, shirt. Humbert is back in his chair, Lolita is on the landing. With a good deal of shuffling and scraping she comes into Humbert's room. She potters around, fidgets, moves variously in the neighborhood of his desk.

LOLITA   (*bending close to him*) What are you drawing?

HUMBERT   (*considering his drawing*) Is it you?

LOLITA   (*peering still more closely – she is somewhat shortsighted*) Is it?

HUMBERT   Or perhaps it is more like a little girl I knew when I was your age.

One of the drawers of the desk comes out by itself in a kind of organic protractile movement, disclosing a photograph of Humbert's first love in a Riviera setting: a sidewalk café near a peopled *plage*.

LOLITA   Where's that?

HUMBERT   In a princedom by the sea. Monaco.

LOLITA   Oh, I know where that is.

HUMBERT   I'm sure you do. Many and many a year ago. Thirty, to be exact.

LOLITA   What was her name?

HUMBERT   Annabel – curiously enough.

LOLITA   Why curiously enough?

HUMBERT   Never mind. And this was me.

Same snapshot, same setting, but now in the photograph the chair next to Annabel is occupied by young Humbert, a moody lad. Morosely, he takes off his white cap as if acknowledging recognition, and dons it again.

Actually it is the same actress as the one that plays Lolita but wearing her hair differently, etc.

LOLITA   She doesn't look like me at all. Were you in love with her?

HUMBERT   Yes. Three months later she died. Here, on that beach, you see the angels envying her and me.

He clears his throat.

LOLITA   (*now bolding the photo*) That's not angels. That's Garbo and Abraham Lincoln in terrycloth robes.

She laughs. A pause. As she bends her brown curls over the picture, Humbert puts his arm around her in a miserable imitation of blood relationship, and still studying the snapshot – which now shows young Humbert alone – Lolita slowly sinks to a half-sitting position upon his knee.

The erotic suspense is interrupted.

CHARLOTTE   (*shouting up from hallway*) Lolita! Will you come down, please?

LOLITA   (*without changing her position*) I'm busy! What d'you want?

CHARLOTTE   Will you come down at once?

At the Foot of the Stairs
Charlotte and Lolita.

CHARLOTTE   Now, firstly I want you to change. Put on a dress: I'm going to the Chatfields, and I want you to come too. Secondly: I simply forbid you to disturb Mr Humbert. He's a writer and should not be disturbed. And if you make that grimace again, I think I'll slap you.

CUT TO:

Humbert Transcribing from Pad to Diary
speaks as he deciphers his jottings.

HUMBERT   (*in a low faltering voice*) The hag said she would slap Lolita, my Lolita. For thirty years I mourned Annabel, and watched nymphets playing in parks, and never once dared—. And now Annabel is dead, and Lolita is alive – my darling – 'my darling – my life and my bride.'

CUT TO:

Dinner with Charlotte

HUMBERT   And where is your daughter tonight?

CHARLOTTE   Oh, I left her at the Chatfields' – she's going to a movie with Phyllis. By the way, I have a glorious surprise for you.

HUMBERT   What surprise? One of your dramatic sweets?

CHARLOTTE   Wrong, Monsieur. Try again.

HUMBERT   A new light bulb.

CHARLOTTE   Nope.

HUMBERT   I give up.

CHARLOTTE   After tomorrow, Lolita is leaving for summer camp.

HUMBERT   (trying to conceal his consternation) Really? This is only June, you know.

CHARLOTTE   Exactly. I think of myself as a good average mother, but I confess I'm looking forward to ten full weeks of tranquility. Another slice of beef? No?

HUMBERT   Toothache.

CHARLOTTE   Oh, you poor man! Let me have Dr Quilty take care of you.

HUMBERT   No, no, don't bother. It will pass. How far is that camp?

CHARLOTTE   About two hundred miles. It was a stroke of genius on Mama's part. I arranged everything without telling little Lolita, who dislikes Phyllis for no reason at all. Sprang it upon her at the Chatfields', so she could not talk back. Ain't I clever? Little Lolita I hope will be mollified by the movie. I just could not have faced her tonight.

HUMBERT   Are you sure she will be happy at that camp?

CHARLOTTE   She'd better. She'll go riding there, which is much healthier than banging a tennis ball against the garage door. And camp will be much healthier than moping here, and pursuing shy scholarly gentlemen. Camp will teach Dolores to grow in many ways – health, knowledge, temper. And particularly in the sense of responsibility toward other people. Shall we take these candles with us and sit for a while on the piazza? Or do you want to go to bed and nurse that tooth?

HUMBERT   Tooth.

He slowly ascends the stairs. Charlotte calls after him.

CHARLOTTE   By the way — I told Lolita you had advised it. I
   thought your authority
      (*crystalline little laugh*)
   would have more weight than mine.

Night. Humbert in His Room at the Window
Car stops at 342 Lawn Street.

CHARLOTTE   Oh, do come in for a moment, Mary. I forgot
   to check a few items on that list for the girls. Do come in.

MRS CHATFIELD   Well, just for a minute.

CHARLOTTE   We excuse you, Dolores. Straight to bed like a
   good girl.

Humbert meets Lolita on the landing.

HUMBERT   (*attempting small talk*) How was the picture?

Without answering, Lolita marches toward her room.

HUMBERT   What's the matter, Lolita?

LOLITA   Nothing. Except that you are revolting.

HUMBERT   I did not do anything. It's a mistake. I swear.

LOLITA   (haughtily) I'm through with you. *Envoyez votre jeune fille au camp, Madame.* Double-crosser!

HUMBERT   I never said that! It's not even French! I'd do anything to have you stay here. I really would.

She slams the door.

CUT TO:

Humbert Dictates His 'Baudelaire and Poe' lecture into the recorder.

HUMBERT   Other commentators, commentators of the Freudian school of thought. No. Commentators of the Freudian prison of thought. Hm. Commentators of the Freudian nursery-school of thought, have maintained that Edgar Poe married the child Virginia Clemm merely to keep her mother near him. He – I quote – had found in his mother-in-law Mrs Clemm the maternal image he had been seeking all his life. What piffle! Listen now to the passion and despair breathing in the letter he addresses to Virginia's mother on August 29, 1835, when he feared that his thirteen-year-old little sweetheart would be taken away to be educated in another home. 'I am blinded with tears while writing this letter . . . My

last, my last, my only hold on life is cruelly torn away . . .
My agony is more than I can bear . . . for love like mine
can never be gotten over . . . It is useless to disguise the
truth . . . that I shall never behold her again . . .'

CUT TO:

Humbert's Alarm Clock Rings
Seven thirty. He hurries to the window.

SHOT FROM ABOVE

The maid helps to put a bag into the car. Lolita is leaving
for camp.

CHARLOTTE   Hurry up, Lolita.

Lolita is now half in and about to pull the car door to, but
suddenly she looks up – and scurries back into the house.

CHARLOTTE   (*furiously*) Dolores, get back into the car
    immediately!

She does not heed her mother's shout. She runs upstairs. She
wears her Sunday frock – gay cotton, with ample skirt and
fitting bodice. Humbert has come out on the landing. She
stomps upstairs and next moment is in his arms. Hers is a
perfectly innocent impulse, an affectionate bright farewell.

As she rises on tiptoe to kiss him, he evades her approaching lips and imprints a poetical kiss on her brow.

CHARLOTTE   (*Blows the horn.*)

Lolita flies downstairs, gestures up to him in a ballerina-like movement of separation, and is gone.

The blond leg is drawn in, the car door slams, is reslammed as the car gathers momentum to the sound of the collie's *Bark*.

CUT TO:

Silence – except for the birds outside and the young Negro maid in the kitchen. The telephone *rings*.

MAID   No, there's no Miss Lee here. You must have got the wrong number. You're welcome.

Humbert has remained standing on the landing between his open door and the open door of Lolita's room opposite.

He surveys her deserted room. Abandoned clothes lie on the rumpled bed. A pair of white shoes with roller skates on the floor. He rolls one on his palm.

There is a full-page advertisement (back cover of magazine) tacked onto the wall: a distinguished playwright solemnly smoking ('I can write without a pen, but not without a Drome'). After a moment's brooding, Humbert goes to his room and incontinently starts to pack. Knock on his door.

The maid Louise knocks on Humbert's door. He opens. She hands him a letter.

LOUISE   Mrs Haze asked me to give you this, Mr Humbert.

Humbert inspects envelope.

LOUISE   I'll be doing the girl's room now. And when I've done I'd like to do yours. And then I'll go.

Humbert, puckering brow at envelope, walks slowly back to his desk.

The neat handwriting of the address turns momentarily into a schoolgirl's scribble, then reverts to the ladylike hand. He opens the letter.

Humbert, in a classical pattern of comments, ironical asides, and well-mouthed readings, scans the letter. In one SHOT, he is dressed as a gowned professor, in another as a routine Hamlet, in a third, as a dilapidated Poe. He also appears as himself.

HUMBERT   'This is a confession, this is an avowal of love.'
No signature – what, no signature? Ah, here it is. Good
God! 'I have loved you from the moment I saw you. I am
a lonely woman and you are the love of my love.' Of 'my
life,' I suppose.

As in a pimp's sample album, Charlotte appears in various
unattractive attitudes and positions.

HUMBERT   'Now, my dearest, *mon cher, cher Monsieur*,' that's a
new one: she thinks it's a term of endearment. 'Now, you
have read this, now you know. So will you please, *at once*,
pack and leave: this is a landlady's order. I shall be back by
dinner time if I do eighty both ways and don't have an
accident. But what would it matter?' I beg your pardon: it
matters a lot *one* way. 'You see, *chéri*,' ah, French improv-
ing, 'if you decided to stay, if I found you there when I got
home, it would mean only one thing – that you want me
as much as I do you – as a lifelong mate; and that you are
ready to link up your life with mine forever and be a
father to my little girl.' My dear Mrs Haze, or rather Mrs
Clemm, I am passionately devoted to your daughter.

Pensively, with a dawning smile, Humbert starts to take out,
one by one, slowly, then faster, the articles he had already
packed. Then he goes into an awkward and grotesque jig

(in striking contrast to his usual mournful and dignified demeanor). Dancing, he descends the stairs.

CUT TO:

Humbert
making a long-distance call.

HUMBERT   Is this Camp Q on Lake Climax?
(*Listens.*)
Is Mrs Haze still there? She brought her daughter today.
(*Listens.*)
Oh, I see. Could I speak to Dolores Haze, Lolita?

He listens, waits.

LOLITA   Hullo?

Now both parties are visible in a montage arrangement, with the camp's various activities illustrated at the corners as in a publicity folder.

HUMBERT   I have news for you.

LOLITA   Hullo?

HUMBERT   This is Humbert. I have news for you.

She is holding a big pup.

LOLITA   Oh, how are you? I have a friend here who wants
to say hullo.

The pup licks the receiver.

HUMBERT   Listen, Lolita. I'm going to marry your mother.
I'm going to propose to her as soon as she's back.

LOLITA   Gee, that's swell. Look, I've got to get rid of this
beast, he's too heavy. One sec. There.

HUMBERT   Will you come to the wedding?

LOLITA   What? I can't hear too well.

HUMBERT   Will you come to the wedding?

LOLITA   I'm not sure. No, I guess, I have to stay here. It's a
fabulous place! There's a water-sports competition sched-
uled. And I'm learning to ride. And my tentmate is the
Ramsdale junior swimming champion. And—

DISSOLVE TO:

The Honeymooners
A month has elapsed. Kitchen at 342 Lawn Street.

Charlotte (radiant and demure, in tight velvet pants and bed slippers) prepares breakfast for two in the cute breakfast nook of the chrome-and-plastic kitchen. Shadows of sun and leaves play on the white refrigerator. Humbert, in the wake of his yawn, enters (dressing gown, rumpled hair).

Charlotte makes him a jocular Oriental bow. His face twitching with neuralgia, he glances at the scrambled eggs and starts clawing at a cupboard.

CHARLOTTE   What are you looking for?

HUMBERT   Pepper.

A tennis ball jumps out of the cupboard.

HUMBERT   I wonder if she can play tennis at that damned camp.

CHARLOTTE   I could not care less. Look what the *Ramsdale Journal* has to say about us. Here. Society Column.

Humbert glances at paper.

CHARLOTTE   Isn't that something? Look at your elegant
bride. 'Mr Edgar H. Humbert, writer and explorer, weds
the former—' I never knew you were Edgar.

HUMBERT   Oh, I called up a reporter and thought I'd inject
a little glamor.

He yawns again.

CHARLOTTE   And what have you explored?

HUMBERT   Madame should not ask vulgar questions.

CHARLOTTE   (very arch) And Monsieur has certainly a grand
sense of humor.

Charlotte Is Showing Bored Humbert
some of her treasures. A lamplit evening at the Humbert
residence.

HUMBERT   (suddenly interested) Hey, a gun.

He examines a small automatic.

CHARLOTTE   It belonged to Mr Haze.

HUMBERT   Hm. And then suddenly it went off.

CHARLOTTE   It's not loaded.

HUMBERT   That's what they all say: 'I did not know it was
    loaded.'

CHARLOTTE   Who – they?

HUMBERT   Boy shoots girl, banker shoots bitch, rapist
    shoots therapist.

CHARLOTTE   I told you many times that I appreciated your
    humor, but now and then it is misplaced. This is a sacred
    weapon, a tragic treasure. Mr Haze acquired it when he
    thought he had cancer. He wanted to spare me the sight
    of his sufferings. Happily, or unhappily, he was hospital-
    ized before he could use it. And this is me just before I
    married him.

In the snapshot Charlotte at twenty-five resembles her
daughter more than she does now. Humbert is moved.

HUMBERT   I like this one tremendously. May I have it?

CHARLOTTE   Oh, my dear, of course! Everything is yours.
   Wait, let me inscribe it.

Charlotte writes on the photo: For my chéri Humbert from
his Charlotte. April 1946 [if it is now 1960.]

CUT TO:

Humbert and Wife in Car
He is driving her to the lake.

HUMBERT   What's that palazzo? A brothel?

CHARLOTTE   That's Jerome McFate's house. He's manager
   of our bank, if you please.

HUMBERT   What a name for a banker.

They leave the car at the edge of the pine forest and walk
through it to the lake. They are sandaled and robed.

CHARLOTTE   Do you know, Hum, I have one most ambi-
   tious dream. I should love to get hold of a real French
   servant like that German girl the Talbots had, and have
   her live in the house.

HUMBERT   No room.

CHARLOTTE   Come.
                    (*with a quizzical smile*)
Surely, *chéri*, you underestimate the possibilities of the
Humbert home. We would put her in Lo's room. I
intended to make a guest room of that hole anyway. It's
the coldest and meanest in the whole house.

HUMBERT   And where, pray, will you put your daughter
when you get your guest or your maid?

CHARLOTTE   (*softly exhaling and raising one eyebrow*) Ah! Little
Lo, I'm afraid, does not enter the picture at all, at all. Little Lo goes straight from camp to a good boarding school
with strict discipline. I have it all mapped out, you need
not worry.

The Brilliant Lake
There is a moored raft some forty yards off the lake shore.
Humbert and Charlotte on the sandy strip. He, sitting, hands
clasping knees, in a dreadful frame of mind; she, serenely
and luxuriously reclining.

HUMBERT   The sand is filthy. Some oaf has been walking
his filthy dog. And there's a chewing-gum wrapper.

CHARLOTTE   Oh, those are just leftovers from Sunday.

There's not a soul anywhere. It's not at all like the east end of the lake where they built the casino.

HUMBERT   One would think there would be some decrepit cripple with a piked stick cleaning up on Mondays.

CHARLOTTE   No, I don't think so. In fact, even on week-ends there is hardly anybody bathing at this end. This is the restricted part. We are alone, sweetheart, you and me. And we'll remain so forever. Just you and me. A red cent for your thoughts.

HUMBERT   I was wondering if you could make it to that raft, or whatever it is. I loathe this dirty gray sand. Out there we could sunbathe in the
                    (wrinkling his nose)
nude, as you genteel Americans say.

CHARLOTTE   I doubt it. This American's back is burnt as it is. Besides, I couldn't swim that far.

HUMBERT   Nonsense. Your merman will be at your side.

CHARLOTTE   How deep would you say it is?

HUMBERT   Twice your height. Two wives.

CHARLOTTE   I'm sure to panic and drown.

HUMBERT   All right, all right. If you don't want to swim, let's go home. This place bores me stiff.

CHARLOTTE   Well, I can always try.

DISSOLVE:

Humbert and Charlotte
reach the raft.

CHARLOTTE   Ah! I thought I would never make it.

HUMBERT   Yes, but there's still the return voyage.

An airplane passes overhead.

CHARLOTTE   That's a private plane, isn't it?

HUMBERT   I've no idea. That guardian angel has been circling above the lake during our entire swim. I think he's leaving now.

A butterfly passes in shorebound flight.

CHARLOTTE   Can butterflies swim?

HUMBERT   (*indistinct answer*)

CHARLOTTE   Shall I risk taking off my bra?

HUMBERT   I don't give a damn.

CHARLOTTE   Will you give a damn if I kiss you?

He grunts. Pause.

DISSOLVE TO:

Another Angle

CHARLOTTE   Not a cloud, not a soul, not a sound.

HUMBERT   Let's swim back.

CHARLOTTE   What – already? We haven't been here ten minutes.

HUMBERT   Come on, let's go in.

CHARLOTTE   Please, Humbert, stop pushing me.

HUMBERT   I'll roll you in the water.

CHARLOTTE   You'll do nothing of the sort. We are going to stay here till the Farlows come.

HUMBERT   They won't be here for another hour.

CHARLOTTE   Relax and enjoy yourself. Tell me about your first wife.

HUMBERT   To hell with her.

CHARLOTTE   You are very rude, sweetheart.

HUMBERT   I'm very bored. Look here. The Farlows will retrieve you. I'm going home. *Au revoir*.

He dives and swims away.

CHARLOTTE   Oh, please. Wait! I'm coming too. Oh, wait!

He swims on without turning his head. Awkwardly, she lowers herself into the water. He is now nearing the shore. She starts swimming and almost immediately is seized with a cramp.

A neat little diagram shows the relative positions of a

drowning person (one arm sticking out of the water), a stationary raft, and the shoreline at equal distance from the sufferer.

For a few seconds, Humbert floats motionless in a vertical position, his chin just above the surface, his eyes fixed on floundering Charlotte. There should be something reptilian and spine-chilling in his expectant stare. Then, as she gasps, and sinks, and splashes, and screams, he dashes toward her, reaching her in a few strokes.

He helps her out onto the beach.

CHARLOTTE   (*still panting*) You know — you know — for one
    moment — I thought you — would not come to save me —
    your eyes — you looked at me with dreadful, dreadful eyes—

He soothes her in a humid embrace.

CUT TO:

Car
They are driving home.

CHARLOTTE   You know, it's so funny. A drowning person is
    said to recollect his entire life but all I remembered was

last night's dream. You were offering me some pill or potion, and a voice said: Careful, Isolda, that's poison.

HUMBERT   Rather pointless – what?

The car pulls up at 342 Lawn Street. They get out.

HUMBERT   Here, take this towel. Oh, blast it! I forgot my sunglasses on that bloody beach.

CHARLOTTE   Were they very expensive?

HUMBERT   (*still searching*) I loved them. They made a kind of taupe twilight. I bought them in St-Topaz, never mislaid them before.

CHARLOTTE   Why don't you drive back to the lake and find them? Kiss?
          (*Humbert obliges.*)
     Meantime I'll tidy up—

CUT TO:

The 'Semi-Studio'
Taking advantage of Humbert's absence, Charlotte lovingly cleans his den. A small key drops out of a jacket. She considers

it for a moment with amused perplexity; then tries it in the lock of a certain small drawer. The treasure turns out to be a little black book, Humbert's dark diary. She flips it open. Her daughter's name leers at her from every page. But the microscopic script is hard to decipher. She snatches up a magnifying glass. In its bland circle Humbert's jottings leap into formidable life:

'. . . but her grotesque mother butted in . . . Friday: She is a bitch, that Haze woman. She is sending my darling away. Alas, Lolita! Farewell, my love! If the old cat expects me to stay on, she is—'

CUT TO:

Humbert
opening the door of his living room. Charlotte, with her back to him, is writing at the desk in the far corner.

HUMBERT   I'm back. Couldn't find them.

Charlotte does not answer but her writing hand stops. She turns slowly toward him revealing a face disfigured by grief and wrath.

CHARLOTTE   'The Haze woman,' 'the old cat,' 'the obnoxious mama,' 'the – the old stupid Haze,' is no longer your dupe.

HUMBERT   But what—

CHARLOTTE   You're a monster, you're a detestable, abominable, criminal fraud! If you come near me, I'll scream out the window.

HUMBERT   But really—

CHARLOTTE   I'm leaving today. This is all yours. Only you'll never, never see that miserable brat again.

HUMBERT   I can explain everything.

CHARLOTTE   Get out of here. Oh, I can see it all now. You tried to drown me, you would have shot me or poisoned me next. You disgusting satyr. I'm applying for a job in Parkington and you'll never see me again.

Furiously, she rummages for the stamps she needs. The convex block of them has fallen on the carpet. Tears off one, two. Fast and furious. Thumps on envelope.

CUT TO:

Humbert
goes swiftly upstairs to his study. There he contemplates the open and empty drawer. He crosses over to the bedroom and starts looking for his diary, which he suspects she has

hidden. After some rapid ransacking, he finds it under her pillow. He walks downstairs again.

CUT TO:

Kitchen
He opens the refrigerator. Its roar, as well as the crepitation of the ice cubes in their cells under warm water, the noisy faucet, the fussing with the whiskey and soda, the banging of cupboard doors, and Humbert's own mutter, drown the *Sounds* from the street (such as the hideous screech of desperate brakes).

HUMBERT   (*muttering*) Tell her . . . Misunderstood . . . Civilized people . . . Brought you a drink . . . Don't be ridiculous . . . Fragments of novel . . . Provisional names . . . The notes you found were fragments of a novel . . .

He has now prepared his defense. Carrying the two glasses he leaves the kitchen.

CUT TO:

Hallway-Door of Living Room Slightly Ajar
As Humbert approaches the *Telephone Rings* on table near door. He places the glasses on the table and lifts the receiver.

VOICE   This is Lesley Tompson, the gardener next door. Your wife, sir, has been run over and you'd better come quick.

HUMBERT   Nonsense. My wife is here—
                    (*Pushes the door open.*)
man saying you've been killed, Charlotte . . .

The room is empty. He turns back, the front door is not shut, the receiver is still throbbing on the table. He rushes out. 'The far side of our steep little street presented a peculiar sight. A big black limousine had climbed Miss Opposite's sloping lawn at an angle from the sidewalk.'

The picture now is a still. Humbert surveys the scene: The body on the sidewalk, the old gentleman resting on the grass near the car, various people attracted by the accident, the unfortunate driver, two policemen, and the cheerful collie walking from group to group.

A photographer from the Traffic Division is taking a picture.

In a projection room it is shown to a bunch of policemen by an instructor with a pointer:

THE INSTRUCTOR   Now, this is the picture of a real accident. To the ordinary spectator who has just arrived on
the scene the situation may seem very, very unusual: it is
not so, really. The lap robe there, on the sidewalk, covers
a dead woman. The elderly person here on the grass is
not dead but comfortably recovering from a mild heart
attack. His nephew, the fat fellow talking to the police
officers, was driving him to a birthday party when they
ran over this woman. This is their car up on the slope of
the lawn where it came to rest after leaving the road. It
was moving down the street like so.

A diagram now appears with arrows and dotted lines.

INSTRUCTOR   The driver was trying to avoid the dog. The
woman was crossing here. She was in a great hurry to
mail a letter but never made it to the mailbox.
                    (*still picture again*)
That man there who stands looking stunned is her
husband.

The still comes to life. A little girl picks up the letter which
Charlotte was about to post and hands it to Humbert. Old
Mr Jung is sobbing uncontrollably. The ambulance arrives.
The Farlows lead Humbert away.

Act Two

The Office of Camp Q, a Stucco Cottage – early afternoon
The camp mistress hangs up and calls a camp counselor.

CAMP MISTRESS (*to counselor*) Mr Humbert has just tele-
phoned. Lolita's mother has been killed in a street accident.

COUNSELOR Oh, my gosh.

CAMP MISTRESS He's on the way here to fetch her. He
asked me to tell her that her mother is sick. Find the girl,
please, and have her get ready to leave. By the way, where's
that lazy son of mine – make him move the garbage cans
to the back of the shed.

CUT TO:

The Search for Lolita
Her name is cried out in different voices and keys at various
points. We pass in review the awfully quaint cabins and tents
in a pine grove. The camera looks behind trees and bushes.

Two shadows hastily unclip in the undergrowth. Distant cries swell and recede.

Lolita! Lolita!

CUT TO:

Dirt Road

leading to cabins and tents. Humbert drives up. Charlie, the camp mistress's fourteen-year-old-son, is rolling an empty garbage can across the road.

HUMBERT   (*out of car window, pointing questioningly*) Is that the office?

Charlie mutely directs him with a jerk of his thumb.

CUT TO:

Camp Office — Humbert and the Camp Mistress

CAMP MISTRESS   (*computing the bill and not raising her eyes from her writing*) What a terrible accident! When is the funeral?

HUMBERT   Oh, that was yesterday. It was decided not to have the child attend. Spare her the shock.

He settles the bill.

CAMP MISTRESS   Thank you. The poor kid. Here's your receipt.

Lolita arrives, dragging and bumping her valise.

LOLITA   Hi.

He lets his hand rest on her head and takes up her bag. She wears her brightest gingham and saddle oxfords.

As Humbert and she walk toward the car, Lolita waves to Charlie.

LOLITA   Good-bye, Charlie boy!

Moodily, not without some regret, he follows her with his pale, fair-lashed eyes.

CUT TO:

The Hot Car (inside)
She settles down beside Humbert, slaps a prompt fly on her lovely knee; then, her mouth working violently on chewing gum, she rapidly cranks down the window. The car speeds through the striped and speckled forest.

LOLITA   (*dutifully*) How's mother?

HUMBERT   It's something abdominal.

LOLITA   Abominable?

HUMBERT   No, abdominal. A stomach ailment. She's been moved to a hospital in the country. Not far from Lepingsville.

LOLITA   Are we going to, what you called it – Lepersville?

HUMBERT   Lepingsville. Yes, I expect we'll have to hang around a bit while she gets better or at least a little better. And then we'll go to the mountains. Is that a peachy idea?

LOLITA   Uh-huh. How far is it to her hospital?

HUMBERT   Oh, two hundred miles. Did you have a marvelous time at the camp?

LOLITA   Uh-huh.

HUMBERT   Sorry to leave?

LOLITA   Un-un.

HUMBERT   Talk, Lolita, don't grunt. Tell me something.

LOLITA   What thing, *Dad?*

HUMBERT   Any old thing.

LOLITA   Okay if I call you that?

HUMBERT   Quite.

LOLITA   It's a sketch, you know—

HUMBERT   A what?

LOLITA   A scream: you falling for my mummy.

HUMBERT   There are also such things as mutual respect and spiritual happiness.

LOLITA   Sure, sure.

(The lull in the dialogue is filled in with some landscapes).

HUMBERT   Look at all those cows on the hillside.

LOLITA   I'll vomit if I see another cow.

HUMBERT   You know I missed you terribly, Lolita Lo. Really and truly.

LOLITA   I didn't. Fact I've been revoltingly unfaithful to you, but it doesn't matter a bit because you've stopped caring for me, anyway. You drive much faster than my mummy, mister.

He slows down from 70 to 50 as seen on speedometer.

HUMBERT   Why do you think I've stopped caring for you?

LOLITA   Well, you haven't kissed me yet, have you?

Humbert wobbles into the roadside weeds and stops. She cuddles up to him. A highway patrol car draws up alongside.

POLICEMAN   Having trouble?

HUMBERT   No, no. I just wanted to look at the map.

LOLITA   (*eagerly leaning across H.H. and speaking with unusual urbanity*) I'm afraid we have parked where we shouldn't but there was some question of taking a short cut, and we thought—

POLICEMAN   Well, if you want to stop there's a picnic area three hundred yards from here.

LOLITA   Oh, thank you.

The beetle-browed trooper gives the little colleen his toothiest smile and glides away. Lolita presses a fluttering hand to her breastbone.

LOLITA   The fruithead! He should have nabbed you.

HUMBERT   Why me, for heaven's sake?

LOLITA   Because the speed limit in this bum state is fifty. No, don't slow down. He's gone now.

HUMBERT   We have still quite a stretch, so be a good girl.

LOLITA   That light was red. I've never seen such driving.

They roll silently through a silent townlet.

HUMBERT   You said you'd been – I don't know – naughty? Don't you want to tell me about that?

LOLITA   Are you easily shocked?

HUMBERT   No. What did you do?

LOLITA   Well, I joined in all the activities that were offered.

HUMBERT   *Ensuite?*

LOLITA   Ansooit, I was taught to live happily and richly with others and to develop a wholesome personality. Be a cake, actually.

HUMBERT   Yes, I saw that in the camp booklet.

LOLITA   We loved the sings around the fire.

HUMBERT   Anything else?

LOLITA   (*rhapsodically*) The Girl Scout's motto is also mine. My duty is to be useful to animals. I obey orders. I am cheerful. And I am absolutely filthy in thought, word, and deed.

HUMBERT   Is that all, young wit?

LOLITA   We baked in a reflector oven. Isn't that terrific? Oh, gee! We made shadowgraphs. We identified the three birds teacher knew. What fun!

HUMBERT   *C'est bien tout?*

LOLITA   *C'est.* Except one little thing that I may tell you later in the dark.

CUT TO:

The Road

A sign by the side of the road says 8 MILES TO ENCHANTED HUNTERS. Further, another sign BRICELAND, ELEV. 759 FEET. Finally a sign at a crossing 3 MILES TO ENCHANTED HUNTERS — YE UNFORGETTABLE INN.

LOLITA   Oh, let's stop at the unforgettable!

HUMBERT   I've reserved rooms in a tourist home at Lepingsville, but—

LOLITA   Oh, please. Let's go to the Enchanted. It's a famous romantic place. We'll make people think you've eloped with me. Please!

. . . And there it was, marvelously and inexorably there, at the top of a graded curve under spectral trees, at the top of a graveled drive — the pale palace of The Enchanted Hunters.

LOLITA   (*getting out of the car*) Wow! Looks swank.

Old Tom, a hunchbacked and hoary Negro, takes out the bags.

It is a large old heavily quaint family hotel with a pillared porch. Humbert and Lolita enter the ornate lounge. Two conventions, a medical one on the ebb and a floral one on the flow, throng the reception rooms.

Lolita sinks down on her haunches to caress a cocker spaniel sprawling and melting under her hand.

HUMBERT   (*At the reception desk talks to Mr Potts, the clerk, indistinctly*)
I want a room for the night.

POTTS   Excuse me, sir?

HUMBERT   I want two rooms or one room with two beds.

POTTS   I'm not sure we can accommodate you. We have the overflow of a convention of doctors from another hotel and we also have a reunion of rose growers just budding. Is it for you and your little girl?

He looks kindly at Lolita.

HUMBERT   Her mother is ill. We are very tired.

POTTS   Mr Swoon!

Swoon, another clerk, appears.

POTTS   What about Dr Love, has he called?

SWOON   He has canceled his reservation.

POTTS   And what about the Bliss family?

SWOON   They are supposed to check out tonight.

POTTS   (to Humbert) Well, I could give you 342. But it has one bed.

HUMBERT   Could you put in a cot perhaps?

POTTS   We have none available at the moment but the situation may improve later.

HUMBERT   Well, I'll register.

POTTS   It's really quite a large
                    (*opens the book*)
   bed. The other night we had three doctors
   sleeping in it, and the middle one was a pretty broad
      (*offers the desk pen to Humbert whose own pen has stalled*)
   gentleman.

Third-Floor Corridor
Uncle Tom, with bags and key, opens the door for Humbert
and Lolita. There is some fussing with the key.

LOLITA   Oh, look! It's the same number as our house. 342.

HUMBERT   Funny coincidence.

LOLITA   Yes. Very funny. You know
                    (*laughing*)
   last night I dreamt mother got drowned in Ramsdale Lake.

HUMBERT   Oh.

CUT TO:

Room
There's a double bed, a mirror, a double bed in the mirror,
a closet door with mirror, a bathroom door ditto, a blue-dark

window, a reflected bed there, the same in the closet mirror, two chairs, a glass-topped table, two bed tables, a double bed: a big panel bed, to be exact, with a Tuscan rose chenille spread, and two frilled, pink-shaded nightlamps, left and right.

Humbert tips old Tom one dollar, calls him back, and adds another. Exit Tom, gratefully grinning.

LOLITA   (*her features working*)
You mean we are *both* going to sleep *here?*

HUMBERT   I've asked them to give me a separate room or at least to put in a cot – for you or me, as you wish.

LOLITA   You are crazy.

HUMBERT   Why, my darling?

LOLITA   Because, my dahrling, when dahrling Mother finds out, she'll divorce you and strangle me.

She stands slitting her eyes at herself contentedly in the closet door mirror. Humbert has sat down on the edge of a low chair, nervously rubbing his hands and leaning toward her pleased reflection.

HUMBERT   Now look here, Lo. Let's settle this once for all. I'm your stepfather. In your mother's absence I'm responsible for your welfare. We shall be a lot together. And since we are not rich, we won't be able
(*Gets up and hangs up his raincoat, which however slips off the hanger.*)
to have *always* two rooms.

LOLITA   Okay. I want my comb.

Humbert tries to embrace her – casually, a bit of controlled tenderness before dinner.

LOLITA   Look, let's cut out the kissing game and get something to eat.

He opens the suitcase with the articles he bought for her.

HUMBERT   By the way – here are some frocks and things I got for you at Parkington.

'Oh, what a dreamy pet! She walked up to the open suitcase as if stalking it from afar, at a kind of slow-motion walk, peering at that distant treasure box on the luggage support.' She raises by the armlets a garment, pulls out the slow snake of a brilliant belt, tries it on. 'Then she crept into my waiting arms, radiant, relaxed, caressing me with her tender, mysterious, impure, indifferent twilight eyes – for all the world like the cheapest of cheap cuties. For that is what nymphets imitate – while we moan and die.' Their kiss is interrupted by a knock on the door. Old Tom enters with a vase of magnificent roses.

HUMBERT   Well! Where do these come from?

TOM   I don't know.

HUMBERT   What do you mean – you don't know? Is it the management?

TOM   I don't know I was given them at the flower counter. For Mister—
                    (*Glances at the card.*)
    Mister Homberg and his little girl.

Exit Uncle Tom, with a quarter.

HUMBERT   (*shrugging it off*) Seems that flower show had a surplus of roses. I detest flowers. And I also detest when my name is misspelt.

LOLITA   Oh, but they are gorgeous!

(The point is, of course, that the bouquet is from an old admirer of little Dolores, Clare Quilty, whom we shall glimpse presently.)

CUT TO:

Dining Room at the Enchanted Hunters
A pretentious mural depicts enchanted hunters in various postures and states of enchantment amid a medley of animals, dryads, cypresses, and porticoes.

LOLITA   (*considering the mural*) What does it mean?

HUMBERT   Oh, mythological scenes, modernized. Bad art, anyway.

LOLITA   What's bad art?

HUMBERT   The work of a mediocre derivative artist. Look at that crummy unicorn. Or is it a centaur?

LOLITA   He's not crummy. He's wonderful.

Waitress brings food.

CUT TO:

End of Meal

Humbert produces a vial of sleeping pills, removes the stopper, and tips the container into his palm. He claps a hand to his mouth and feigns swallowing.

LOLITA   Purple pills – what are they?

HUMBERT   Vitamin P. Purple seas and plums, and plumes of paradise birds. And peat bog orchids. And Priap's orchard.

LOLITA   And double talk. Gimme one quick!

HUMBERT   Here.

Out of his fist the pill he had palmed is slipped into her gay cupped little hand.

LOLITA   (*swallowing*) I bet it's a love philter.

HUMBERT   Good gracious! What do you know about philters?

LOLITA   Just a movie I saw. *Stan and Izzie*. With Mark King. Oh, look who's here.

A man in a loud sports jacket comes into the dining room and walks to a distant table. It is Quilty. He recognizes Mrs Haze's fascinating little girl but except for a glance of amused appraisal does not pay any attention to Humbert and her.

LOLITA   Doesn't he look exactly, but exactly, like Quilty?

HUMBERT   (*frightened*) What? Our fat dentist is here?

Lolita arrests the mouthful of water she has just taken and sets down her dancing glass.

LOLITA   (*with a splutter of mirth*) 'Course not. I meant the writer fellow in the *Drome* ad.

HUMBERT   O Fame, O Femina.

WAITRESS   What would you like for dessert? We have ice cream – raspberry, chocolate, vanilla and let me see—

LOLITA   Chocolate and raspberry for me.

HUMBERT   And for me just a cup of coffee. And the check,
   please.

Lolita shakes her curls trying to dismiss somnolence.

HUMBERT   When did they make you get up at camp?

LOLITA   Half past
                    (*She stifles a big yawn.*)
   six.
                 (*yawn in full swell, shiver of all her frame*)
   Half past six.
                    (*throat fills up again*)
   I went canoeing this morning, and after that—

WAITRESS   We did not have the raspberry after all.

DISSOLVE TO:

The Elevator
Enter Humbert and Lolita; three rose-growing ladies each
looking like a rock garden; two old men; and the elevator
girl. Humbert and Lolita face each other closely, then still
more closely as others crowd in. The two men get out. Lolita
somnolent and sly, pressed against Humbert, raises her eyes
to him and laughs softly.

HUMBERT   What's the matter?

LOLITA   Nothing.

The three smiling matrons get out. There is now sufficient room for H. and L. to stand apart.

OPERATOR   Watch your step, please.

CUT TO:

Corridor to Room 342

LOLITA   You ought to carry me as they do in cartoons. Oh, I'm so sleepy. Guess I'll have to tell you how naughty Charlie and me have been.

CUT TO:

Room 342

LOLITA   This bed sleeps two.

HUMBERT   It's yours.

LOLITA   Where is your room?

Yawning, she sits on the edge of the bed, removes her shoes and peels off one sock.

HUMBERT   I don't know yet. Brush your teeth or whatever you're supposed to do and go to bed.

                    (Opens her overnight case.)

Here are your things. I want you to be asleep when I come back. I'm going downstairs. Please, Lolita. No, that's the closet. The bathroom is there.

LOLITA   Mirror, mirror—

She laughs drowsily and exits.

CUT TO:

Humbert Leaves the Room and Walks Downstairs
As he nears the lobby and turns a corner he is brushed by the shoulder of a lurching, elated man (Quilty).

Humbert asks a bellboy the way to the bar.

BELLBOY   There is no bar.

HUMBERT   I wonder where that lush got his liquor.

BELLBOY   Oh, that's Mr Quilty, sir. And he would not want to be bothered. He comes here to write.

HUMBERT   I see. Can you direct me to the washroom.

BELLBOY   To your left and down.

CUT TO:

Humbert
emerging from the lavatory. A hearty old party, Dr Braddock, on the way in, greets him.

DR BRADDOCK   Well, how did you like Dr Boyd's speech? Oh, I'm sorry. I mistook you for Jack Bliss.

Humbert passes a group of women who are bound for the Rose Room. He consults his watch. He lingers for a moment in the lobby. Mr Potts, noticing him but by him unnoticed, lifts a finger, then calls old Tom and gives him an order. Humbert consults his watch again and continues his restless loitering. He strolls out onto the dimly lit pillared porch. To one side in the darkness two or more people are sitting. We distinguish vaguely a very old man, and beyond him another person's shoulder. It is from these shadows that a voice (Quilty's) comes. It is preceded by the rasp of a screwing off, then a discrete gurgle, then the final note of a placid screwing on.

QUILTY'S VOICE   Where the devil did you get her?

HUMBERT   I beg your pardon?

QUILTY'S VOICE   I said: the weather is getting better.

HUMBERT   Seems so.

QUILTY'S VOICE   Who's the lassie?

HUMBERT   My daughter.

QUILTY'S VOICE   You lie – she's not.

HUMBERT   I beg your pardon?

QUILTY'S VOICE   I said: July was hot. Where's her mother?

HUMBERT   Dead.

QUILTY'S VOICE   I see. Sorry. By the way, why don't you two lunch with me tomorrow. That dreadful crowd will be gone by then.

HUMBERT   We'll be gone, too. Good night.

QUILTY'S VOICE   Sorry. I'm pretty drunk. Good night. That child of yours needs a lot of sleep. Sleep is a rose, as the Persians say. Smoke?

HUMBERT   Not now.

CUT TO:

Humbert Leaves the Porch
Sufficient time has elapsed. He tries not to display any hurry. As he makes his way through a constellation of fixed people in one corner of the lobby near the dining room, there comes a blinding flash, as beaming Dr Braddock and some matrons are photographed.

DR BRADDOCK   (*pointing to part of the mural which continues around the corner*) And here the theme changes. The hunter thinks he has hypnotized the little nymph but it is she who puts him into a trance.

Humbert Walks up the Stairs
and turns in to the corridor. The door key with its large unwieldly hangpiece of polished wood is dangling from his hand. He takes off his coat. He stands for a moment

immobile before door 342. It is a moment of wholesome hesitation. From the service elevator old Tom, the gray-haired Negro, hobbles out trundling a folded cot. Humbert turns guiltily.

TOM   342. I've brought you the cot, sir.

HUMBERT   Oh? Yes, yes, of course. But I'm afraid she is fast asleep. She has had a strenuous day.

TOM   That's quite all right. We'll put it in gently.

Humbert opens the door. Soft and slow, the rhythm of the young sleeper's respiration is kept ajar for ten seconds.

HUMBERT   Please, very quietly. I don't want the child to be disturbed.

Crablike, crippled old Tom unfolds the cot alongside the bed and shuffles out. Once out, he performs very slowly the act of closing a creaky door but at the last moment (the poor devil being somewhat spastic) he bangs it shut. Lolita does not wake up. Humbert (now in pajamas) tests and retests the security of her drugged sleep. He turns on the radio. She does not stir. A fist pounds on the wall. He shuts off the radio and touches her shoulder. Still she sleeps. That drug certainly works. He is about to take advantage of this safe sleep, but as the moon reaches her face, its innocent helpless fragile infantine beauty arrests him. He slinks back to his cot.

CUT TO:

Humbert Lying on His Cot supine, traversed by pale strips of moonlight coming through the slits in the blinds. Clouds engulf the moon.

'There is nothing louder than an American hotel; and, mind you, this was supposed to be a quiet, cozy, old-fashioned, homey place – "gracious living" and all that stuff. The clatter of the elevator's gate – some twenty yards northeast of my head but as clearly perceived as if it were inside my left temple – alternated with the banging and booming of the machine's various evolutions and lasted well beyond mid-night. Every now and then, immediately east of my left ear, the corridor would brim with cheerful, resonant, and inept exclamations ending in a volley of good nights. When *that* stopped, a toilet immediately north of my cerebellum took over. It was a manly, energetic, deep-throated toilet, and it was used many times. Its gurgle and gush and long afterflow shook the wall behind me. Then someone in a southern direction was extravagantly sick, almost coughing out his life with his liquor, and his toilet descended like a veritable Niagara, immediately beyond our bathroom. And when finally all the waterfalls had stopped, and the enchanted hunters were sound asleep, the avenue under the window of my insomnia, to the west of my wake – a staid, eminently residential, dignified alley of huge trees – degenerated into the despicable haunt of gigantic trucks roaring through the wet and windy night.'

In the first antemeridian hours there is a lull. The sky pales. A breeze sighs. A bird discreetly twitters. Lolita wakes up and yawns (a childish, cozy, warm yawn). Humbert feigns sleep.

LOLITA   (*sitting up, looking at him*) What d'you know! I thought you got another room. Hey! Wake up!

Humbert gives a mediocre imitation of that process.

LOLITA   I never heard you come in. Oh, you're handsome in bed, Hum. Is that cot comfortable?

HUMBERT   Awful.

LOLITA   Come and sit here. Shall we eat that fruit in the brown bag? You need a shave, pricklepuss.

HUMBERT   Good morning, Lolita.

LOLITA   My tan is much darker that yours. Say, I have a suggestion. Are you listening?

HUMBERT   Yes?

LOLITA   It's something we did at the camp, Charlie and
me. It's fun.

HUMBERT   Yes?

LOLITA   Gosh, how your heart is thumping! Shouldn't you
see a doctor? You aren't dying?

HUMBERT   I am dying of curiosity. What was that suggestion?

LOLITA   It's playing a game. A game we played in the
woods – when we should have been picking berries. I did
it strictly for kicks, but oh well, it was sort of fun. It's a
game lots of kids play nowadays. Kind of fad. Still don't
get it? You're dense, aren't you?

HUMBERT   I'm dying.

LOLITA   It's – sure you can't guess?

HUMBERT   I can't.

LOLITA   It's not tiddledywinks, and it's not Russian roulette.

HUMBERT   I'm a poor guesser.

With a burst of rough glee she puts her mouth to his ear (could one reproduce this hot moist sound, the tickle and the buzz, the vibration, the thunder of her whisper?).

    She draws back. Kneeling above recumbent Humbert (who is invisible except for a twitching toe), she contemplates him expectantly. Her humid lips and sly slit eyes seem to anticipate and prompt an assent.

HUMBERT'S VOICE   I don't know what game you children played.

In an eager gesture, she brushes the hair off her forehead and applies herself again to his tingling ear.

HUMBERT'S VOICE   (faintly) I never played that game.

LOLITA'S VOICE   Like me to show you?

HUMBERT   If it's not too dangerous. If it's not too difficult. If it's not too – *Ah, mon Dieu!*

CUT TO:

Various Rooms in the Enchanted Hunters

The CAMERA glides from room to room at dawn, with some of the guests still fast asleep. The purpose of these shots is to construct a series of situations contrasting with the atmosphere in Room 342. The movement of the CAMERA reveals the following scenes, all of very brief duration:

Room 13:   Mr Potts, the hotel clerk, old, chubby, and bald, is awakened by his alarm clock, which he knocks over in his fussy attempt to stop its ringing.

Room 180:   Dr and Mrs Braddock – the snoring lustily; she is awakened by two pigeons on the window sill.

Room 423:   The playwright Quilty, dead to the world, sprawls prone among the emblems of drunkenness.

Room 342:   (balcony) Pigeons. Early sunlight effects. A truck rumbles by below. From the inside of the room comes the laughter of a child (Lolita!).

Room 344:   The laughter of a child in the neighboring room rouses Dr Boyd, who looks at his watch and smiles.

Room 442: A very large woman, Miss Beard, has risen and indulges in some ponderous exercises causing the flowers to shake in her small room.

Room 342: Lolita, sitting up in her tumbled bed, looks up at the loud ceiling. She is messily consuming a peach. A banana skin hangs from the edge of the bed table. The cot is empty. Humbert is in the bathroom, the door of which is ajar. The faucet whines.

Room 242: Mr Rose is shaving in the bathroom. The faucet in the bathroom above whines. Mrs Rose urges her daughter, a dark-haired child Lolita's age, to get up.

Murals in the dining room: The hunters are still in a trance.

Corridor on third floor: Negro maids load a wagon with linen.

The morning grows in brightness and blare. The elevator is active. It is now around 9 A.M. One of the maids attempts to open the door of 342. Humbert's nervous snarl from within.

CUT TO:

Room 342

Lolita combs her hair before the mirror.

HUMBERT'S VOICE   I love you. I adore you . . .

LOLITA   Oh, leave me alone now. We must get dressed.

HUMBERT'S VOICE   Lolita, Lolita, Lolita! Please, not yet,
    Oh, my darling. This is—

CUT TO:

Hotel Dining Room

DR BRADDOCK   (*pointing out details of mural to the Rose family*)
    This is paradise, or at least a pagan shadow of paradise.
    Note those ecstatic flowers and things sprouting every-
    where. In this corner we have one of the enchanted
    hunters courting a young nymph. The coloration of the
    sky is dreamlike. I knew well Lewis Ruskin who painted
    this remarkable mural. He was a gentle soul, a melan-
    choly drawing master who eventually became the head
    of a select girls' school in Briceland. He developed a
    romantic attachment for one of his young charges and

committed suicide when she left his school. She is now married to a missionary.

MRS ROSE   How very sad. Don't you just love those three maidens dancing around the sleeping hunter? And that shaggy animal with the mauve horn?

MRS ROSE'S LITTLE DAUGHTER   Why has one of the girls a bandage on her leg?

CUT TO:

Lounge to Dining Room
Humbert, followed by Lolita, drifts in. She acquires a movie magazine which she reads throughout breakfast, and continues to read as they trail out, and reads it in the lounge while Humbert is paying the bill.

A VOICE   Hullo there, Lolita!

She looks around. There is no one. Humbert joins her. Old Tom carries out the bags.

CUT TO:

The Highway to Lepingsville

They drive in silence. A queer dullness has replaced Lolita's cheerfulness.

HUMBERT   (*attempting small talk*) My, my. I wonder what Mrs Chatfield would say if she discovered the things her pretty Phyllis did with your filthy Charlie.

LOLITA   (*making a weeping grimace*) Look, let us get off the subject.

Silence. Some landscape.

HUMBERT   Why are you fidgeting like that? What is the matter?

LOLITA   Nothing, you brute.

HUMBERT   You what?

She turns away.

They drive on in silence. 'Cold spiders of panic crawled down my back. This was an orphan . . .'

CUT TO:

Receding Road

LOLITA   Oh, a squashed squirrel! What a shame.

HUMBERT (*hopefully*) Yes, isn't it? The little animals are imprudent. You know, there should be—

LOLITA Stop at the next gas station. I want to go to the washroom.

HUMBERT Righto. Tummy-ache?

LOLITA (*smiling sweetly at him*) You chump, you creep, you revolting character. I was a daisy-fresh girl and look what you've done to me. I ought to call the cops and tell them you raped me. Oh, you dirty, dirty old man!

Humbert frowns, sweats, glances at her askance.

LOLITA (*wincing and making a sizzling sound as she intakes through parted lips*) You hurt me. You've torn something inside.

CUT TO:

A Filling Station
She scrambles out and disappears. Slowly, lovingly, the old mechanic soaps and wipes the windshield, etc. Lolita reappears.

LOLITA Look, give me some dimes and nickels. I want to call Mother at that hospital. What's the number?

HUMBERT   Get in. You can't call.

LOLITA   Why?

HUMBERT   Get in and slam the door.

The old garage man beams. They swing onto the highway.

LOLITA   Why can't I call my mother if I want to?

HUMBERT   Because your mother is dead.

CUT TO:

Lepingsville — a Travel Agency on Main Street
A thick smear crayon traces across a map the itinerary which Humbert and Lolita will follow through three or four mountain states, to Beardsley, Idaho. Besides the folding map, they are given a strip map and a tour book.

CUT TO:

Humbert and Lolita Shopping in Lepingsville
The purchases are: a beribboned box of chocolates, comic books, toilet articles, a manicure set, a travel clock, a ring with a real topaz, field glasses, a portable radio, chewing

gum, a transparent raincoat, various playsuits and summer frocks. She remains rather sullen throughout though some of the purchases do provoke a transient gleam in her gloom.

CUT TO:

A Forest Road at Nightfall
They have stopped by the side of the road.

HUMBERT   We must have taken the wrong turning. This is awful.

He gets the map and a torch light.

LOLITA   Give me that map.

HUMBERT   We should have turned left half an hour ago and taken 42 south, not north.

LOLITA   We? Leave me out of it.

HUMBERT   (*over her shoulder*) I am sure we'll find some place to stop, if we just drive on.

He nuzzles her tentatively.

LOLITA (*flinching*) Leave me alone. I despise you. You deceived me about Mother. You took advantage of me.

CUT TO:

We see the Car moving on
This is the first, rather ominous, lap in their trip. Things will pick up, however – and then degenerate again.

It is assumed that Humbert and Lolita are traversing by car a distance of some three thousand miles, including side trips, from Lepingsville (which is anywhere between Massachusetts and Minnesota) westward through several mountain states to Beardsley, a college town in Idaho. Their journey is a leisurely, sightseeing tour, so that it takes them not less than two or three weeks to reach, in mid-September, their destination. All along their route there is an evolution of the motel theme, illustrated by six examples beginning with the modest log cabin (Acme Cabins), through cottages in a row (Baskerville Cottages), garage-connected units (Crest Court), fused units (Dymple Manor), and the patio-and-pool type (Eden Lodge), to the fancy two-story affair (Foxcreek Ranch), a gradation which, if pursued further, would lead us back to the country hotel. There is also a (shorter) series of eating places, from the breakfast counter of the Truckers Welcome, through the coffee-shop type, to the more or less smart restaurant.

While the accommodations improve, and their preten-
tions climb, Lolita's attitude takes an opposite, downward,
course, starting with a forlorn semblance of affection and
passing through a gamut of deterioration, to end in the
wretchedness of their last night before reaching Beardsley.

We have now put up at The Humble Log Cabin, where
Humbert and Lolita will conclude a pathetic pact – soon to
be broken.

CUT TO:

*Acme Cabins – a Modest Cabin, One of Five, Higgledy-piggledy in a Pine
Forest*
None has a bath. The separate privy is garlanded with wild
roses. A brisk, buxom, unkempt woman shows our tired
travelers the wood-burning stove and the two dissimilar
beds, separable by a curtain on rings. There is a Bible on the
chest of drawers. A fly buzzes drowsily. Above Humbert's bed
there is the picture of a girl garlanded with wild roses.

Humbert, in his curtained-off section, sits on the bed
with his face between his fists in mournful meditation. Presently, he puts out the light and lies down; silence. The moon
rises, a disturbed fly buzzes and is still again. Humbert lies
in the mottled dark with eyes open, his arms under his nape.

A child sob sounds and is followed by more. He sits up, listening. The curtain is drawn aside.

Lolita with tears streaming down her face, her nightgown white and infantine in the moonlight, comes to be comforted. He gently caresses her hair, as she weeps on his shoulder.

HUMBERT   I beseech you not to cry. I love you. I cannot exist without you. Everything will be all right.

LOLITA   (with a snuffle and a wail) Nothing will ever be all right.

HUMBERT   I'm sure we are going to be very happy, you and I.

LOLITA   But everything has changed, all of a sudden. Everything was so – oh, I don't know – normal: the camp, and the lake, and Charlie, and the girls, and the – oh, everything. And now there is no camp, and no Ramsdale, nothing!

There is the patter of some little night beast on the roof.

HUMBERT   I don't want you to cry. We'll see things, we'll go places.

LOLITA   There's no place to go back to.

HUMBERT   We'll find a new home.

LOLITA   But there's no old one. And I've left all my things there.

HUMBERT   What, for instance?

LOLITA   My roller skates, my — oh, lots of things.

HUMBERT   You silly darling, why didn't you tell me in Lepingsville?

LOLITA   (*tearfully*) I forgot.

HUMBERT   We'll get every blessed thing you want. It's over two thousand miles to Beardsley but we've got a month before the fall term begins. We can dawdle as much as you want.

LOLITA   But what next? Oh, where is that handkerchief?

HUMBERT   Next you'll go to school in Beardsley, and have a wonderful time there. I love you. I'm also going to cry if you don't stop. Remember, I'll die if you ever leave me.

LOLITA   Leave you? You know perfectly well I have no where to go.

CUT TO:

Baskerville Cottages
Ten white-washed cottages in a row, with a vast well-kept lawn in front, separating them from the highway.

Lolita and Humbert in a Leafy Spot not far from their cottage. Humbert with a book on the grass. Lolita in an old garden swing, swinging gently.

HUMBERT   You have been a very sweet child so far. It would be a pity to break the precious rhythm we have now established. I suggest we spend another night here, in this fairy-tale cabin. We shall ramble and read. Do you know, these notes on Edgar Poe that I have prepared for Beardsley College always remind me of Ramsdale and the first time I touched you. Come here, sit down beside me. I'll read you my favorite poem.

LOLITA   (*in the swing, just behind him*) I want to sit here.

HUMBERT   All right, but don't make it creak. I want you to follow very closely the intonation, the inner construction of these lines.

It was night in the lonesome October

Of my most immemorial year

Marvelous emphasis on 'immemorial.' Makes you step up from one dim rim to a dimmer one.

It was hard by the dim lake of Auber,

In the misty mid region of Weir

Notice how nicely the 'dim' is read back and becomes 'mid' – 'misty mid region'?

(The swing creaks.)

HUMBERT   Darling, please don't do that. I skip a few stanzas. Now listen again:

Thus I pacified Psyche and kissed her

And tempted her out of her gloom . . .

And we passed to the end of the vista,

But were stopped by the door of a tomb

. . . And I said: 'What is written, sweet sister? . . .

She replied: Ulalume, Ulalume!

LOLITA   I think that's rather corny.

HUMBERT   Really? What exactly do you object to?

LOLITA   Vista-sister. That's like Lolita-sweeter.

HUMBERT   Oh, that's true. A very fine observation.

(A more or less tame rabbit stops, nibbles, lopes on.)

HUMBERT   In my class you'd get an A-plus and a kiss. But
    what I'm really driving at is that there is a certain intona-
    tion in this poem which is so much more original and
    mysterious than the rather trivial romanticism of Anna-
    bel Lee. (*He turns his head and notices the swing is empty.*)

HUMBERT   (*getting up to his feet*) Lolita!

(She has disappeared)

HUMBERT   Lolita, where are you hiding?

He looks for her among the trees and shrubs. He is in a state
of distress and distraction hardly warranted by the circumstances. (She has wandered away in dim-smiling, stooping
pursuit of the soft elusive rabbit)

HUMBERT   (*emerging from a thicket*) Lolita!

She is crouching behind the circumspect bunny. A very low-
class young couple with an unattractive baby are on the back
porch of a cabin. They talk to Lolita. The young man is not

unlike (and should be played by the same actor as) Lolita's future husband.

THE YOUNG MAN   I guess he doesn't want to be caught.

Humbert, excited and angry, appears on the scence.

HUMBERT   Will you please come at once. I've been calling you for hours. This is preposterous.
              (*Does not quite know what he is saying.*)

Lolita turns and walks back to their cabin, followed by Humbert and the CAMERA. She stops near their parked car, and jiggles the door handle.

LOLITA   Unlock, please.

HUMBERT   Darling, you must forgive me.

LOLITA   You've insulted me in front of those people.

HUMBERT   I lost my head. I was reading a poem. I got the nightmare notion that you had disappeared for good — that perhaps you never existed. Don't be mad at me, my love. I'll unlock if you like, but don't be mad. Your mother once told me that when you were quite small and wanted to sulk, you'd get into the family car all alone.

LOLITA   I don't care. You can't do this to me.

HUMBERT   I know, I know. I'm asking your pardon. It won't happen again. I'm a fool. I thought you were gone.

LOLITA   I've nowhere to go.

CUT TO:

Breakfast Counter in a Diner Called TRUCKERS WELCOME
A very plain place with a deer head and adman's visions of celestial sundaes on the wall. At the counter, Lolita has Humbert on her right and a tremendous trucker with hairy forearms on her left. The trucker and Lolita wear identical clothes: dungarees and T-shirts. The man is messily finishing his meal. Humbert and Lolita are waiting for theirs.

CUT TO:

Lolita, Humbert, Driving on
The road is bordered by hilly farmlands and then winds through sparsely settled country interspersed with pine groves.

CUT TO:

Crest Court – a semicircle of stucco units connected by narrow garages

The lawn in front is shaded by ample maples. Inside, two identical pictures (stylized dahlias) hang over the twin beds. The hideous drone of an air-conditioning apparatus provides a constant sonic background.

CUT TO:

Long Shot – Humbert and Lolita Arriving

It is the ordinary procedure. They both get out of the car in front of the office. The woman who runs the motel cries out, 'I'll be with you in a moment,' as she hurriedly escorts some other people back to the office from the room they have seen. It is now Humbert's and Lolita's turn. They follow the sidewalk in the wake of the bustling woman. She shows them the room. Humbert nods his head. Listless, Lolita drops into a low chair. Humbert follows the woman back to the office and registers there.

HUMBERT Where can I get some soft drinks round here?

THE WOMAN It's just one block down the road.

Humbert walks out to follow her directions but then thinks

better of it and returns to the room, where Lolita is sprawling in the chair with a magazine.

HUMBERT   We'll be going out in five minutes for a bite. Do lay aside that old magazine and come talk to me.

Lolita scans magazine without replying.

HUMBERT   Do you hear me, darling? I want a little chat with you, *mon petit chat*. Please.

LOLITA   If you give me a dime. From now on I am coin operated.

She continues to read.

Humbert, who has taken off his shirt, notices the approach of the motel woman and steps into the bathroom. The woman enters bringing a jug of ice cubes.

THE WOMAN   There. You can have a nice cold drink, dearie. Long way from home?

LOLITA   Home? Yes, I guess so. Very long way.

WOMAN   Must be fun to travel all alone with your daddy?

LOLITA   Oh, I dunno—

WOMAN   Depends on what you call fun?

LOLITA   Uh-huh.

WOMAN   Left your mama up at the farm?

LOLITA   Uhn-uhn. We don't have a farm.

WOMAN   Get along with your daddy?

LOLITA   Yah.

WOMAN   You don't talk the way he does. I mean, he talks
    foreign, and you don't.

LOLITA   Oh, well – I went to school in this country.

WOMAN   And he didn't? Is he French Canadian?

LOLITA   Sort of.

WOMAN   Look, there's a Canadian couple living across the
    road. Maybe you'd like to talk to them?

LOLITA   Why?

HUMBERT   (*from the threshold of the bathroom*) Yes – why indeed?

WOMAN   Oh, I thought you had gone out for a drink.

HUMBERT   By the way, can you stop that ventilator, or whatever you call it? I can't stand that whirr.

CUT TO:

Another Stretch of Road
For the first time sagebrush and juniper appear. There is some uncertainty whether it is a bank of clouds or a range of mountains that have started looming just above the horizon. By the side of the road, a granite obelisk commemorates a bloody battle – the defeat of Blue Bull.

A Crowded Coffee Shop
A hard-working harried young waitress is doing her best to satisfy too many customers.

LOLITA   (*to Humbert*) Give me a coin for the juke box. Oh, they have my song.

She starts the juke box. The following song is produced:

> Lolita, Lolita, Lolita!
> For ever tonight we must part:
> Because separation is sweeter
> Than clasping a ghost to one's heart.
>
> Because it's a maddening summer,
> Because the whole night is in bloom,
> Because you're in love with a strummer
> Who brings his guitar to your room.
>
> You know he's a clown and a cheater,
> You know I am tender and true —
> But *he* is now singing, Lolita,
> The songs I've been making for you!

CUT TO:

The Route now offers spectacular scenery
as it snakes up a gigantic mountainside. At the top of the pass, tourists take pictures and feed the marmots. In the next valley we inspect the collection of frontier lore in a Ghost Town museum. We have a little trouble when the car stalls on a steep incline but some kind youths help. The radiator grill is plastered with dead butterflies.

CUT TO:

A Dirt Road in a Canyon
Humbert pulls up at the bloomy and lush wayside.

HUMBERT   I should not have attempted to take a short cut. We're lost.

LOLITA   Ask that nut with the net over there.

The Butterfly Hunter. His name is Vladimir Nabokov. A fritillary settles with outspread wings on a tall flower. Nabokov snaps it up with a sweep of his net. Humbert walks toward him. With a nip of finger and thumb through a fold of the marquisette Nabokov dispatches his capture and works the dead insect out of the netbag onto the palm of his hand.

HUMBERT   Is that a rare specimen?

NABOKOV   A specimen cannot be common or rare, it can only be poor or perfect.

HUMBERT   Could you direct me—

NABOKOV   You meant 'rare species.' This is a good specimen of a rather scarce subspecies.

HUMBERT   I see. Could you please tell me if this road leads
    to Dympleton?

NABOKOV   I haven't the vaguest idea. I saw some loggers
    (*pointing*) up there. They might know.

CUT TO:

Dymple Manor — twenty units firmly fused together in a Row
The screen doors never cease banging as people come in and
out, and the only way to confound one's neighbor's canned
music is to start one's own full blast. Sprinklers irrigate the
parched-looking lawn and its border of trembling petunias.
In the adjacent lot a bulldozer is at work, and another motel
is rising.

LOLITA   Give me a quarter for the TV.

HUMBERT   It's free, my pet, in this, as they say, joint.

A notice under glass says PETS ACCEPTED.

LOLITA   I need a quarter anyway.

HUMBERT   My pet must earn it.

CUT TO:

The Television Screen
A commercial is melting:

A FRUITY VOICE   . . . soft, soft as the bloom on a peach.

SUPREMELY HAPPY ANNOUNCER   And now we return
   to Act One of *The Nymphet*

LOLITA'S VOICE   Oh, I saw it at home last winter. It's good.

On the TV screen, an art collector is seen examining a mini-
ature statue: a tiny bronze nude.

HIS SUBDUED NARRATIONAL VOICE   I had bought it on a
   hunch; but now, as I stroked each curve, I knew it was a
   unique masterpiece.

CLOSE-UP of the statuette, which is called 'Playing Hooky.'
A teen-age girl is about to take a dip, her dress and school
books are lying at the foot of a gnarled willow.

NARRATIVE UNDERVOICE CONTINUES   I knew that the
   artist who made it was traveling in a distant country with
   his young wife. A strange urge possessed me. Next day I
   was flying over the jungle.

HUMBERT'S VOICE   Must we look at this trash?

LOLITA'S VOICE   It's not trash. It will get quite exciting. He finds the girl and he shoots her.

CUT TO:

High Altitude

We stop at Sapphire Lake. Snow banks and wild flowers. Two boys from another car engage Lolita in a snowball fight. Humbert, who has incongruously put on rubbers, slips on an icy patch and ignominiously lands on his back. Lolita and the boys laugh at his discomfiture. A scenic drive takes our travelers to the Pueblo dwellings. A rodeo is advertised in the next town.

CUT TO:

Eden Lodge

We are now in the patio-and-pool belt. The arrangement of fused whitewashed units brackets a square of green grounds with a heated swimming pool in the middle. The rooms are smarter and more expensive than at Crest or Dymple; unfortunately, a tented roller-skate rink on the opposite side of the road impairs Eden's elegancy with a sustained blare of rowdy music.

In the Room

LOLITA   (*reading a notice*) Children free. Goody-goody.

HUMBERT   (*laughing tenderly*) No quarter tonight, free child.

LOLITA   That's what you think. From now on this child is paid half a dollar.

HUMBERT   My Persian peach.

LOLITA   And moreover – moreover you must promise you'll let me go roller-skating – no, wait a sec – it's not only that, but you must promise you'll not supervise me – I mean, you may wait outside, or at the chuck wagon, but the inside is reserved for teen-agers. See?

HUMBERT   My carissa, my liquidambar, my early delicious.

CUT TO:

Swimming Pool

At poolside Lolita (satin pants, shirred bra) and two other nymphets (one dark, with a striped ball in her scanty lap, the other fair, with a long scar on her leg) recline. A lad of their age, in bathing trunks, sits on the cement brink, paying not the slightest attention to the three maidens.

FAIR (*in response to Lolita's index finger*) Rock climbing in Pink Pillar Park. Skinned my fanny too. That's a cute bracelet you've got.

LOLITA   Thank you.

DARK   You can't be Spanish, Lolita?

LOLITA   (*smile, shrug*)

FAIR (TO DARK)   Are your folks like mine – playing cards all day?

DARK   My father is an admiral, and my mother's an actress.

FAIR   Good for you. (*pause*) That character there (*pointing with her bare toe at owlish Humbert, who at some distance beyond the pool is sitting in a shadow-dappled garden chair*), I know why *he* wears sunglasses.

(Dark girl and Lolita exchange a glance, and both laugh.)

DARK   It's her dad, bright kid.

FAIR   I'm sorry.

All three wince as the lad dives, splashing them.

FAIR   And who's the nitwit?

DARK   He belongs to this motor court.

Humbert, in the dappled distance, raises his hand beckoning Lolita. She makes a grimace of resignation, and leaves the poolside.

DARK   (to Fair) I bet her folks are divorced.

FAIR   (to Dark) Yah. She looks like one of those mixed-up kids you see on TV.

CUT TO:

Poolside

HUMBERT   (closing his book) I see from this point of vantage they have finished cleaning up our room. I therefore suggest we retire for a brief siesta, my love.

LOLITA   I want a hamburger first.

HUMBERT   And then a humburger.

LOLITA   Those two bitch girls are watching us.

HUMBERT   A propos: I don't mind your playing with girls of your age. In fact, I rather welcome it if I can be present. You may exchange wisecracks with them to your heart's content. But I must repeat: be careful.

LOLITA   Telling me what to say – huh?

HUMBERT   Telling you what not to say.

CUT TO:

The Motel Room

HUMBERT   Now let me rub this in. I may well be a middle-aged morals offender, *d'accord*, but *you* are a minor female who has impaired the morals of an adult in a respectable inn. I go to jail – *d'accord*. But what happens to you, neglected incorrigible orphan? Let me tell you: a nice grim matron takes away your fancy clothes, your lipsticks, your life. For me, it is jail. But for you, little waif, it is the correctional school, the bleak reformatory, the juvenile detention home where you knit things, and sing hymns, and have rancid pancakes on Sundays. Oh, horrible! My poor wayward girl (come, give me a kiss) should realize, I think, that under the circumstances she'd better be very careful, and not talk to strangers too freely. What were you giggling about with those two girls?

CUT TO:

A Roadside Sign: PINK PILLAR NATIONAL MONUMENT. Another sign further on: SADDLE HORSES. PERSONALIZED TOURS.

DISSOLVE TO:

A Slow Cavalcade of Tourists
weaving along a bridle trail, topped by digitate and phallic cliffs. Lolita is bobbing at a walking pace immediately behind the leader, a lanky ranger who keeps turning to her and kidding the cocky lass. A fat dude rancher in a flowery shirt rides behind her, then come two small boys, then a Mrs Hopson, and then Humbert.

Edda Hopson (her name is on her back) takes advantage of a widening in the path to fall back and engage reluctant Humbert in polite conversation (oh, shade of Charlotte!).

MRS HOPSON   What a lovely child you've got! I kept admiring her last night in the lounge. Those cheekbones! That virgin bloom on her arms and legs! I'm a bit of an artist, and in fact have exposed. Keep her pure! I do hope she has a good heart. I used to hurt my parents as a savage hurts dumb animals. Is she kind to you? Does she love you?

HUMBERT   No.

MRS HOPSON   Ah, teen-agers are dreadfully cruel. And such a little beauty! A word of advice: don't let that redhaired brute of a ranger tease her the way he is doing. I rode with him alone once, and he exhibited his – well, emotion most shamelessly. I must say I thought it rather thick: knowing I was a divorcee and taking advantage.

CUT TO:

A Fairly Good Restaurant
Tablecloths and napkins. Waiters. A three-man orchestra. Lolita and Humbert sit at a table in shaded light.

LOLITA   (*to Humbert*) What's a roast caponette?

HUMBERT   Chicken.

LOLITA   No. I'll have the charcoal-broiled filet mignon.

The orchestra plays 'Lolita, Lolita, Lolita.' Humbert has ordered half a bottle of wine.

LOLITA   Give me some.

HUMBERT   If nobody's looking. Well, here's to your health, my life and my bride.

LOLITA   Okay, okay.

HUMBERT   I'm so anxious to make you happy. Just don't know what to suggest. I'm rather awkward and sometimes a brute. But I adore every inch of you. I'd like to kiss your kidneys and fondle your liver. Tell me, what shall we do tomorrow? Let's stay here a couple of days longer and take in Phantom Lake and perhaps hire a boat there. Would you like that?

LOLITA   A boat? What do you know about boats?

HUMBERT   Why are you laughing?

LOLITA   I just remembered. One day we went in the rowboat, Phyl, Agnes, and me, and we found a cove, and went for a swim, and Charlie came out of the wood just like that. And of course he was not supposed to go swimming with us, and Phyllis said—

THE WAITER   Would the young lady like some more milk?

LOLITA   Yes, I guess so.

HUMBERT   So what did Phyllis say?

LOLITA   Nothing.

HUMBERT   I had hoped I was getting another racy account of your camp activities.

LOLITA   No, that's all.

Three days are spent in this region, and some side trips are made. Humbert photographs Lolita among the rocks of the Devil's Paint Box – hot springs, baby geysers, bubbling mud, pouting puddles. Another trip takes them to Christmas Tree Cavern, a deep damp place where Humbert shivers and is rude to the guide. A long drive toward a disappointing objective – the display of a local lady's home-made sculptures – does not improve Lolita's mood. She feigns gagging. They traverse an incredibly barren and boring desert. Timbered hills rise again.

CUT TO:

Foxcreek Ranch
This is the last and most pretentious motel of the series, a two-story affair, very fancy and ugly, in the heart of the train and truck traffic. The office is brightly illumined. The time is rather late at night.

THE MANAGER   Well, all I have left is this one room with a double bed.

Lolita is examining some Indian souvenirs on the counter.

LOLITA   (to Humbert, who is about to register) I want this money purse.

HUMBERT   Wait a moment, my dear.

LOLITA   I want this purse.

HUMBERT   *Mais c'est si laid.*

LOLITA   *Si laid* or not *si laid* — I want it.

HUMBERT   All right, all right.

MANAGER   (giving Humbert his change) Fifteen, and — let me see — three ninety-five for this. One silver dollar and one new nickel. Would the young lady like her monogram upon it?

LOLITA   Yes. It's D.H.

MANAGER   Aha. Very well. Where did my old dad put those initials? Dad! Oh, here they are.

LOLITA   D.H. Dolores Haze.

Humbert has started to write his name on a register slip. He has got as far as 'Humbert Hu.' With great presence of mind he changes 'u' to 'a,' and adds 'ze.'

MANAGER   Ask your dad for that dollar, Dolores. That's a tongue twister – dollar doll – isn't it?

CUT TO:

Front of Hacienda
The manager shows Humbert where to park.

CUT TO:

Room
Wall-to-wall carpeting and floor-to-ceiling picture windows; dressing alcove; ceramic-tiled bath; trucks and trains accompany the dialogue.

HUMBERT   That 'Haze' was a bad slip of your adorable little tongue. While we put up at hotels, you are – remember – Dolores Humbert. Let's keep 'Haze' for the reformatory.

LOLITA   Meaning that school at Beardsley?

HUMBERT   You're going to an extremely good private school at Beardsley. But one hot whisper to a girl friend, one stupid boast, may send me to jail and you to a juvenile detention home.

LOLITA   By the way, you said 'private.' Is it a girls' school?

HUMBERT   Yes.

LOLITA   Then I'm not going there. I want to go to an ordinary public school.

HUMBERT   Let's not fight and argue tonight. I'm fagged out. We have to start quite early tomorrow. Please, Dolly Humbert.

LOLITA   I loathe your name. It's a clown's name: Humlet Hambert. Omelette Hamburg.

HUMBERT   Or plain 'Hamlet.' I daresay, you hate me even more than my name. Oh, Lolita, if you knew what you are doing to me. Some day you'll regret.

LOLITA   That's right. Just go clowning on and on.

HUMBERT   Well, let's struggle with these blinds. The war with Venice. I can't do anything with these slats and slits.

LOLITA   I'm not listening to you, you know.

HUMBERT   Pity. This is our last night on the road. I wonder what kind of house the Beardsley people have prepared for us. I hope it's brick and ivy.

LOLITA   I could not care less.

HUMBERT   But don't you think it has been an enchanting journey? Tell me, what did you like best of all? I think, yesterday's canyon, eh? I think I've never seen such iridescent rocks.

LOLITA   I think iridescent rocks stink.

HUMBERT   (*affecting a good-natured laugh*) Have it your way.

She takes off her shoes. Her movements are slumber-slow.

LOLITA   I'm thirsty.

HUMBERT   There's ice in this jug.

Tinkle.

LOLITA   (*hazily*) I want a soda.

HUMBERT   Shall I bring you one from the Coke dispenser?

LOLITA   (*yawns and nods*)

HUMBERT   Grape? Cherry?

LOLITA   Cherry. No, make it grape.

She yawns.

CUT TO:

Spacious Patio, Neon-flooded Solitude
Humbert walks to the vending machine which is outside the motel office. Dime. Bottle. Repeat performance. He opens both bottles on the cap-bite.

AN OLD MAN'S VOICE   The missus thirsty?

It is the deaf old father of the hotel manager sitting and smoking in the shadows.

HUMBERT   I beg your pardon?

OLD MAN   Women sure get thirsty.

HUMBERT   It's my daughter . . .

OLD MAN   What's that?

HUMBERT   . . . who wants a drink.

OLD MAN   No, thank you, very kind of you.

HUMBERT   (*after a moment's hesitation*) Well, good night.

OLD MAN   My wife was also like that – but *her* drink
was beer.

Chuckles, mumbles, expectorates in the dark.

CUT TO:

Humbert

walking back to his door with the two bottles. He reaches
the door. He has not got the key. As he frees his hand to
knock, the telephone rings somewhere in an adjacent room
and for a moment the shadow of a past combination of

memorable details is imposed upon the present ('. . .better come quick. . .') Humbert taps gently on the door. No answer.

HUMBERT   (*not too loud*) Lolita!

No answer. He taps again, then peers through the slits of the Venetian blind. A blurry light is on in the room. Lolita, half undressed, lies supine on the bed, fast asleep.

It is hopeless. Humbert is disinclined to get the manager to come and unlock: the nymphet's sleep is not that of an acceptable child.

CUT TO:

Humbert
mouth open, asleep in the car. It is dawn. From one of the motel rooms there gradually emerges a big family – sleepy children, portable icebox, accepted pet, crib – and fills a big station wagon which has the stickers of various resorts and natural marvels affixed to it: a summary also of Humbert's honeymoon. One of the children turns on the radio.

Act Three

Beardsley School

A private school for girls at Beardsley, Idaho. It is a sunny spring day. There are catkins in all the vases. We are in the music room of the school. It is here that the drama classes are held. Several girls, including Lolita, mostly in gym suits, some barefoot, sit around, some on the floor. Miss Cormorant, a lean faded Lesbian, is discussing the play which they will stage at the Spring Festival of Arts.

MISS CORMORANT   For our Spring Festival next month, we are going to do a play by Clare Quilty. When I taught at Onyx, Mr Cue, as we called him, would sometimes drive over from Briceland to direct a dance pantomime. The girls adored him. One day he told me that he and a famous painter, the late Lewis Ruskin, were engaged in writing a play for children. Eventually, Mr Quilty published it under the intriguing title, *The Enchanted Hunters*. And this is the play we are going to do. Why are you laughing, Lolita? Did I say anything hilarious?

197

LOLITA   No, Miss Cormorant.

CORMORANT   The play is a charming fantasy. Several hunt-
    ers are lost in a wood, and a strange girl they meet puts
    them into a kind of trance. They fraternize with mythical
    creatures. Of course, later the girl turns out to be a stu-
    dent at a nearby Institute for Extra-Sensorial Studies, and
    all ends quite plausibly. Mr Quilty will be giving a lecture
    at Beardsley College at the end of this month, and I'm
    sure he'll help us to rehearse.

CUT TO:

*Beardsley College (A coeducational institution where Humbert Humbert
teaches)*
The flowers that were budding in the first scene are now
opening. A shrill whirring bell rings through the corridors.
Students are leaving the classroom, where Humbert is collecting his notes. Miss Shatzki, an intense unkempt young
woman in a formless sweater, speaks to him.

HUMBERT   Yes, I see what you mean, Miss Shatzki.

MISS SHATZKI   I would also like to ask you about Poe's
    other love affairs. Don't you think—

CUT TO:

College Corridor with moving sunlight at the far end
Humbert walks down this long passage toward the exit. At one point various publicity items are tacked onto a cork board hanging on the wall. Humbert's glance passes across:

MISS EMMA KING, PIANO LESSONS

SPRING IS HERE — SAY IT WITH ADELE'S DAFFO-
DILS AT THE CAMPUS FLOWER SHOP

FOUND: : A GIRL'S LEATHER BELT FRIDAY,

8 P.M., MAIN AUDITORIUM FAMOUS PLAYWRIGHT
CLARE QUILTY WILL LECTURE ON THE LOVE OF ART

CUT TO:

Campus — Humbert
walks across the turfy expanse toward the parking lot, a small group issues from the college library. An instructor of English and a couple of students have been conducting a distinguished visitor, Quilty, and his constant companion, Vivian Darkbloom, on a tour through the stacks. Vivian is a stylish, bob haired, lanky lady in a well-tailored suit, with striking exotic features marred by a certain coarseness of

epiderm. The following scene is accompanied by a strong spring wind blowing across the campus.

INSTRUCTOR   (to Quilty)
    Next week the Department of Anthropology is arranging a special exhibition in the Rare Books department. It will feature some rugs, and, I think, sacred pictures, which Professor and Mrs Brooks brought back from Moscow.

QUILTY   Fascinating.

INSTRUCTOR   (noticing Humbert, who is passing by) Oh, Professor Humbert!

Humbert stops.

INSTRUCTOR   Mr Quilty, this is Professor Humbert, our visiting lecturer in Comparative Literature.

QUILTY   I don't think we have actually met – or have we? Seen you a couple of times in Ramsdale and elsewhere. Happy occasions.

He mumbles and smirks.

VIVIAN DARKBLOOM *(very distinctly)*
   And I am Vivian Darkbloom.

QUILTY *(his sparse hair and necktie stirring in the strong wind)* My
   collaborator, my evening shadow. Her name looks like an
   anagram. But she's a real woman – or anyway a real person. You're an inch taller than me, aren't you, m'dear?

VIVIAN *(training her brilliant smile upon Humbert)* My niece Mona
   goes to Beardsley School with your daughter.

HUMBERT Step.

QUILTY *(addressing the instructor and the two students)* You know
   the first thing people usually say when I'm introduced to
   them is how much they like, or simply adore, my *Nymphet*
   on TV.

HUMBERT I do have a vague recollection . . .

QUILTY Good for you. I often wonder what is technically
   more vague – a vague recollection or a vague premonition.
                    (to Vivian)
   This is a philosophic question, my dear, way above
   your pretty head. Ghouls of the past or phantoms of
   the future – which do we choose?

HUMBERT   Some of my best friends are phantoms.

QUILTY   Sense of humor, I see. What a wind! *Quel vent!*
Lucky I'm not wearing my toopee. Have a cigarette.

Humbert declines.

QUILTY   It should have been a Drome, but it is not. It's a
very special Spanish brand made especially for me, for
my urgent needs.
(*Dissolves in ghoulish giggles.*)
Does it always blow like this on your campus?

A photographer and a reporter, led by a lion-haired faculty
member, are seen approaching across the wind-rippled lawn.

FACULTY MEMBER   Mr Quilty, the town paper would like
a picture of you.

REPORTER   How long will you be staying in Beardsley?

QUILTY   Oh, I don't know. A week. Perhaps longer.

REPORTER   You're on your way from the East to Arizona.
Correct?

QUILTY   Yes. I share a ranch there with a few merry companions.

REPORTER   You are lecturing here on the Love of Art. How do you define 'Art'?

Front of Humbert's Rented House
in Thayer Street, Beardsley. It is a two-story brick-and-stucco affair, with an unkempt dandelion-invaded lawn which is in striking contrast to the adjacent neat garden of Miss Fenton Lebone, whose name is on the mailbox. She is inspecting the progress of certain bulbs when Humbert drives up. As he walks past her along the gravel path to his porch, the sound track registers his rapid mental supplication: Don't let Lebone notice me, don't have Miss Fenton Lebone talk to me, please don't let—. But the old lady's hawk eye has followed her neighbor's passage, and now she greets him sternly from behind her frontier of lilacs and laurels.

MISS LEBONE   Good afternoon, Professor.

HUMBERT   Oh. Hallo. (*Attempts to reach the safety of his door, but she will not be shaken off.*)

MISS LEBONE   I hate to intrude but don't you think you should do something about that jungle (*denouncing the dandelions*).

HUMBERT   (*trying a feeble quip*) Kindness to flowers. They are immigrants. We all are in a sense.

LEBONE   I'm certainly not. Couldn't I lend you my mower?

HUMBERT   Yes. Thanks. Perhaps Sunday.

LEBONE   You look exhausted.

HUMBERT   Yes, lots of work.

LEBONE   Incidentally, are you sure your pretty little girl gets enough sleep? I notice the light in her bedroom off and on, off and on, at all hours of the night. That *is* her bedroom window, isn't it? There's a string dangling from your pocket.

HUMBERT   Oh, thank you. Every time I undo a parcel I put the string in my pocket. So stupid.

LEBONE   Now tell me – why doesn't your Dolly come over to my house, any time, and curl up in a comfortable chair, and look at the *loads* of beautiful books my dear mother gave me when I was a child. Wouldn't that be much more wholesome than having the radio at full blast for hours on end?

HUMBERT   Certainly. By all means. We'll do that. (*He reaches the porch.*)

HUMBERT   (*mental monologue*) Should have said, as we all are refugees in this world. Staircase wit. Abominable woman!

CUT TO:

The Humbert Home
There is a depressing atmosphere of disorder and neglect in every room of the house.

HUMBERT   (*calling*) Lo! Lolita! Not in.

Leaning against the hallway telephone there is an empty Cola bottle with its straw. In the living room, a stool is askew, pushed away from the easy chair with a medley of magazines spilled on the floor; a plate with crumbs stands on the TV; a heap of bluebooks (ruins of a college examination) have been left by Humbert on and around the divan. On a small table there are the implements from Lolita's manicure set: a bottle of nail polish has stuck to the varnished top of the table where it leaves a bald spot when removed; one ballet shoe sits on the piano, its mate lies sole up on the threshold to the next room. In the kitchen there is a mountain of dirty dishes in the sink; bottle caps strew the table where flies stroll around a chicken drumstick.

CUT TO:

Hallway — Lolita with her school chum, Mona Dahl
(a smartly dressed, experienced-looking, cool brunette), and two boys come in and troop into the living room, where with magic instantaneousness, as if awaiting them, music starts mewing and moaning. Humbert comes out on the upper landing from his study.

HUMBERT   (*calling down*) Lolita? Who's that?

LOLITA   (*climbing the stairs*) It's me, and Mona, and Roy, and Rex.

HUMBERT   Where have you been?

LOLITA   Oh, at the candy bar. And now I've come to fetch my sweater and swimsuit.

HUMBERT   What for?

LOLITA   (*pulling on the sweater, which she finds on the banister*) We are going to the BB River Club.

HUMBERT   The *what?*

LOLITA   (*laughing as she emerges Bardotesquely disheveled through the neckhole*) The Beach and Boat Club. Roy's father's a member.

HUMBERT   Now, first of all I don't want that racket in the living room. And in the second place, it's much too windy on the river today.

LOLITA   Oh, maybe we'll just hang around—

HUMBERT   Besides, my pet, the theme of boating has not been a particularly fortunate one in your young life.

LOLITA   Okay, okay, there are other things we can do there—

HUMBERT   You are not going.

LOLITA   They have a bowling alley and table tennis—

HUMBERT   You have your homework to do. And house-work!

LOLITA   Jees—

HUMBERT   You tell your friends you're not going.

LOLITA   I'll do nothing of the sort.

HUMBERT   Then I will.

He clears his throat and descends the stairs. From the land-ing Lolita sees him entering the living room. The music stops, stunned. Swearing under her breath, Lolita runs down the steps toward her friends, as they are herded into the hallway from the living room by Humbert, whose con-strained nervous smile and jaunty manner cannot mask his awkward boorishness.

MONA   Really, sir, we would not stop long out there.

HUMBERT   No-no-no.

ROY   I'm sure, sir, you have nothing to worry about.

HUMBERT   I'm sorry, children, but it will be some other time.

He dismisses them and ascends the staircase repeating that rasping sound in his throat. In the hallway, Lolita talks to her friends as they file out into the sun.

LOLITA   Well, you see – this is the way it is.

MONA   I'll call you later, Dolly. I think your sweater's dreamy.

LOLITA   Thank you. It's virgin wool.

MONA   The only thing about you that is, kiddo.

Mona's husky laugh recedes as Lolita closes the door after her. Humbert from the stairs has heard that exchange. Lolita runs up past him to her room. She fumbles for the key to lock herself in. Humbert, rumbling, follows her.

CUT TO:

Lolita's Very Untidy Bedroom

HUMBERT   I've removed that key long ago, my dear. There is no place in the world where you could—

LOLITA   You get out!

HUMBERT   You have no reason to be mad at me. Yes, I shall leave you to your meditations, but first I want to say something about that girl, Mona.

LOLITA   You can't have her. She belongs to a marine.

HUMBERT   I shall ignore that idiotic remark. What I mean to say is − can it possibly be that you have betrayed me to her?

LOLITA   Very melodramatic.
                    (*Clowns.*)
You make me sick.
                    (*in a quieter smaller voice*)
Why can't I have fun with my friends?

HUMBERT   Because, Lolita, whenever you leave me, whenever you go somewhere without me, I start imagining all sorts of things.

LOLITA   So I never can have *any* fun?

HUMBERT   But you do have fun. You asked for a bicycle − I gave you one. You wanted music lessons − I got you Miss Emperor, I mean, Miss King, who is the best pianist in town.

LOLITA   I want to act in the school play.

HUMBERT   My darling, we went into that before. Can't you see, the more exposed you are to contacts, to people, the more dangerous it all becomes. You and I have to guard our secret constantly. You say you want to act in a play. You *are* in a play as it is. In a very difficult play where you have the part of an innocent schoolgirl. Stick to that role. It's quite big enough for one little performer.

LOLITA   Some day . . . Some day you'll be sorry.

HUMBERT   I know it's all very simple really. You don't love me. You never loved me. Isn't that the main problem?

LOLITA   Will you let me act in the play?

HUMBERT   Do you love me just a little, Lolita?

She looks at him, mysterious and meretricious, pondering whether to get what she wants by granting or by refusing.

CUT TO:

Living Room
Lolita is rehearsing. Mimeos of her part litter the furniture. From the kitchen threshold, Humbert tenderly observes her. She, like a hypnotic subject or a performer in a mystic rite, touches mirages of make-believe objects with her sly, slender, girl-child hands.

211

LOLITA   (in romantic monotone) Sleep, hunter. Velvet petals
flutter down upon you. In this bower you will recline.

She gestures toward an invisible partner – and then, with a
more normal movement, forehead puckered, searches for
the rest of her part on a mimeographed sheet.

HUMBERT   (gently) If you have finished, come and have
something to eat.

LOLITA   (continuing her incantations) I'll recite to you, hunter,
a lullaby song about the mourning dove you lost when
you were young. Listen!

> Gone is Livia, love is gone:
> Strong wing, soft breast, bluish plume;
> In the juniper tree moaning at dawn:
> doom, doom.

HUMBERT   What an ominous last line. A perfect spondee
but how depressing.

LOLITA   Lay off, will you? And now sleep, hunter, sleep.
Under the raining rose petals, sleep, hunter.
(to Humbert)
What do you want?

HUMBERT   A five-minute pause. I want you to forget Mr Hunter whoever he is.

She goes on with her tactile make-believe, stroking the air before her with kneading fingers.

HUMBERT   What are you doing? Plucking a fruit?

LOLITA   Look – what does it matter to you?

HUMBERT   One would like to know.

LOLITA   Suppose I'm stroking the horn of my pet unicorn – what the heck is it to you?

HUMBERT   Okay, Hecuba.

LOLITA   Will you go, please? I'll come in a minute.

He looks at her with dewy eyes, in an ecstasy of tenderness and adoration. She, exasperated, bangs her fist on the piano keys and falls into an easy chair, her legs sideways over the armrest.

LOLITA   You will never leave me alone, is that it?

He goes down on his knees literally crawling toward her, adumbrating an amphoric embrace, almost like a lover of yore.

LOLITA   Oh, no! Not again.

HUMBERT   My love, my mourning dove! I'm so miserable! There is something gathering around us which I cannot understand. You are not telling me all, you—

Doorbell

LOLITA   Get up! Get up from the floor! It's Mona. I quite forgot. Let her in. I'll be down in a sec.

She rushes through the kitchen, picking up the wedge of pizza on the way, and runs upstairs to her room. From the upper landing she cries down to Mona, whom Humbert has let in:

LOLITA   I'm changing and coming down!

CUT TO:

Living Room
Mona saunters in, followed by Humbert.

HUMBERT   Are you going to rehearse? She's been at it all day.

MONA   Well, no. I'm driving Dolly to her piano lesson.

HUMBERT   But today's Saturday? I thought Miss Emperor had changed the hour to Monday afternoon.

MONA   It's been changed back again.
                    (*picking up a book*)
Is this novel as good as some people say?

HUMBERT   Oh, I don't know. It's just an old love story with a new twist. Superb artist, of course, but who cares? We live in an age when the serious middlebrow idiot craves for a literature of ideas, for the novel of social comment.

MONA   I wish I could attend your lectures at Beardsley College, sir. We young people of today are so much in need of spiritual guidance.

HUMBERT   Tell me, young person of today, how was that party at your aunt's the other night?

MONA   Oh, it was sweet of you to allow Dolly to come.

HUMBERT   So the party was a success?

MONA   Oh, a riot, terrific.

HUMBERT   Did Dolly, as you call her, dance a lot?

MONA   Not a frightful lot. Why?

HUMBERT   I suppose all the boys are mad about her?

MONA   Well, sir, the fact is Dolly isn't much concerned with mere boys. They bore her.

HUMBERT   What about that Roy what's-his-name?

MONA   Oh, him.

A languorous shrug.

HUMBERT   What do you think of Dolly?

MONA   Oh, she's a swell kid.

HUMBERT   Is she very frank with you?

MONA   Oh, she's a doll.

HUMBERT   I mean, I suppose you and she—

Lolita runs into the room.

MONA   Dolly, your piano lesson is today. Remember? Not Monday. I came to fetch you as we agreed. Remember?

HUMBERT   Eight o'clock punctually, Lolita.

The two girls leave.

CUT TO:

The School Auditorium
A gauze curtain has just come down and the young performers are taking a last bow. Quilty's pudgy hands are briefly seen meatily clapping, as Lolita dreamily smiles across the footlights. Vivian Darkbloom, darkly blooming, blows her a kiss. The applause gradually subsides.

CUT TO:

Backstage
An atmosphere of exuberant success. Miss King, the piano teacher, greets tuxedo-clad Humbert.

HUMBERT   Glad to see you, Miss Emperor.

MISS KING   King.

HUMBERT   Yes, of course. Miss King. A thousand excuses. I keep thinking of the piano teacher in *Madame Bovary*. Well, I must thank you for giving Lolita so much time.

MISS KING   So much time? Why, on the contrary, she seems to have been much too busy with rehearsals. Let me see: she must have missed at least four lessons.

Lolita emerges from the greenroom. She is glamorous. She is excited. She has not yet shed her wings.

LOLITA   (*to Humbert*) You can go home now. Mona is taking me to her aunt's place for refreshments.

HUMBERT   You're coming with me. Home. At once.

LOLITA   I've promised Mona. Oh, please!

HUMBERT   No.

LOLITA   I'll do anything if you let me go.

HUMBERT   No.

LOLITA   I love you.

HUMBERT   Love me? With that lethal hate in those painted
    eyes? No, my girl, you'll come home and practice the
    piano.

He grasps her by the hand. A struggle would be indecorous.
Exeunt.

CUT TO:

Car
It pulls up. Humbert and Lolita come out in front of their
house. Lolita attempts to move away.

HUMBERT   Where are you going? Come here.

LOLITA   I want to ride my bike. I need some fresh air,
    you brute.

HUMBERT   You're coming in with me.

LOLITA   For Christ's sake—

CUT TO:

Hallway

HUMBERT   I know you are unfaithful to me. There's a tangled web around me. But I will not surrender. You cannot torment me like that. I have a right to know, I have a right to struggle.

LOLITA   Finished?

HUMBERT   And that's all you can answer?

LOLITA   If you've finished, I'll get something to eat. You cheated me out of a luscious supper.

CUT TO:

The Kitchen

Lolita has finished her sandwich and is messily fishing out slippery peach halves from a can. Humbert, throbbing with rage, makes himself a drink. She eats, reading a comic book and scratching her calf.

HUMBERT   What a fool – what a fool, this Humbert! Giving little Lolita numberless humbertless opportunities! Dreamy

bicycle rides, sunsets, lovers' lanes, piano lessons, rehearsals, ditches, garages, coal sheds.

Lolita, having finished her meal, walks to the door.

CUT TO:

Living Room
Lolita sprawling in an overstuffed chair. She bites at a hang-
nail and mocks Humbert with her heartless eyes. She has
placed one outstretched shoeless foot in coarse white sock
on a stool which she rocks with heel and toe.

LOLITA   Well, speak, lover.

Humbert paces the room rubbing his cheek with his fist in
a tremor of exasperation.

LOLITA   Because, if you don't want to speak to me, in a
    couple of minutes, I'll go riding my bicycle.

Humbert sinks down in a chair facing her. She continues to
stare at him and to rock the stool.

HUMBERT   I doubt you'll be using your bicycle much
    longer now.

LOLITA   Oh, yah?

He controls himself and tries to speak calmly but in the course of his speech his voice gradually rises to a hysterical pitch. And the window is open with the lilacs listening.

HUMBERT   Dolores, this must stop right away. You are ruining our relationship and jeopardizing your own safety. I don't know, nor wish to know, what young hood-lum, Roy or Foy, you are dating in secret. But all this must stop or else anything may happen.

LOLITA   Anything may happen, huh?

He snatches away the stool she is toe-heel rocking, and her foot falls with a thud.

LOLITA   Hey, take it easy!

Humbert grabs her by her thin wrist as she attempts to run out of the room.

HUMBERT   No, you'll listen to me! I'll break your wrist, but you'll listen. Tomorrow – yes tomorrow – we'll leave, we'll go to Mexico, we'll start a completely new life.

She manages to twist out of his grip and runs out of the house.

Humbert rushes out into the street and sees her pedaling townward. With one hand pressed to his palpitating heart, he makes for the corner, and then continues to the familiar drugstore. In the lamplight her bicycle, self-conscious and demure, is leaning against a post. Humbert enters the drugstore. At its far end, Lolita is revealed through the glass of a telephone booth, a little mermaid in a tank. She is still speaking. To whom? Me? Cupping the tube, confidentially hunched over it, she slits her eyes at Humbert, hangs up, and walks out of the booth.

LOLITA   (*brightly*) Tried to reach you at home.

HUMBERT   You did? That's odd. I saw you speaking, I saw your lips move.

LOLITA   Yes, I got the wrong number. Look, I don't want you to be mad at me any more. Everything is going to be all right from now on. I've reached a great decision.

HUMBERT   Oh, Lolita. If only I could still believe you.

She smiles at him and straddles her bike.

Thayer Street, leading home

A glistening night. Along the damp pavement Lolita half-rides her bike, pushing against the curb with one foot, waiting for Humbert to catch up, and then propelling herself again. He walks behind, agitated, moist-eyed, jerkily trying to keep up with her. A dog strains on its leash, and its owner allows it to sniff at a lamppost. The CAMERA follows Humbert and Lolita as they approach the house. Lilacs in bloom. The neighbor's lighted window goes out.

CUT TO:

Hallway. Lolita and Humbert enter

LOLITA   Carry me upstairs. I feel kind of romantic tonight.

He gathers her up. The telephone rings.

LOLITA   (*raising her index finger*) Telephone.

HUMBERT   Oh, let it ring!

LOLITA   Put me down, put me down. Never disappoint a telephone.

HUMBERT   My aphoristic darling! All right.

On the telephone Quilty speaks in a disguised muffled croak-voice.

QUILTY   How are you, Prof?

HUMBERT   Fine. May I—

QUILTY   Sorry to disturb you at such a late hour. Are you enjoying your stay at Beardsley?

HUMBERT   Yes. May I inquire who's calling?

QUILTY   This is the best time of the year but we might do with some rain.

HUMBERT   Sorry – who's calling?

QUILTY   (with a pleasant laugh) We haven't actually met but I've been keeping a friendly eye on you. Could I talk to you on the phone for a minute?

HUMBERT   Are you connected with the college?

QUILTY   In a way. I am a kind of extramural student. You see, I am studying your case.

HUMBERT   What case? I don't understand.

QUILTY   Is Dolores in bed?

HUMBERT   Oh, that's what it is. Are you disguising your voice, Roy Walker?

QUILTY   No, no. You are mistaken.

HUMBERT   Well, all I can tell you is that neither she nor I welcomes calls from strangers.

QUILTY   (*very suavely*) This is a complete misunderstanding. The group I represent is merely anxious that children should not keep late hours. You see, Mr Humbert, I am a private member of the Public Welfare Board.

HUMBERT   What's your name?

QUILTY   Oh, it's an obscure unremarkable name. My department, sir, wants to check some bizarre rumors concerning the relationship between you and that pretty child. We have certain plans for her. We know an elderly gentleman, a bachelor of independent means, who would be eager to adopt her.

In the course of this speech Humbert takes a pillbox out of his waistcoat and swallows a tablet.

HUMBERT   This is ridiculous.

QUILTY   Have you adopted her? Legally, I mean?

HUMBERT   Well, I—

QUILTY   Have you filed a petition? Your stutter proclaims you have not.

HUMBERT   I assume that a stepfather is a relative and that a relative is a natural guardian.

QUILTY   Are you aware that the word 'natural' has rather sinister connotations?

HUMBERT   Not in my case, no.

QUILTY   But you agree that a minor female must have a guardian?

HUMBERT   I suppose so.

QUILTY   And that she is not merely a pet?

HUMBERT   I really—

QUILTY   You moved here from Ramsdale, Professor?

HUMBERT   That's right. But—

In the meantime Lolita has crept into the hallway and enlaced Humbert with her bare arm.

QUILTY   Are you aware that some states prohibit a guardian from changing the ward's residence without an order of the court?

HUMBERT   Which states?

QUILTY   For example, the state you are in: a state of morbid excitement. Have you seen your psychiatrist lately?

HUMBERT   I neither have nor need one.

QUILTY   You are classified in our files as a white widowed male. Are you prepared to give our investigator a report on your present sex life, if any?

HUMBERT   Investigator?

Humbert nervously strokes caressive Lolita's wrist.

QUILTY   Yes. We intend our Dr Blanche Schwarzman, a
very efficient lady, to visit you at your convenience.

HUMBERT   I'm afraid I have nothing to tell her.

QUILTY   'Afraid' is Freudian lingo.

HUMBERT   I do not follow you. Give me your address and
I shall write you.

QUILTY   That's unnecessary. After tomorrow our doctor
will examine you and your protégée. I now hang up.

DISSOLVE TO:

Living Room
Humbert walking about nervously.

HUMBERT   It's a hoax. It's a hoax. But that's immaterial.
Rumors, he said. Oh, mon Dieu!

LOLITA   We must go away.

HUMBERT   We must flee as in an old melodrama. Out saf-
est bet is to go abroad.

LOLITA   Okay – let's go to Mexico. I was conceived there.

HUMBERT   I'm sure I'll find a lecturing job there. Marvelous! I know a Spanish poet in Mexico City. He is full of
black bulls and symbols, and as corny as a matador. But
he is influential.

LOLITA   One condition. This time I am going to trace out
our route. I want to take in Arizona. I want to see the
Indian dances in Elphinstone.

HUMBERT   (*weeping*) I'm in your hands, your hot little
hands, my love.

It is assumed that from Beardsley (which is situated in
Idaho) to the Mexican border (via Arizona) the distance is
at least 1,000 miles. Our fugitives start Wednesday morning.
Humbert, who is eager to reach with the least delay Borderton, S. Arizona (and thence, Mexico's West Coast Highway)
intends to be there Friday morning. In a naive effort to be
inconspicuous he plans to sleep two nights in the car (the
first, within the parking area of a trailer court and the
second, somewhere in the Arizona desert). It is further

assumed that Quilty, using three or four different rented cars, so as to avoid identification and confuse his victim, pursues Humbert from Idaho, through Nevada (or Utah), to Arizona. Quilty's plan is to have Humbert transport the minor female across two state lines down to Elphinstone, Arizona, where he will kidnap her and take her to his ranch in that vicinity. During the journey, there arises the problem how to get Lolita's luggage out of the car. This is attempted at the stop in Waco, Thursday morning (and successfully brought off on the following Monday, with the unplanned help of Lolita's hospitalization). The glimpses Humbert has had of Quilty before (e.g., in Briceland and Beardsley) had been too casual and brief to allow recognition. Quilty takes care to remain a fleet shadow, a ghostly predator, as he keeps up with Humbert on the road, now overtaking him, now awaiting his passage. Humbert's anxiety and rage are increased by his not quite knowing if it is a sleuth or a suitor.

CUT TO:

Humbert's Eyes in the Rearview Mirror
He and Lolita are driving along a canyon into the small burg of Cottonwood: three poplars and alfalfa fields.

LOLITA   We'll crash into something if you keep looking back.

HUMBERT   What a bizarre situation!

LOLITA   You're telling me. I've been riding with a nut all day.

HUMBERT   – bizarre because there's no general way of dealing with this kind of case. That car has been following us, on and off, for the last two hundred miles. I can't very well complain to the highway patrol.

LOLITA   (laughing) You certainly can't!

HUMBERT   But I can try to give him the slip.

LOLITA   Not with this jalopy.

HUMBERT   (going through a changing light in Cottonwood) Ah, the red light will stop him.

LOLITA   You'll get arrested if you do that.

HUMBERT   And here we'll turn and hide for a minute. In this nice little lane.

LOLITA   It's a one-way little lane.

HUMBERT   True.

He backs out.

LOLITA   Besides it's illegal to play games with other cars on the road.

HUMBERT   Will you stop chattering. I almost hit that van.

LOLITA   Look. Let's get back to the highway and just ignore the whole business.

CUT TO:

The Highway Again — evening of the same day — low blinding sun
Lolita is eating a banana in the moving car.

CUT TO:

Service Station
Needing a pair of new sunglasses, Humbert leaves Lolita in the car and walks into the office of the station. His pursuer quietly pulls up just across the street while Humbert is selecting the glasses. He glances through a side window.

CUT TO:

Humbert's Car

Quilty has walked up to it and Lolita is leaning out and talking to him rapidly, her hand with outspread fingers going up and down, as it does when she is very serious and emphatic. Humbert is struck by the voluble familiarity of her manner. The conversation is not heard (except, perhaps, for the word 'Elphinstone'), and Quilty's face is not seen. He bolts back to his convertible, which disappears as Humbert comes out of the office.

CUT TO:

Humbert's Car moving up a steep grade

HUMBERT   What did that man ask you, Lo?

LOLITA   (*studying a road map*) Man? Oh, that man. Oh, yes. Oh, I don't know. He wondered if I had a map. Lost his way, I guess.

A pause.

HUMBERT   Now listen, Lo. I don't know if you are lying or not. I don't know if you are insane or not – but that person has been following us all day, and I think he is a cop.

LOLITA   (*laughing*) If he's really a cop the worst thing we
    could do would be to show that we are scared. Oh, look:
    all the nines are changing into the next thousand. When
    I was a little kid I used to think they'd stop and go back to
    nines if only my mother would agree to back the car.

CUT TO:

Market

HUMBERT   Let me see – we wanted—

He broods among the fruit, a rotting Priap, listening to a
melon, questioning a peach, pushing his wire cart toward
the lacquered strawberries. Lolita has been loitering near the
window where the magazine rack is. She sees Quilty haunt-
ing the sidewalk. Satisfying herself that Humbert is engrossed
in his shopping, she slips out. Presently, burdened with his
cornucopian paper bag, Humbert comes out of the store
looking around for Lolita. He leaves the bag in the parked
car, locks it again, and then paces the sidewalk peering into
various shops as he proceeds along a series of Drugs, Real
Estate, Auto Parts, Café, Sporting Goods, Real Estate, Furniture, Drugs, Western Union, Cleaners, Appliances, Betty's
Beauty Parlor. As he walks back, in pain and panic, he
suddenly descries her trying to retrieve her new coat and

traveling case out of the car; but the doors are locked, and she can't pull out her things through the three-quarters closed window (Quilty the shadow is ambushed in a side street, the idea being that she join him with some of her treasured possessions). She notices Humbert approaching – and, slitting her eyes, walks toward him with feigned nonchalance.

LOLITA   Oh, there you are.

For a few seconds Humbert looks at her in grim silence.

LOLITA   What's the matter?

HUMBERT   You were gone twenty minutes. I cannot toler-
    ate these vanishing acts. I want to know exactly where
    you've been – and with whom.

LOLITA   I ran into a girl friend.

HUMBERT   Really?

LOLITA   You calling me a liar?

HUMBERT   Her name, please.

LOLITA   Oh, just a kid I went to school with.

HUMBERT   Beardsley School?

LOLITA   Yes. Oh, yes. Beardsley.

HUMBERT   Her name?

LOLITA   Betty. Betty Parker.

HUMBERT   Perfect. Here, in this little black book, Volume 2, I have a list of your schoolmates. Let's see. Hm. There's a Mary Paddington, and a Julia Pierce. But no Parker. What say you?

LOLITA   She was not in my group.

HUMBERT   That's the entire school I have listed here.

LOLITA   She enrolled just before we left.

HUMBERT   Well, let's try another angle. Where exactly did you meet her?

LOLITA   Oh, I saw her from the grocery. She was just loafing around like me.

HUMBERT   And what did you do next?

LOLITA   We went to a drugstore.

HUMBERT   And you had there—?

LOLITA   Couple of Cokes.

HUMBERT   Careful, my girl. We can check that, you know.

LOLITA   At least, she had. I had a glass of water.

HUMBERT   The anonymous fluid. I see. Very good. Was it that place over there?

LOLITA   Sure.

HUMBERT   Good. Come on, we'll grill the soda jerk.

LOLITA   Wait a sec. Come to think, it might have been the other store, on the corner.

HUMBERT   Confrontation delayed. But it's all right. We'll try both.

LOLITA   Or perhaps in one of the side streets.

HUMBERT   We'll find it. Here, let's go into this telephone booth. You rather like telephone booths, don't you? Now, let's consult the directory. This dirty book. This chained and battered book. Dignified Funeral Service. No, we don't need that yet. Here we are. Drugists, Retail. Hill Drug Store. Corner Drug Store. Cypress Lane Drugs. And Larkin's Pharmacy. Well, that's all they have around here. And we'll check them one by one.

LOLITA   Go to hell.

HUMBERT   My dear, rudeness will get you nowhere.

LOLITA   You are not going to trap me. Okay. So we didn't have a pop. We just talked and walked, and looked at dresses in show windows.

HUMBERT   That window, for example?

LOLITA   Yes, that window for example.

HUMBERT   Oh, Lolita! Let us look closer at it.

CUT TO:

The Show Window of a dress store.

A man, on his hands and knees, is rearranging the carpet on which a wedding group stands in a more or less dismantled state ('as if a blast had just worked havoc with them'): one wigless and armless figure is naked except for white spats. Another, a sexless little nude, stands in a smirking pose, with a posy, and would represent, when clothed, a flower girl of Lolita's size. The taller, lavishly veiled bride is complete but lacks one arm. On the floor, where the employee crawls, there lies a cluster of three bare arms and a blond wig. Two of the arms, not necessarily a pair, happen to be twisted and seem to suggest a clasping gesture of horror and supplication. Humbert, tense and bitter, his face twitching, points out these details to sullen Lolita.

HUMBERT   Look, Lolita. Look well. Isn't this a gruesome symbol of something or other? Doesn't it make your delicate flesh creep a little?

CUT TO:

A Highway, low sun, Shadow of Car running and fluctuating on a rock bank – a Sign:

ELPHINSTONE 20 M.

Lolita is ill. She covers her eyes with her hand, throws her head back, moans.

HUMBERT   Tired?

She does not respond.

HUMBERT   Would you like me to stop? You might nap for an hour or two.

She shrugs her shoulders.

HUMBERT   Don't you feel well?

LOLITA   I feel utterly rotten.

HUMBERT   Why, what's the matter, my darling? Tummy?

LOLITA   Everything. I want to stop at Elphinstone for the night.

HUMBERT   Oh, but we'll never make Borderton at this rate.

LOLITA   I'm dying, you dope. We'll spend the night in Elphinstone.

HUMBERT   I wanted to avoid motels.

LOLITA   Well, this time we'll go to the best one in Elphinstone.

I underlined it in the AAA book. Dream Hacienda. Oh, I've never felt so awful in all my life! You're sitting on my sweater.

HUMBERT My poor darling! What a setback. Tsk-tsk. I know what we'll do. At the next turnout I'll take your temperature. I have a thermometer in my overnight bag.

CUT TO:

Turnout — a sheer cliff rising on the far side of the highway and a misty abyss melting just beyond the rim of the turnout Lolita, her head on the nape rest, eyes closed, endures the thermometer stuck in her mouth. The CAMERA gingerly inspects the litter receptacles with their cans and containers, and a small child's sneaker forgotten on the stone parapet. Humbert consulting his wristwatch.

HUMBERT Well, I think we can peep now.

Tenderly he removes the glass tube from her mouth. She licks her parched lips and shivers. Humbert tries to make out the level of the mercury.

HUMBERT These tricky American thermometers are meant to conceal their information from the layman. Ah, here we are. Good God, one hundred and three. I must take you straight to a hospital.

Quilty has pulled up at the next turnout.

CUT TO:

Dream Hacienda Motel at Elphinstone, Arizona – a fine morning Humbert is seen coming out of his unit with several books under his arm and a bunch of rather straggly wild flowers. The landlady talks to him as he goes to his car.

LANDLADY   I hope she's much better today.

HUMBERT   Well, I'm driving over to see. The doctor said that in this kind of flu there's a distinct drop in temperature on the fourth day, and indeed she had hardly any fever yesterday.

LANDLADY   She'll love the flowers.

HUMBERT   I picked them in the ravine at the back of your place. Cold breeze today. Is it the elevation?

LANDLADY   Oh, it's hot enough for me.

HUMBERT   I'm not feeling well. Guess I'll lie down when I return.

LANDLADY   Wait a minute. I'll remove this basket of linen so you can turn more easily.

CUT TO:

A Sunny Private Room in the Elphinstone Hospital

Lolita, looking happy and innocent, lies in her neat bed with a magazine, her lips freshly painted, her hair brilliantly brushed. There is a white telephone, a topaz ring, and one rose in a glass with bubble-gemmed stem on the bedside table. Mary Lore, a plump, comely, arrogant young nurse who is in cahoots with the nymphet, is folding very rapidly a white flannel blanket as Humbert enters with his pathetic bouquet and books.

HUMBERT   *Bonjour, mon petit.*

LOLITA   What gruesome funeral flowers. Thanks all the same. But do you mind cutting out the French, it annoys everybody.

Her eyes go back to her magazine.

HUMBERT   Temperature normal? Well, that's splendid. Who gave you that rose?

LOLITA   Mary.

MARY LORE   (*glancing window-ward at the yard below*) You can't park there, Mister. You have to go around to the other end.

HUMBERT   Sorry. I was in a hurry – and I don't feel too well.

MARY   There is a sign saying 'staff only.'

HUMBERT   All right, all right.

Exit Mary with blanket.

LOLITA   Mary was trying to be helpful.

HUMBERT   Mary is arrogant and nosy. I would not wonder, my dear, if you two had swapped every kind of crummy confession. That rump of hers must make interns pant.

LOLITA   Your English is showing vahst improvement, my deah. You'll be using delinquent lingo next.

A pause.

HUMBERT   I brought you some rather fascinating books: *The History of Dancing. The Romantic Poets* by my friend Professor Behr. *Flowers of the Rockies*, with excellent illustrations. And *Carmen* by Mérimée – not a very good translation, I'm afraid, but do read it, it's a marvelous melancholy story.

Lolita emits a grunt of indifferent gratitude and continues to consume her magazine. Mary Lore bustles in again.

HUMBERT   (*picking up a pair of sunglasses from the top of a chest of drawers*) Oh – whose are these? Not mine, not yours.

MARY   (*after exchanging a quick glance with Lolita*) Then it's a visitor left them.

HUMBERT   Visitor? You had a visitor, Lolita?

MARY   (*pocketing the glasses*) Another patient had. I found them in the corridor and thought they might be yours.

HUMBERT   *Est-ce que tu ne m'aimes plus, ma Carmen?* My Carmen does not love me any more?

LOLITA   There we go again.

She flips through her magazine, finds the continuation, and reads on.

HUMBERT   The thermometer broke in the glove compart-ment but I took my pulse this morning and it was one hundred and ten. I shall soon leave you and go to bed. Don't you want to look at the nice books I brought you?

Lolita emits again her neutral grunt and picks her nose as she plunges deeper into 'They called me a Harlot.' Humbert lowers himself into a cretonne chair, opens the botanical work he has brought her, and attempts to identify his flowers. This proves impossible.

HUMBERT   (with a sigh) I'll be going away in a minute. I'm not feeling well at all. Don't you want to talk to me?

LOLITA   What?

HUMBERT   I said don't you want to talk to me? You'll read your magazine when I'm gone.

LOLITA   What do you want me to tell you?

Mary Lore reenters with a vase for the flowers.

HUMBERT   I'm wondering if you should not leave the hospital tomorrow. You look the image of radiant health.

MARY   She will stay till Tuesday. Doctor's orders. Horse mint, poison oak. And this goldenrod will give her hay fever.

HUMBERT   Oh, throw them out, throw them out.

MARY   Yes, I think I had better remove them.

She exits.

HUMBERT   Lolita! My love! Just think – Tuesday if we start early we'll be in Mexico by noon. No mysterious agents, no ghosts, no ghouls will follow us any longer. We shall be free to live as we like, my Lolita. I'll make you a formal proposal. An old priest will bless us, and we shall live happily forever after, in lovely Rosamorada.

Both realize that Mary Lore is again in the room.

LOLITA   He's reciting poetry. Don't mind him, Mary.

HUMBERT   Yes, poetry. The only reality on this earth. Well, I'll be on my way.

LOLITA   I want all my things. The brown bag, mother's blue one, the car sack, everything.

HUMBERT   They are still in the car. I did not take them to the motel.

LOLITA   Well, I want them right now.

HUMBERT   Couldn't you wait till Tuesday? I mean, you don't want *all* your frocks immediately.

LOLITA   That's for me to decide. Where's that hand mirror, Mary?

HUMBERT   I don't feel strong enough to carry all that luggage.

MARY   Oh, we'll have Joe do it, don't you worry.

HUMBERT   All right. I think I'll go now. Well, good-bye, Lolita.

LOLITA   (*looking at herself in the hand mirror*) Bye-bye.

HUMBERT   Girl with a Hand Glass. Artist unknown.

He considers her, softly swinging the car keys he holds. Mary waits at the door.

CUT TO:

Motel Room

Humbert is asleep asprawl on one of the twin beds. He is in the throes of a virus infection and has been drinking freely from the bottle of gin beside him. The bedside telephone rings. It takes him some time to come out of his sick slumber.

VOICE   Hi there, Professor.

HUMBERT   Who's calling?

VOICE   Are you all right?

HUMBERT   Not exactly.

VOICE   Not feeling too good, eh?

HUMBERT   No. Who is it?

VOICE   Not enjoying your trip? That's too bad.

HUMBERT   What d'you want?

VOICE   I'm not sure what to call it. Cooperation? Surrender to fate?

HUMBERT   All right. If you are not a hallucination, not a mere tinnitus—

VOICE   A *what?*

HUMBERT   Tinnitus – a singing in the ears, because I have a high fever—

VOICE   Frankly, I'm also nursing some sort of bug. Guess, we both caught it from her.

HUMBERT   From her? What d'you mean?

VOICE   Oh, lots of things are feminine – cars, carpets, car pets, haha! I've even heard a fireman refer to a fire as she.

HUMBERT   If you're not my delirium—

VOICE   Skip it. Look, Bertie, I just wanted to make sure you're safe in bed. Good-nitus.

HUMBERT   If I'm not fancying things, then you must be the person who's been following me.

VOICE   Well, that's all finished now. You're not followed any more. I'll be leaving in a minute with my little niece. (Aside: You stay out of this.)

HUMBERT   Wait!

VOICE   Good-nitus, good-nitus. (*with a laugh*) I know exactly what you'll do as soon as I hang up.

He hangs up. Humbert frantically searches for the scrap of paper on which he has jotted down the telephone number connecting him with Lolita at the hospital. Finds it and dials. A nurse's voice answers, but is engulfed in Quilty's rich baritone.

VOICE   I'll take it. It's for me. Well, isn't that pat. I told you I knew you would do it. Sorry I can't talk now. She's in my lap and quite lively.

Hangs up guffawing.
Humbert is about to dial again – but thinks better of it and in a frenzy of horror and hurry pulls on some clothes and stumbles out.

CUT TO:

The Vestibule of Elphinstone Hospital — a spacious lobby with a staircase on either side and offices at the farther end.

There are several people around. Joking Joe, a robust male nurse, is in the act of wheeling a mummylike patient out of the elevator. Nurse Mary Lore is preening herself on the first landing. Doctor Blue is coming out of the x-ray department perusing a cloudy picture, the galaxy of a lung. Two old men in a corner are playing chess, and a third old-timer is inspecting the titles of several books (*Flowers of the Rockies*, etc.) heaped on a chair. As Humbert rushes in and launches into his dramatic, drunken, sick, hysterical expostulations, the various people around freeze in various positions.

HUMBERT   Lolita! Lolita! Lolita!

MARY LORE   (*tripping down the steps*) We don't want a scene—

HUMBERT   Where is she?

MARY   You know perfectly well that her uncle was to come for her today.

HUMBERT   I know nothing of the sort.

DR BLUE   Take it easy. What's the matter, Mary?

MARY   He's sick and doesn't know what he's saying. The girl's uncle just took her away.

HUMBERT   It's hellish conspiracy.

MARY   She warned me her stepfather had a feud with the rest of the family.

HUMBERT   A hellish lie! Where is she? I demand an answer.

DR BLUE   Now, now, don't get excited.

Humbert tries to get hold of Mary Lore. He almost manages to clutch her. She gives a melodious yelp and twists free. The patient, who has been wheeled out by Joe, rises like Lazarus and joins Joe and Dr Blue who are subduing Humbert.

CUT TO:

Psychiatrist
speaking (this is Dr Ray who appears in the Prologue and will appear again at the very end of Act Three):

PSYCHIATRIST   As we now know from his notes, Humbert

Humbert spent many a dismal month trying in vain to locate his lost Lolita and to establish the identity of her mysterious abductor. His quest merely resulted in impairing his health. At the sanatorium where he was treated for a heart condition, attention was also given to his mental state. The present speaker and two other psychiatrists endeavored to help Mr Humbert but dissimulation had become second nature with him. My assistants and I tried to open channels of communication for the patient by providing a background of refinement and ease, soft music, amusing hobbies, and a permissive atmosphere in which he might dare express his most dangerous thoughts. However, the patient not only refused to indulge in voluptuous or vengeful fantasies, but insulted the therapist by calling him 'the rapist of Psyche the Soul.' He sneered at cooperation. He was abusive, he was taciturn. And Dr Christina Fine, a lovely lady and a very strong analyst, complained that the patient kept trying to hypnotize her and make her divulge her innermost cravings. I am happy to say she is now my wife.

By the beginning of the following year, the patient's physical condition had improved so much that he was able to check out and join again the faculty of Beardsley College.

CUT TO:

A Neutral Place

The detective whom Humbert had hired to look for Lolita is reporting to him for the last time.

DETECTIVE   I'm afraid we'll have to give it up.

HUMBERT   Couldn't you go on? You said you would investigate the New Mexico clue.

DETECTIVE   Proved a dud. Dolores Hayes, H, A, Y, E, S, is a fat old dame selling homemade Tokay to the Indians.

HUMBERT   What about Canada?

DETECTIVE   What about the wide world? She might be a model in Brazil or a dancer in Paris.

HUMBERT   But isn't it merely a question of time? Can't *everybody* be tracked down finally?

DETECTIVE   Look, mister. We don't even have good pictures of her, she's just a kid in them. By now she may have three babies of her own.

HUMBERT   You are sure you could not keep trying?

DETECTIVE   It would just mean taking your money.

HUMBERT   I want the photos back.

DETECTIVE   We'll keep one or two in our files just in case. This one, in fancy dress, for instance.

He returns a number of photographs to Humbert. They should give a brief pictorial summary of Lolita's past life with him: Kneeling, half-naked, in a patch of sun on a mat; standing beside her mother on the dappled lawn; attending a school ball in full-skirted flamingo dress; in bluejeans and T-shirt, sprawling with a comic book; in dirty shorts, getting into a canoe (Charlie handing her a paddle from the bushy bank); in the passenger seat of Humbert's car; feeding a chipmunk; riding a pony; wearing black tights; in fancy dress on the stage.

CUT TO:

Beardsley College
Men and women students are seen streaming out into a courtyard. Humbert, with books and papers under his arm, walks to the parking lot. Mrs Fowler, a lean, elegant,

forty-year-old flirt, the wife of the Head of the Department, calls out to Humbert from inside her car.

MRS FOWLER   Hullo, Humbert.

HUMBERT   Hullo, Diana.

MRS FOWLER   Do you know if my husband is through with his seminar?

HUMBERT   Yes, I think I saw him going to his office.

MRS FOWLER   He said he would finish a little earlier. We are to pick up a niece of mine at the airport. The poor kid lost her mother last year, and now her father has cancer.

HUMBERT   Oh.

MRS FOWLER   I am so sorry for the child. We'll take her to the Riviera in spring. When is your sabbatical, Humbert?

HUMBERT   Alas, I've been here only two years.

He stands leaning with his elbows on the sill of her car. She puts her hand on his.

MRS FOWLER   You must come to see us more often. Frank will be away on a lecture tour next month, and I will be very lonesome. Would you teach me chess? I think it's such a glamorous medieval game.

Frank Fowler comes up.

MRS FOWLER   (to her husband) I was telling Humbert we must get together soon.

FOWLER   Yah. What about Sunday? Come have dinner with us.

CUT TO:

The Fowlers' Living Room
Bourgeois abstract art on the walls. They are having preprandial drinks with their guests. Frank Fowler gulps down the contents of a tall tumbler.

FOWLER   (to Humbert) Another Scotch? Well, I think I shall.

MRS FOWLER   No, Frank, that's enough before dinner.

FOWLER   How does it feel to be a bachelor, Humbert? Must be a heavenly sensation.

HUMBERT   I was twice married.

MRS FOWLER   Oh, were you?

HUMBERT   My second wife died four years ago. I inherited a stepdaughter.

MRS FOWLER   But that's fascinating, Humbert. How old is she?

HUMBERT   Oh, she must be quite old by now. More than seventeen. She's living her own life somewhere. I've lost track of her.

A nymphet comes in.

MRS FOWLER   This is Nina, my niece.

In the course of the following dialogue Humbert pays no attention to the child, and only at the last moment, as she turns away, and he sinks back into his chair with a tidbit picked from a remote plate, does he permit himself one brief, sad, ember-hot, tiger-quick glance.

MRS FOWLER   When is Rosemary coming to fetch you?

NINA   I dunno. Soon, I guess.

MRS FOWLER   What picture are you going to see?

NINA   Oh, some western. I don't care.

MRS FOWLER   (*smiling*) Okay. Run along.

Nina indolently leaves.

MRS FOWLER   She is twelve and in her blasé period, if you please.

FOWLER   I think I'll spank her if she perseveres in that droopy style.

MRS FOWLER   Oh, she'll be all right after we take her to Europe.

FOWLER   What's your vacation going to be, Humbert, m'boy?

HUMBERT   I have no definite plans.

FOWLER   Come with us to Cap Topaz. It's the best spot on the Riviera.

HUMBERT   I know it well. My father owned a big hotel not
far from there. The Mirana. It has degenerated now into
an apartment house.

MRS FOWLER   Will you come, Humbert? We'll gamble at
the casino.

HUMBERT   I dare not gamble any more.

MRS FOWLER   Well, Frank and I will, and you can sprawl
on the *plage*, and build sand castles with Nina. Is that a
deal? Will you come?

HUMBERT   What again? The old pang? The perilous magic?
No. I'm not coming with you. The excitement would be
too much. I have a weak heart, you know.

MAID   Dinner is served.

CUT TO:

An Exchange of Good Nights
on the lighted steps of the Fowler home. Humbert walks off.
His steps resound on the deserted sidewalk.

HUMBERT   I'm very lonely and I'm very drunk. The old

262

magic. Kill Frank Fowler, marry Diana, drown Diana, inherit Nina, kill self. Oh, my Lolita, Lolita, Lolita . . .

Next Day.

CUT TO:

Lecture Hall
Humbert has just finished his routine lecture and is collecting his notes. A male student comes up to the lectern.

STUDENT   I've been auditing your lectures, Professor. My name is Shatzki, Norbert Shatzki, you had my sister in your class three years ago, she sends you her kindest regards.

HUMBERT   Oh yes. Yes.

SHATZKI   She's married now. I was wondering, sir, if you would also cover Edgar Poe's other loves?

In the meantime, another student, a girl, has entered the classroom.

GIRL   May I audit your lectures, Professor Humbert?

HUMBERT   (*absentmindedly, paying little attention to either of them, still collecting his notes*) If you like. No, I'll ignore his other romances.

GIRL   I'm taking philosophy, but I hope to enroll in your courses next year.

HUMBERT   Yes. Yes.

He is now ready to leave.

GIRL   I see you don't recognize me at all, at all, monsieur.

HUMBERT   Good God – Mona!

MONA   It has been three years since we met. Time certainly flies.

HUMBERT   Let's walk across the campus and have some coffee at The Den.

MONA   I'm afraid I have a class in ten minutes.

HUMBERT   Well, let's go to my office. It's right opposite.

CUT TO:

Humbert's Office

HUMBERT   Three long years . . .

MONA   You don't live on Thayer Street any more?

HUMBERT   Oh no. I've a room in Clemm Hall. And you —
how have you been?

MONA   Oh, fine. I left Beardsley School at the same time
as – as – anyway, I mean, I never finished Beardsley School.

HUMBERT   I see.

MONA   Your temples are a little gray, which is most becom-
ing.

HUMBERT   You don't ask me an obvious question, Mona.

MONA   Sorry. Have you remarried, sir?

HUMBERT   You haven't changed. Evasive Mona, strange girl.

MONA   I'm not strange. I merely know life rather well.
Okay: how's Lolita?

HUMBERT   She's attending a school, a kind of junior college in Europe.

MONA   Oh, so it's true. That's what one of your colleagues
told me. What college exactly?

HUMBERT   You would not know it. A small college in Paris.

MONA   Oh.

A pause.

HUMBERT   Old schoolmates seldom write to each other –
isn't that so?

MONA   It depends.

HUMBERT   Naturally. Well, let's chat – let's reminisce, as
Americans say. Why do you look at me like that?

MONA   Mr Humbert . . . My parents sent me to Europe,
too; I, too, went to school in Paris. It's odd that I never
ran into Dolly.

HUMBERT   She never gave you her address, did she?

MONA   Oh, I knew you were still teaching in Beardsley. I could always reach her through you, couldn't I?

HUMBERT   But you didn't.

MONA   Well, no.

HUMBERT   And you completely lost track of her?

MONA   Why don't you give me her address?

HUMBERT   It's hardly worth while: she'll be leaving next week. As a matter of fact, she may be already in this country.

MONA   You are still very fond of your stepdaughter, sir?

HUMBERT   Still? What do you mean – 'still'?

MONA   Everybody loves a child, but the child grows up, and something fades, something diminishes.

HUMBERT   Philosophy major.

MONA   But isn't it true? Or would you say that nothing changes?

HUMBERT   Nothing.

MONA   And you'd still be ready to forgive—?

HUMBERT   Forgive? Forgive what?

MONA   We are taking a purely abstract case. Assuming she had done something wrong—

HUMBERT   Mona, will you stop acting the impenetrable vamp?

MONA   Why, everything is crystal clear now. I'm very fond of Dolly, and it's such a comfort to know that you always intend to be kind to her.

HUMBERT   Did she write you? Please, tell me.

MONA   Doesn't she write to *you*?

HUMBERT   She's a poor correspondent – but that's not the point.

MONA   Oh, the point is clear, sir. I'm afraid I must be going now.

HUMBERT   She did write you? You *do* know where she is?

MONA   In those faraway schools we were talking about, in those schools one can be very unhappy, their lamps are dim, but one learns a good deal. I'm sure you needn't worry about our Dolly. I've got a class now.

The bell violently rings announcing the beginning of the next class period.

It should now have been established that Mona has had a letter from Lolita, apparently asking her to find out if it is safe for her, Lolita, to write to Humbert.

CUT TO:

University Post Office – The time is 8:55 A.M.
Professor Fowler takes out his letters. Humbert comes up and tweaks open *his* pigeonhole.

PROFESSOR FOWLER   If your mail is as dull as mine, I'm sorry for you, Humbert.

HUMBERT   I never expect anything – that's my advantage. This is a circular. This is from a Mrs Richard Schiller – some graduate student, I presume. This is a fenestrated bill. This is a publisher's list. And this is not for me but for Professor Humphries.

FOWLER   Not gay, as the French say.

HUMBERT   Well, I must be rushing to my exam. Room 342,

(*repeats*)

342.

CUT TO:

The Door with That Number
He stares at it for a moment.

HUMBERT   How strange.

CUT TO:

A Large Classroom
The questions have been handed out by a monitor, and the examination is under way. Humbert from his lectern morosely observes the bent heads. A crew-cut footballer shoots up an arm, and then buoyantly walks up to the lectern.

FOOTBALLER   It says here, 'How did Poe define the Poetic

Sentiment'? Do you want us to give a general answer, or actually quote the poem?

HUMBERT   I don't think there is any specific poem implied.

FOOTBALLER   (*utterly at his wit's end but with optimism unshattered*) I see. Thank you, sir.

He buoyantly walks back to his seat. Humbert, sitting at the lectern, takes his mail out of his pocket and scans it. The monitor turns to the blackboard to write on it '9:10.' The footballer, gratefully but mutely, receives from his neighbor a secret note which reads 'Poetry is the sentiment of intellectual happiness.' The letter that Humbert has opened begins talking to him in a small, matter-of-fact, agonizingly familiar, voice:

LOLITA'S VOICE   Dear Daddy, how's everything? I'm married. I'm Mrs Richard Schiller. I'm going to have a baby. I guess he's going to be a big one. I guess this is a hard letter to write. I'm going nuts because we don't have enough to pay our debts and get out of here. Dick is promised a big job in Alaska, in his specialized corner of the mechanical field. That's all I'm told about it but it's really grand. Please, do send us a check, Dad. We could manage with three or four hundred, or even less. Anything is welcome. I have gone through much sadness and hardship. Your expecting Dolly (Mrs Richard F. Schiller).

Most of the students having filled a bluebook page in the same number of minutes simultaneously turn it, which makes a brief whistling rustle.

Humbert has risen from his chair, dazed and unstable. He leaves the room followed by all eyes.

CUT TO:

Coalmont — a bleak foggy town

CUT TO:

Hunter Road — a dismal district
all dump and ditch, and wormy vegetable garden. Clapboard shacks line the wasteland. An old man is shoveling mud by the roadside. Humbert speaks to him from his car.

HUMBERT   Would you know if the Schillers live around here?

OLD MAN   (*pointing*) It's the fourth house after the junk-yard.

CUT TO:

Humbert

driving up to the fourth house. Sounds of hammering and of two male voices exchanging loud but indistinct comments come from the back of the shack. Humbert turns off the motor and for a few seconds sits motionless. A shaggy dog with a muddy belly comes out and woofs. Humbert fingers his pistol, transfers it to a handier pocket, gets out of the car, slamming the door.

DOG   (perfunctorily) Woof.

Humbert presses the bell button, keeping one hand in his pocket.

DOG   Woof, woof.

A rush and a shuffle – the door explodes – and Lolita stands on the threshold. She wears glasses. She has a new heaped-up hairdo, new bare ears. She is frankly pregnant. Her pale arms and neck are bare. But neither the maternity dress nor the sloppy felt slippers can disguise her Botticellian grace.

LOLITA   (after a pause, exhaling with all the emphasis of wonder and welcome) We-e-ll!

HUMBERT   (*in a croaking voice*) Husband home?

LOLITA   Come on in.

She lets him pass, crucifying herself against the open door.

LOLITA   (*to the dog*) No, you stay here.

CUT TO:

A Small, Shabby, Meagerly Furnished Parlor with the connubial bed disguised as a couch
Lolita, emitting interrogatory 'hm's,' makes familiar Javanese gestures with her wrists, offering her guest a choice between the couch and the rocker. He chooses the latter.

LOLITA   Dick's mending the back porch with a pal. I'll call him.

She goes out. 'Dick!' Dick and a friend come lumbering in. Humbert's hand comes empty out of his trouser pocket. How disappointing!

LOLITA   (*in a resounding violent voice*) Dick, this is my step-father, Professor Humbert.

DICK   How do you do, Professor.

LOLITA   (*to Humbert*) Dick is very deaf. Speak loud, please. Oh, and this is our kind neighbor, Bill Crest.

BILL   Glad to meet you, Prof.

LOLITA   This calls for a celebration. I'll get some refreshments.

BILL   Let me help you, Dolly.

They go out. Humbert sits in a rocker, Dick on the edge of the couch. He wears overalls, has a shock of dark hair, a nice boyish face. He needs a shave and a hearing aid.

DICK   This is a grand surprise, Professor. Hope you're here to stay. You'll have this couch.

Humbert shakes his head.

DICK   No trouble. We can sleep on a spare mattress in the kitchen.

HUMBERT   I'm on a lecturing tour . . .

Lolita and Bill have reentered.

LOLITA   (*very loud*) He's on a lecturing tour. He chanced to visit this town. I wrote him to look us up.

DICK   (*nodding sagely*) I see, I see.

There is a pause. Beer is quaffed. Nobody knows what to say. Lolita greedily crunches potato chips. Bill signals to Dick.

DICK   Well
                    (*slapping his knees and rising*)
I guess, you two have a lot to talk about. Come along, Bill. Back to work.
                    (*to Lolita*)
You just holler, sweetheart, when it's time for K.P.

HUMBERT   That's not the fellow I want.

LOLITA   Not *who?*

HUMBERT   You know very well. Where is the swine you eloped with?

LOLITA   (*inclining her head to one side and shaking it in that position*)
Look, you are not going to bring that up.

HUMBERT   I certainly am. Three years – during three years I've been trying to find him. Who is he? Where is he?

LOLITA   I should never have written you. Oh, it was a great mistake. Now you are going to spoil everything.

HUMBERT   Could your husband give me that information?

LOLITA   (*blazing and bristling*) Leave out Dick! See? Leave out my poor Dick. He does not know a thing about the whole mess. He thinks I ran away from an upper-class home just to wash dishes in a diner. Why should you make things harder by raking up all that muck?

HUMBERT   Be a sensible girl – if you expect help from me. Come, his name!

LOLITA   (*Half turns away, fumbling for something on a crowded table.*) I thought you had guessed long ago.
              (*with a mischievous and melancholy smile*)
    It's such a sensational name. You would never believe . . .
    I can hardly believe it myself – and there's no one I can brag to about it.

HUMBERT   His name, please.

LOLITA   Skip it. It does not matter now. Want a cigarette?

HUMBERT   No. His name.

LOLITA   (*Lights up, shakes her head firmly*) It's too late now to
raise hell.

HUMBERT   All right. I'm afraid I must be on my way.
Regards to your husband. Nice to have seen you.

LOLITA   Oh, you are so silly to insist. I really should not tell
you. On the other hand – do you want to know it that
badly? Well, it was—

Softly, confidentially, arching her thin eyebrows and puckering her parched lips, with a note of fastidious, not untender,
mockery, she emits in a kind of muted whistle, the name:

LOLITA   – Quilty.

Humbert regards her with stupefaction.

LOLITA   Yes, Clare Quilty, the playwright. Oh, you must
have seen his face lots of times in those cigarette ads! And
he was staying at that cute hotel at Briceland – remember?
And he wrote that play we chose for the Beardsley School
show. And he came to rehearsals. And he followed our
car in that absurd fashion for miles and miles. Do you
know the word 'cynic'? Well, that sums him up – a bold

278

laughing cynic. Yes, that's him all over. Clare Quilty. The only man I was ever crazy about.

HUMBERT   There is also Dick.

LOLITA   Oh, Dick is a lamb. We are very happy together. I meant something quite different.

HUMBERT   And I? I have never counted, of course?

Lolita considers him for a moment as if trying to grasp the tedious and confusing fact that Humbert had been her lover. That poor romance is dismissed by her like a dull party, a gray picnic, a raindrop of boredom.

He manages to jerk his knee out of the range of a sketchy tap – one of her acquired gestures.

LOLITA   Don't be dense. The past is the past. You've been a good stepdaddy, I guess. Watch your step, Daddy – remember that joke?

HUMBERT   No, that must have been after my time. Where can I find him?

LOLITA   Clare Quilty? Oh, what does it matter? Up in Parkington, I guess. He's got a house there, a regular old castle.

(*Gropes and rummages in a pile of magazines on the
lower shelf of a console.*)
There was a picture of it somewhere.
(*Pulls out a bedraggled issue of* Glance.)
Yes, here it is.

The magazine opens in her slender hands revealing a photograph of Pavor Manor as shown in the first shot of the
Prologue. She says with a deep sigh:

LOLITA   This world is just one wild gag after another. If
somebody wrote up my life nobody would believe it.

She directs the dart of her cigarette toward the hearth, index
rapidly tapping as her mother used to do. Lolita had never
smoked under Humbert the Terrible.

HUMBERT   No. I suppose not. Well, let's recapitulate. So it
was in Beardsley that you betrayed me.

LOLITA   Betrayed? No. In fact, Cue – everybody called him
Cue, you know – Cue was very understanding and sym-
pathetic toward you. You must not tell anybody but many
years ago he actually was questioned once by the police
about some kid who had complained. So you see you

were among friends. Oh, he knew everything about you and me, and it tickled him no end.

She smiles, exhales smoke, shakes her head, darts her cigarette.

LOLITA   You know – that guy saw through everything and everybody. He was not like you or me – he was a genius. He had an Oriental philosophy of life. He believed in Life. Oh, he was – wonderful. Funny – I speak of him in the past as though we were all dead.

HUMBERT   Where exactly did he take you when you gave me the slip?

LOLITA   Yes, that was awfully mean, I must admit that. He took me to a dude ranch near Elphinstone. DukDuk Ranch. Silly name.

HUMBERT   Where exactly? What highway?

LOLITA   No highway – a dirt road up a small mountain. Anyway – that ranch does not exist any more. Pity, because it was really something. I mean you can't imagine how utterly lush it was, that ranch, I mean it had every-thing, but everything, even an indoor waterfall. You know when Cue and I first came the others had us actually go through a coronation ceremony.

HUMBERT   The others? Who were they?

LOLITA   Oh, just a bunch of wild kids, and a couple of fat old nudists. And at first everything was just perfect. I was there like a princess, and Cue was to take me to Hollywood, and make a big star of me, and all that. But somehow nothing came of it. And, instead, I was supposed to cooperate with the others in making filthy movies while Cue was gadding about the Lord knows where. Well, when he came back I told him I wanted him and not that crowd of perverts, and we had a fight, and he kicked me out, and that's all.

HUMBERT   You could have come back to me.

LOLITA   (smile, shrug) Oh, well ... I suppose I was afraid you'd kill me. And anyway I was a big girl now, on my own. So – worked in motels, cleaning up and that sort of job, and in roadside cafés. And then after a year I could not stand it any longer, and thumbed my way back to the place where the ranch should have been. But it just was not there any more, it had burned down completely. So strange.
                    (Smokes meditatively.)
Well, I drifted back to cheap diners, and one day on the

highway Dick picked me up, and we both were lonesome, and so it began.

She closes her eyes leaning back on the cushions of the couch, her belly up, one felted foot on the floor.

'I knew all I wanted to know. I had no intention of torturing my darling. Somewhere, beyond the shack, an afterwork radio had begun singing of folly and fate, and there she was with her ruined looks, and her adult rope-veined hands, there she was, my Lolita, hopelessly worn at seventeen – and I looked and looked, and knew that I loved her more than anything I had ever seen, or imagined, or hoped for . . . She was only the dead-leaf echo of my nymphet – but thank God it was not that echo alone that I worshipped. I loved my Lolita, this Lolita, pale and polluted, and big with another's child, but still gray-eyed, still sooty-lashed, still auburn and almond, still Carmencita, still mine. "Changeons de vie ma Carmen, allons vivre quelque part où nous ne serons jamais séparés" [this is a quotation from Mérimée's novel], no matter, even if those eyes of hers would fade to myopic fish, and her nipples swell and crack – even then I would go mad with tenderness at the mere sight of your dear worn face, at the mere sound of your raucous young voice, my Lolita.'

HUMBERT   Lolita, this may be neither here nor there, but

I have to say it. Life is very short. From here to that old car there are twenty-five paces. Make them. Now. Right now. Come just as you are. Take that plate of peanuts with you. And we shall live happily ever after.

LOLITA   You mean you'll give us some money only if? Only if I go to a motel with you? Is *that* what you mean?

HUMBERT   No, you got it all wrong. I want you to leave your incidental Dick, and this awful hole, and come to live with me, and die with me, and everything with me, eternally . . .

LOLITA   (*her features working*) You're crazy.

HUMBERT   Think it over, Lolita. I'll wait for any length of time if you want to think. There are no strings attached – except that – well, that a life would be spared. But even if you refuse to come you shall still get your dowry.

LOLITA   No kidding?

HUMBERT   Here. Here's three, four hundred in cash – and here's a check for nine thousand six hundred.

Gingerly, uncertainly, Lolita takes the money, and speaks with agonized emphasis.

LOLITA   You mean you are giving us ten thousand bucks?

He covers his face and breaks into tears. They trickle through his fingers down his chin, his nose is clogged, he can't stop. He gropes for a handkerchief. She touches his wrist. He draws back abruptly.

HUMBERT   I'll die if you touch me. You are sure that you are not coming with me? Is there no hope of your ever coming?

LOLITA   No, honey, no.

His shoulders heave. She provides him with a paper napkin.

LOLITA   No, it's quite out of the question. I'd sooner go back to Quilty. I mean—

HUMBERT   I know. *He* broke your heart. I merely broke your life.

LOLITA   Oh, but everything is so wonderful now. I think it's so utterly grand of you to give us all that dough. It settles everything. We can pay all our debts. We can fly to Alaska tomorrow. Stop crying, please. You should understand. Let me get you some more beer. Oh, don't cry. I'm so sorry I cheated so much – but that's the way things are.

He wipes his face. She smiles at the money.

LOLITA   (*exulting*) May I call Dick?

HUMBERT   No, no. Please don't. I don't want to see him at all. I must leave in a moment.

LOLITA   Oh, don't go yet.

HUMBERT   I love you and this is sheer torture. By the way – about these money matters. There'll be more coming. I must go now.

LOLITA   It has been nice—

HUMBERT   All right, all right.
                              (*evading her hand*)
Yes, good-bye, I have a piece of very important business to take care of. A ragged, raw, horrible piece.

CUT TO:

The Front Porch
A remote sound of voices and hammering comes from the back of the house. The song 'Lolita, Lolita, Lolita' is repeated. Lolita and the shaggy dog see Humbert off.

LOLITA   What do you know – the same old car.

HUMBERT   One last word. Are you quite, quite sure that – well, not tomorrow of course, and not after-tomorrow, but some day, any day – you'd not come to live with me? I'll create a brand-new God and thank him with piercing cries, if you give me that small hope.

Lolita smiles, shakes her head in smiling negation.

HUMBERT   It would have made all the difference.

He hurries toward the car.

LOLITA   Good-bye. There's a bad storm coming.

HUMBERT   What?

LOLITA   A storm. Take care of yourself.

Her cry and the sound of the motor attract Bill followed by Dick, as Humbert drives off, with the old shaggy dog loping heavily alongside the car, and soon giving up. We dissolve briefly to Lolita's delirious cry of joy and to Dick's incredulous stare at the gift she brandishes.

CUT TO:

Desolate Road — Storm brewing

Humbert drives off, but a little way down the road, stops and weeps uncontrollably, slumped over the wheel, with the windshield wipers vainly warring against a cloudburst.

A NARRATIONAL VOICE (Dr Ray's) Poor Lolita died in childbed a few weeks later, giving birth to a stillborn girl, in Gray Star, a settlement in the remote Northwest. She never learned that Humbert finally tracked down Clare Quilty and killed him. Nor did Humbert know of Lolita's death when shortly before his own dissolution he wrote in prison these last words of his tragic life's story:

HUMBERT'S VOICE (*clear and firm*) . . . While the blood still throbs through my writing hand, you are still as much part of blest matter as I am. I can still talk to you and make you live in the minds of later generations. I'm thinking of aurochs and angels, the secret of durable pigments, prophetic sonnets, the refuge of art. And this is the only immortality you and I may share, my Lolita.

THE END

VLADIMIR NABOKOV

Revised December 1973   Summer 1960

Montreux   *Los Angeles*

The Tragedy of
Mister Morn

Translation by
ANASTASIA TOLSTOY and THOMAS KARSHAN

Introduction by
THOMAS KARSHAN

Introduction

The Tragedy of Mister Morn was Vladimir Nabokov's first major work, and the laboratory in which he discovered and tested many of the themes he would subsequently develop in the next fifty-odd years: the elusiveness of happiness; the creative and destructive playfulness of the imagination; courage, cowardice, and loyalty; the truth of masks; the struggle of freedom and order for possession of the soul; the sovereignty of desire and illicit passion; and what one character calls 'that likeness which exists / between truth and high fantasy' (I.ii.59–60), a likeness under whose inspiration Nabokov would take reality, fancy, art, and impossibility, and twist them together into the four-dimensional knots of *Lolita, Pale Fire*, and his other great novels.

Yet *Morn*, which Nabokov wrote in Prague in the winter of 1923 to 1924, when he was only twenty-four years old, was never performed or published in his lifetime, though several readings of the play did take place in Berlin, then Nabokov's home, in the spring of 1923. The opportunities in Berlin for staging a Russian play by a nearly unknown writer were limited, and publication cannot have seemed financially attractive to the émigré publishing houses that would later print Nabokov's novels. In America, and then in Switzerland, Nabokov translated most of his Russian fiction, but not his early plays, and when he died, in 1977, the typescript and fair copy of Morn still lay dormant in his personal archive in Montreux. Then, in 1997, Zvezda, a Russian literary journal, published the complete Russian text of Morn; and in 2008 the play finally became available to a wider (Russian-reading) audience when a revised version of the text was published in book form by Azbuka Press of St Petersburg. These publications have in turn made possible this current edition – the first translation of Morn into English.

While Morn is in many respects the seedbed for Nabokov's major novels, there are also elements in it which are fascinatingly unlike anything in his later work, and which reflect issues in Nabokov's life at the time of writing. Most prominent of these is revolution. Nabokov came from a distinguished liberal family in St Petersburg: his father, V. D. Nabokov, had been one of the ministers in the short-lived Kerensky government which ruled between the fall of the Tsar and the ascent to power of Lenin and the Bolsheviks in 1917. That year, the Nabokov family fled St Petersburg, first for Yalta, then for London, and, eventually, Berlin – where the young Nabokov would rejoin them in 1922, after completing his degree at Cambridge. Even in Berlin, however, the Nabokov family was not safe from the extremist ideologies of right and left which had vied for power in Russia after the failure of the liberal centre, and on 28 March 1922 Nabokov's father was shot dead by a Monarchist assassin who was in fact aiming not at him but at another émigré politician.

Nabokov's hatred of the Soviet regime is directly expressed in much of his writing, most prominently his novels *Invitation to a Beheading* (1935/6) and *Bend Sinister* (1947). But he would never again write anywhere nearly so directly about the moment of revolution itself, or so probingly about ideology, as he did in *Morn*. In the play's two main revolutionaries, Tremens and Klian, Nabokov depicts a politics and poetics of nihilism which, it is implied, was the driving force behind the Russian Revolution. In this Nabokov was refining a critique of revolutionary ideology which can be traced back as far as Turgenev's *Fathers and Sons* (1862) and Dostoevsky's *The Possessed* (1872). He would articulate this critique again in his last, and greatest, Russian novel, *The Gift* (1937/8), whose fourth chapter is a mocking biography of Nikolai Chernyshevsky – the revolutionary thinker of the 1860s who was the object of Turgenev's and Dostoevsky's conservative critiques, and would become Lenin's hero. But in *Morn* Nabokov explores more fully and explicitly than he ever would again what he saw as the origins of the revolutionary impulse in a death-instinct and passion for destruction. When Ganus, who had once been a revolutionary, returns from exile and discovers the happiness that the masked King has brought to the kingdom, he asks Tremens why he is not now satisfied. Tremens pours scorn on him. Neither happiness nor equality is Tremens's purpose, he explains; rather, he is seeking to imitate the violent destructiveness of life itself, which 'rushes headlong / into ash, [and] destroys everything in its way' (I.i.287–8). 'Everything,' Tremens explains, 'is destruction. And / the faster it is, the sweeter, the sweeter . . .' (I.i.295–6). To him, this destruction is beauty:

> Did you see,
> one windy night, by moonlight, the shadows
> of ruins? That is the ultimate beauty –
> and towards it I lead the world.
>
> (I.i.267–70)

Tremens cites as one aspect of that destructiveness the sexual drive itself, in the figure of 'the maiden, who prays for the blow of a man's love' (I.i.294), and one distinctive quality of the play is an unblushing erotic candour to which Nabokov would not fully return until *Lolita* (1955). Thus Klian, the violent-minded revolutionary poet who serves as Tremens's factotum, tells his fiancée Ella that

> . . . To enter you, oh, to enter,
> would be like entering a tight and searing
> sheath, to gaze into your blood, to break
> through your bones, to learn, to grasp, to touch,
> to press your being in between my palms! . . .
>
> (I.ii.122–6)

This anticipates Humbert Humbert in Chapter 2, Part Two of *Lolita* saying that 'my only grudge against nature was that I could not turn my Lolita inside out and apply voracious lips to her young matrix, her unknown heart, her nacreous liver, the sea-grapes of her lungs, her comely twin kidneys.' Yet, as with so many aspects of the play, in the sphere of desire Nabokov explores opposite poles of experience. Against Klian's dark vision of sexual appetite is set a more salubrious expression of love's idealizing power – in the faith that Midia, and the other citizens, place in Morn's nearly magical beneficence, and in Ella's idea of love as a force that coalesces experience:

> . . . all is one: my love and the raw sun,
> your pale face and the bright trickling icicles
> beneath the roof, the amber spot upon
> the porous sugary snow mound, the raw sun
> and my love, my love . . .
>
> (III.ii.190–94)

This, and the tenderly specific attention paid to the minutiae of Ella's hair, clothes, and make-up, seem to attest to the fact that Nabokov wrote *Morn* soon after meeting and falling in love with Véra Slonim, who would become his wife – and the play's typist. With her girlishness, humour, and idealism, Ella ranks alongside Lolita as one of Nabokov's few fully realized female characters.

If, in its treatment of revolutionary ideology, death, and desire, *Morn* shows us elements that Nabokov would not develop again, or not for a long time, there is one respect in which it stands very obviously as the source of Nabokov's immediately subsequent writing, and this is in its exploration of the twin themes of happiness and make-believe. In 1924, Nabokov would begin writing his first novel, *Happiness*. The novel was aborted and its drafts are now lost, but there is no question that its title expresses one of the central themes of Nabokov's oeuvre, in which happiness is a mysterious variable, 'the zany of its own mortality', as Sebastian Knight calls it, no sooner found than lost, but always something much more profound than anything 'happiness' means in modern use, where it merely names the mirage evoked by the goals we set ourselves. As for make-believe, it is central to Nabokov's work that any reality worth caring about is one freshly imagined, that, as he puts it in *Strong Opinions* (1973), 'average reality begins to rot and stink as soon as the act of individual creation ceases to animate a subjectively perceived texture', and therefore that, as Vadim's aunt tells him in Chapter 2 of Nabokov's final complete novel, *Look at the Harlequins!* (1974), it is a fundamental imperative for every person that in art and life he should 'Play! Invent the world! Create it!' The theme of make-believe also links *Morn* to two other verse-plays which Nabokov had written in 1923 before embarking on *Morn*, the one-act closet dramas *Death* and *The Pole*, which together mark out the two poles between which *Morn* moves: in the first, a cynical intellectual related in mentality to Tremens presses the view of illusion as arrant deceit; while the second heroizes Captain Scott, the quixotic Antarctic explorer, a Morn-like figure whose steadfast courage inspires and sustains his followers, who always seems to be playing, even in the face of death, and who is, like Morn, recognized by his laughter.

In *Morn* Nabokov gave these themes a political significance more explicit than any we find in his later work. Against the revolutionary politics, grounded in the ideals of equality, sameness, and even death, that Tremens and Klian embody, Nabokov postulates a conservative politics, animated by an ideal of happiness. As Morn says, he

> . . . created
> an age of happiness, an age of harmony . . . God,
> give me strength . . . Playfully, lightly I ruled;
> I appeared in a black mask in the ringing hall,

before my cold, decrepit senators . . . masterfully
I revived them – and left again, laughing . . .
   (III.i.131–6)

Morn's example has aestheticized the world, restoring order
by turning it into a fairy tale or a play: if even the King is an
actor, then all identity is not something sovereign but something performed, and he shows people how to act as they
would wish to be. He is a fantasy of the Foreigner, a mysterious figure who enters at the beginning and the end of the
play and comes from the real world of revolutionary Russia:

     . . . In our country all is not well,
not well . . . When I wake up, I will tell them
what a magnificent king I dreamt of . . .
   (V.ii.98–100)

The implicit argument of *Morn* is that for the sake of order,
morality, and happiness in the real world, people must
make-believe in the possibility of an ideal world. The play
takes place in an imaginary kingdom repeatedly described
as having the air of a *skazka* or fairy tale. In a synopsis of the
play, Nabokov described this atmosphere as 'neoromanti-
cism', saying that the setting of the play took 'something
from the 18th Century Venice of Casanova and from the 30s
[the 1830s] of the Petersburg epoch'. It also borrows from

Shakespeare, for in *Morn*, as in Shakespeare's history plays such as *Richard III*, the state is, necessarily, a play or pageant; a secret passage leads from the throne-room to the theatre. This is one of the many details that Nabokov would reuse nearly forty years later in his most metafictive work, *Pale Fire* (1962), in which an imaginary poet and imaginary king conjure with each other's existences. Kinbote, the imaginary King of Zembla, or semblance, may have assassinated Shade, the imaginary poet, just as in *Morn* Tremens says: 'it's a shame, Dandilio, that the imaginary / thief did not destroy the made-up king!' (V.i.188–9). But in *Morn*, as later in *Pale Fire*, this kingdom of imagination is all too precarious: Tremens is determined to unmask Morn's happy reign of make-believe as a cynical fraud, and to tear down the civic order it supports. He succeeds in doing so, until a false rumour that Morn fled for love, not cowardice, reignites the romanticism of the people. It is to defend that illusion that Morn, ultimately, must kill himself.

This idea of kingship as theatre, or as a work of imagination, is one of the many respects in which *Morn* is indebted to Shakespeare. The heavy crown is a symbol of the burdensomeness of power, as it is in Shakespeare's history plays, such as *Henry IV, Part 2*, towards the end of which Prince Henry stares uneasily at the crown lying on his dying father's pillow, 'so troublesome a bedfellow', which, he says, 'dost pinch they bearer', and 'dost sit / Like a rich armour worn in heat of day, / That scalds with safety' (IV.v.22, 29–31). In *Morn*, too, the 'fiery crown' burns and squeezes with 'its diamond pain', and Morn complains that

> . . . The stupefied mob
> does not know that the knight's body is dark
> and sweaty, locked in its fairy tale armour . . .
> (V.ii.124–6)

From Shakespeare, too, Nabokov drew a series of metaphors for civic order which could be deployed to warn against the rash alterations of Bolshevism. The kingdom is like the human body, so that Tremens's fever symbolizes the convulsions he wishes upon the state, as, again, in *Henry IV, Part 2*, where the Archbishop of York declares that

> . . . we are all diseased,
> And with our surfeiting and wanton hours
> Have brought ourselves into a burning fever,
> And we must bleed for it.
> (IV.i.54–7)

Or the kingdom is like music, as Ganus argues when he says that 'The power of the King / is living and harmonious, it moves me now / like music' (I.i.231–3), echoing an idea most famously expressed in a speech given by Ulysses in Shakespeare's *Troilus and Cressida*. The same idea is implicit in *The Tempest*, a play with which *Morn* is associated through the kinship between Prospero and Morn, both of them magician-kings. But the Shakespeare play most obviously linked to *Morn* is *Othello*: Ella dresses Ganus up as Othello so that he can visit Midia unobserved, and she twice quotes the lines Desdemona utters when Othello is about to smother her (the first time slightly misquoting them). *The Tragedy of Mister Morn is* less concerned with doubling, and with the duality of human nature, than Nabokov's later works. But here already, it is clear that when Ganus wears Othello's face, he discovers in himself a shadow side, a dark jealousy like that which blackened and distorted Othello. Conversely, Morn, by wearing a mask, becomes a nameless sovereign, King X, as Nabokov calls him in the synopsis, the variable upon which a lucky people can project their fantasies of happiness and order; and when he is unmasked by his cowardice, he betrays not only the ideals of his people and his own self-respect but even the identity and integrity he had once seen when he gazed into the healing silver of the mirror.

But in *Morn* Nabokov was trying to emulate Shakespeare not only at the level of image and symbol, but also of character and drama, register and rhythm. The simplest expression of this is that *Morn* is written in the iambic pentameter of Shakespearean tragedy, though Nabokov is more strictly regular in his rhythmic patterns than Shakespeare. Though Morn's prosody alludes to Shakespeare, it does so through the mediation of Pushkin's 'little tragedies' (all written in 1830, the most famous of which is Mozart and Salieri). More specifically Shakespearean − and un-Pushkinian − is the language of Morn, which, especially in the philosophic speeches of Tremens, Klian, Morn and Dandilio, is densely metaphorical and highly compressed in the manner of late Shakespeare. So Morn, saying farewell to Midia, justifies the aberrations of fate by comparing life to music, before suddenly shifting the already difficult metaphor into another key, comparing the music of existence to the structure of a building whose details can detract from an appreciation of its overall harmony:

> But, you see − the moulded whimsy of a frieze
> on a portico keeps us from recognizing,
> sometimes, the symmetry of the whole . . .
>   (IV.235−7)

Or Dandilio compares moments of life, good and bad, to pearls which a deep-sea diver must clutch up indiscriminately in his brief breathless moments at the bottom of the ocean, and pursues the metaphor to a visionary limit far beyond any which the mind can easily grasp:

And he who seeks only pearls, setting aside
shell after shell, that man shall come to
the Creator, to the Master, with empty hands –
and he will find that he is deaf and dumb
in heaven . . .
    (I.ii.38–42)

The conceits are often as whimsical as those in Shakespeare, defying that Enlightenment ideal of rhetorical decorum according to which Shakespeare's imagination was deplored as savage and untutored. So Tremens declares that

        . . . The soul is like a tooth, God
wrenches out the soul – crunch! – and it is over . . .
What comes next? Unthinkable nausea and then –
the void, spirals of madness – and the feeling of being
a swirling spermatozoid – and then darkness,
darkness – the velvety abyss of the grave . . .
    (II.208–13)

Or, earlier, he remembers an evening in which he 'shook with fever, / rippling like a reflection in an ice-hole' (I.i.93–4). One is reminded of a line in Chapter 26 of Nabokov's pen-ultimate novel, *Transparent Things*, which was finished nearly fifty years after *Morn*, in 1972, about 'an African nun in an arctic convent touching with delight the fragile clock of her first dandelion'. Such wild conceits, yoking together hot fancy and cold reason, are common in Nabokov's mature style. They derive, as *Morn* helps us to see, from Shakespeare, and mark the rebellion of Nabokov's genius against the decorousness of the Age of Reason.

Equally Shakespearean is Nabokov's subtly reasoned orchestration of many different voices and registers. At one extreme, we have the high-toned rhetoric of Tremens, Klian, Morn, Dandilio, and Ganus, each of whom Nabokov endows with an individual voice that speaks of their desires, values, and condition. The first note struck is that of Tremens's feverish rhetoric, tightly coiled upon itself, thickly patterned with spite and self-pity, and embroidered with antique curses: 'Begone, fever, you snake!' (I.i.7). In Klian, the court poet of Tremens's revolution, that destructiveness finds a sexual urgency which takes his rhetoric to the very limit of intelligibility. In our translation, we have allowed many of his speeches to remain as obscure in English as they are in the original Russian, where they seem to evince his commitment to the revolutionary poetics of violence upon the word associated with such poets as Vladimir Mayakovsky (1893–1930), on whom he may be modelled.

At the other pole of the play's rhetoric are Morn and Dandilio: in Morn there is a noble purity and simplicity of speech – 'radiant', to identify it by one of Morn's own favourite words. Although Morn is not a poet, he has the champagne-like effervescence he himself identifies with creativity, and it is definitive of him that when Ganus attacks him he responds with the carefree laughter which gives him his power. Dandilio shares with Morn this equanimity, which is not to be mistaken for a Buddhist absence of will or desire: on the contrary, Dandilio urges that life be embraced without scruple or discrimination. He is a snuff-taking eighteenth-century Optimist of the kind Voltaire famously satirized in *Candide*, and whom Nabokov would reprise in the figure of *Pale Fire*'s John Shade. He believes that all in the world is well, good and evil, Morn and Tremens alike. In the compressed aphorisms of his speeches the sententious gravity of the Age of Reason is combined with the intermittently childlike and singsong tenor of its thought.

Indeed, memories of childhood, and especially of the pains and illnesses of childhood, stud the play, introducing into it a domestic counterpoint to the stagy rhetoric, in something like the way that Shakespeare typically sets tavern against court, and prose against verse. (The Old Man who enters to clean up after Edmin and Morn have fled is, with his rustic speech, closely reminiscent of such Shakespearean characters as the Porter in *Macbeth*.) Dandilio says that life assuages all pain, like a mother rushing in to kiss better a child who has scratched itself (II.340–45); Midia says her soul is attached to Morn like a child's tongue to the metal it has licked on a frosty day (I.ii.253–6); and the feel of a cold gun muzzle pressing up against his chest reminds Morn, at a moment when he is considering suicide, of the 'lacquer tube' a doctor once pressed against his chest (III.i.119–22). In Ella that domesticity is articulated with a freshness that is essential to the total effect of the play, and it is telling that she often expresses herself in gestures – twirling, stroking the air – rather than in the destructive speechifying of Tremens, Klian, and Ganus.

As all of the above indicates, *Morn* presents some extraordinary difficulties to its translators. The task of translating it is all the more daunting because Nabokov was himself one of the most prominent modern critics of lazy and careless translation. As a young man, Nabokov had written elegant, readable translations of a range of English and French authors, from Carroll and Keats to Ronsard, Byron, and Shakespeare. In America, in the 1940s, he also produced verse translations into English of some of Pushkin's little tragedies, of Fyodor Tyutchev, Mikhail Lermontov, and Afanasy Fet. Yet he began to stress the near-impossibility of successful translation, describing it in Chapter 7 of his 1947 novel *Bend Sinister* by the following extravagant analogy:

> It was as if someone, having seen a certain oak tree (further called Individual T) growing in a certain land and casting its own unique shadow on the green and brown

ground, had proceeded to erect in his garden a prodigiously intricate piece of machinery which in itself was as unlike that or any other tree as the translator's inspiration and language were unlike those of the original author, but which, by means of ingenious combinations of parts, light effects, breeze-engendering engines, would, when completed, cast a shadow exactly similar to that of Individual T – the same outline, changing in the same manner, with the same double and single spots of suns rippling in the same position, at the same hour of the day.

Or, as he put it still more tersely, and (to a translator) intimidatingly, in his poem 'On Translating "Eugene Onegin"' (1955):

> What is translation? On a platter
> A poet's pale and glaring head,
> A parrot's screech, a monkey's chatter,
> And profanation of the dead.

That translation of Pushkin's *Eugene Onegin*, which was published in 1964 alongside three volumes of commentary, is famous, or notorious, for its defiant fidelity to rendering the exact and complete meaning of the original text at the expense of readability or elegance in English – a fidelity that Nabokov called 'the servile path'.

Our policy has been to prioritize accuracy to Nabokov's language, wherever possible, but we have not sought to produce a crib, as Nabokov did in his translation of *Eugene Onegin*. Rather we have aimed to find words, phrases, and rhythms which do justice both to the exact shades of meaning and to the very various tones and registers of Nabokov's *Morn* – and to finish with a text that recreates at least some of the power and beauty of the original, both in private reading and in performance. Our goal has been to produce a text that does not sound like a translation, but like the play that Nabokov would have written had he written *Morn* in English in 1923. That ideal is not entirely speculative, given that we do have some poems and essays which Nabokov wrote in English in the early 1920s, as well as the example of his own translations of his early Russian work into English, and his own writings in English. Nabokov read and wrote English from an early age, studied in Cambridge from 1919 to 1922, and was regarded by the other Russian émigrés as strongly oriented towards England and the English language. There are places in *Morn*, especially in the speeches of the title character, where the Russian hints of English – as, conversely, in *Pnin* and *Lolita*, Nabokov writes an English which sounds distinctly foreign. There are also many places in the text, and especially in Tremens's and Klian's speeches, where the Russian language is being deliberately wrenched into a revolutionary strangeness.

We have throughout resisted all temptations to tame or normalize Nabokov's language, which often sounds as distinctive and peculiar in Russian as in our translation – or, for that matter, as in Nabokov's own English. Indeed, there are moments in the text where we were able to draw on Nabokov's own translation of a phrase. So, for instance, when Midia has left Morn, he uses the curious phrase *letuchii dozhd*' – literally, 'flying rain'. We might have been tempted to make this 'fleeting rain', were it not for the fact that one of Nabokov's first poems, from 1917, is entitled '*Dozhd' proletel*', which Nabokov himself translated as 'The Rain Has Flown', adding in a note printed in *Poems and Problems* (1970) that 'The phrase *letit dozhd*', "rain is flying", was borrowed by the author from an old gardener (described in *Speak, Memory*, Chapter 2 *et passim*) who applied it to light rain soon followed by sunshine.' In the opening speech of the play, we have sought to preserve Tremens's warlock-like tones and his elliptical, highly compressed images. So, too, when Ella in the same scene addresses the coals burning in the fireplace, she uses a strange and archaic phrase – '*Chur – goret*'!' – which we have translated by a phrase equally strange and archaic: 'Fain burn!' (I.i.39). In this case we were influenced by the modern associations of the word 'fain' with Shakespeare. In his translation of Pushkin, Nabokov often sought out the phrases in such poets as Byron which Pushkin had reworked into Russian; we have done the same in trying to retain the shimmering pale fire of Shakespeare's language which is often glimpsed in Nabokov's original Russian. This Shakespeareanism is always dominant but it often in turn absorbs and transforms the echoes of other literary exemplars, so that in Dandilio the terse aphorisms of a Voltaire or a Pope acquire Shakespearean vividness and whimsy, a richness of imagery which, conversely, deepens the fractured, syntax-defying Futurist speeches of Klian. In short, the play contains a range of registers and discourses, often overlain, and we have had to try to reproduce this in our translation.

In a few, though not very many, instances, we have permitted ourselves to travel a fair way beyond the original Russian, where reproducing it would have resulted in entirely the wrong feel and tone, though always with the intention of expressing the essential meaning. In Act Two, Tremens declares: '*Segodnia otkryvaiu / moi nebyvalyi prazdnik*' – literally, 'Today, I will open [or, inaugurate] / my unprecedented [or, fantastic] festival [or, holiday].' Any combination of these possibilities in English would have sounded clumsy and silly; at least as importantly, none of the words in English capture the full semantic range of the Russian words, especially *nebyvalyi*, which dictionaries translate as 'unprecedented' and 'fantastic'. 'Fantastic' was out because it has come in modern English to mean something excellent and admirable. What was needed was a word which would express the idea of a revolutionary rupture in history, and an element of the improbable. We finally landed on 'monstrous', which derives from the Latin *monstra* – nature- and history-rending portents, of the kind Tremens himself embodies. Likewise, 'festival' and 'holiday' both carry excessively positive and pleasurable connotations which do not do justice to *prazdnik* in this context. 'Carnival', we felt, with its hints of flesh and anarchy, would complement the animal idea of the 'monstrous' while contrasting with its implication of the unprecedented; just as, in the Russian, there is a paradox latent in the idea of a *prazdnik*, usually an annual festival, being *nebyvalyi* – unprecedented. We therefore arrived at our solution: 'Today I shall unleash my monstrous carnival' (II.54).

A smaller example comes from the final scene of the play, in which Morn says that the crowd does 'not know that the poor Eastern bride / is barely alive beneath her tasselled weight' (V.ii.128–9), where 'tasselled weight' stands for *tiazhest'iu kosmatoi*, which would more literally be translated as 'shaggy weight'. Not only would 'shaggy' have sounded comical, it would have made an obscure passage still more unclear: Morn here is looking for a female parallel to the image, in his previous speech, of a knight who seems glorious to the crowd but is hot and sweaty inside his armour (as Morn is dying within the prison of his fairy tale). The 'Eastern bride' looks beautiful to the crowd but is suffocating within her heavy ornamental marriage robes. By 'tasselled' we sought to translate *kosmatoi* in a way that would make this idea, if not obvious, at least accessible.

All our work was, however, doubled, if not tripled, by the demands of translating Nabokov's pentameter line. It was essential that Morn, with its high tragic ambition, remain a verse-play, but we soon decided against trying to reproduce Nabokov's own fairly strict iambic pentameter. It would have been impossible to do so without straying a long way from our primary goal of reproducing Nabokov's own nuances of sense. We opted instead for a loose five-stress line, evaluating the total rhythmic pattern of the line according to where the stresses seemed to us naturally to fall, in context. We have also tried if at all possible to pay respect to the integrity of each individual line and to avoid meaningless line-endings and awkward enjambments. Therefore we have not simply broken each line after ten or eleven syllables, and have looked to create lines whose beginnings, endings, and progressive syntactic pattern are part of their poetic meaning.

We feel, nevertheless, that we have achieved a steady beat throughout the play, and we have tried to make the rhythms relevant to the sense and tenor of a particular speech. As is, indeed, the established practice of English pentameter, the ear will, once it is accustomed to the five-stress pattern, hear lines as five stresses even where they are a syllable or two over or under the established measure. Such 'hypermetric' syllables are common in Shakespeare. In the case of split lines, we have allowed ourselves greater liberty – as also with lines ending with an ellipsis (three dots), where the idea is that the line should seem to trail off, so that there is a good reason for a stress to go missing. Some characters' speeches, especially those of Dandilio and Tremens, the play's two most grandiloquent orators, seemed naturally to unfold into many-syllabled lines which verge on the hexameter – appropriately, perhaps, in a play which gestures towards a lost grandeur. Ganus thinks of the vanished King, saying that

> .... His footsteps
> linger in the palace, like the step of a hexameter
> dwindling in one's memory . . .
> (III.ii.116–18)

Contrastingly, when Morn is reduced by his cowardice to the lowly state of a bourgeois 'mister', he muses that

> .... I, I am Mister Morn –
> that is all; an empty space, an unstressed
> syllable in a poem without rhyme.
> (IV.177–9)

Such a slackening of rhythmic pressure characterizes the speeches of characters when they drop out of the high heroic mode; and we have attempted to capture this Shakespearean contrast of prosody and prose.

Lastly, a word on the edition we have translated. *Morn* survives in a typewritten copy and in a handwritten fair copy; neither is entirely complete, with a few passages missing in Act V. These texts were edited together by Serena Vitale and Ellendea Proffer for the 1997 *Zvezda* edition, and re-edited by Andrei Babikov for the 2008 Azbuka edition. It is this latter edition on which our translation is based.

Thomas Karshan, 2012

Further Reading

The Tragedy of Mister Morn was first published in 1997 in *Zvezda*, a Russian literary journal, as 'Tragediia Gospodina Morna' ('The Tragedy of Mister Morn'), edited by Serena Vitale and Ellendea Proffer and with an introduction by Vadim Stark (*Zvezda*, no. 4 (1997), pp. 6–98). This Penguin translation is based on the play as it subsequently appeared in book form: *Tragediia Gospodina Morna* (St Petersburg: Azbuka Press, 2008), edited by Andrei Babikov and containing the Russian text of Nabokov's other plays.

Many if not all of Nabokov's other writings cast light on Morn. Of especial interest, however, are the early Russian writings, included in the volumes of his collected works in Russian: *Sobranie sochinenii russkogo perioda v piati tomakh* (Collected Works of the Russian Period in Five Volumes), with various editors and an introduction to each volume by Alexander Dolinin (St Petersburg: Symposium, 1999–2000). For readers without Russian, many of Nabokov's other early plays are translated by Dmitri Nabokov in *The Man from the* USSR & *Other Plays* (Bruccoli Clark/Harcourt Brace Jovanovich: San Diego, 1985), which also contains his important essay on drama, 'The Tragedy of Tragedy'. Early poems which offer comparisons with *Morn* are translated in Nabokov, *Collected Poems*, edited by Thomas Karshan (London: Penguin, 2012). Early short stories, many of which bear on *Morn*, are translated in *The Stories of Vladimir Nabokov* (New York: Knopf, 1995). This last volume contains the two short stories 'Ultima Thule' and 'Solus Rex', which Nabokov wrote in 1939–40 and which are the only surviving remnants of a novel that would clearly have re-developed the themes of *Morn*. Traces of that project are also to be found in Nabokov's 1947 novel *Bend Sinister*, and still more so in the 1962 *Pale Fire*, the work in which Nabokov most directly re-addressed the images, themes, and ideas of *Morn*.

The definitive biography of Nabokov is the two-volume work by Brian Boyd, whose first volume deals with the period in which Nabokov was writing *Morn* and contains a critical analysis of the play: *Vladimir Nabokov: The Russian Years* (London: Chatto & Windus, 1990). Critical analysis is also offered, for those who read Russian, in Andrei Babikov and Vadim Stark's introductions to their respective editions of *Morn*. Apart from these, there has been little critical analysis of *Morn* to date. Exceptions are: Gennady Barabtarlo, 'Nabokov's Trinity: On the Movement of Nabokov's Themes', in *Nabokov and His Fiction: New Perspectives*, edited by Julian Connolly (Cambridge: Cambridge University Press, 1999), pp. 109–38;

Siggy Frank, 'Exile in Theatre/Theatre in Exile: Nabokov's Early Plays, *Tragediia Gospodina Morna* and *Chelovek iz SSSR*', in the *Slavonic and East European Review*, vol. 85, no. 4 (October 2007), pp. 629–57; A. Iu. Meshchanskii, '"Tragediia Gospodina Morna" kak predtecha russkoiazychnoi prozy V.V. Nabokova', in *Voprosy filologii*, no. 11 (2002), pp. 100–108; and R. V. Novikov, '"Tragediia Gospodina Morna" V. Nabokova: k poetike "p'esy-snovideniia"', in *Maloizvestnye stranitsy i novye kontseptsii istorii russkoi literatury XX v.: Materialy mezhdunarodnoi nauchnoi konferentsii, Moskva*, edited by L. F. Alekseeva and V. A. Skripkina (Moscow: Moscow State Open University, 2003), pp. 181–7.

Much has been written about Nabokov more generally. Excellent starting points are *The Cambridge Companion to Nabokov*, edited by Julian Connolly (Cambridge: Cambridge University Press, 2005) and the encyclopaedic *Garland Companion to Vladimir Nabokov*, edited by Vladimir Alexandrov (New York: Routledge, 1995). Other recent critical studies include: Vladimir Alexandrov, *Nabokov's Otherworld* (Princeton, NJ: Princeton University Press, 1991); Julian Connolly, *Nabokov's Early Fiction: Patterns of Self and Other* (Cambridge: Cambridge University Press, 1992); Leland de la Durantaye, *Style is Matter: The Moral Art of Vladimir Nabokov* (Ithaca, NY: Cornell University Press, 2007); Alexander Dolinin, *Istinnaia zhizn' pisatelia Sirina* (St Petersburg: Academic Project, 2004); Thomas Karshan,

Vladimir Nabokov and the Art of Play (Oxford: Oxford University Press, 2011); Leona Toker, *Nabokov: The Mystery of Literary Structures* (Ithaca, NY: Cornell University Press, 1989); and Michael Wood, *The Magician's Doubts: Nabokov and the Risks of Fiction* (Princeton, NJ: Princeton University Press, 1995).

Dramatis Personae

MAIN CHARACTERS

TREMENS

ELLA

GANUS

KLIAN

FOREIGNER

MIDIA

DANDILIO

MISTER MORN

EDMIN

OTHER CHARACTERS

SERVANTS

GUESTS (including FIRST GUEST, SECOND GUEST, LADY,
GRAY-HAIRED GUEST, SECOND VISITOR, THIRD VISITOR)

OLD MAN

FOUR REBELS

CAPTAIN AND FOUR SOLDIERS

Act One

SCENE ONE

A room. The curtains are drawn. A fire blazes. TREMENS *sleeps in an armchair by the fire, wrapped up in a spotted blanket. He awakens heavily.*

TREMENS:
Dream, fever, dream; the soundless changing
of two sentinels standing at the gates
of my powerless life . . .
                              On the walls
the floral patterns form mocking faces;
the burning hearth hisses at me, not with fire   5
but with a serpent chill . . . O heart, O heart,
blaze up! Begone, fever, you snake! . . . Helpless
am I . . . But, O my heart, how I would like
to lend my trembling sickness to this fair
and careless city, so that the Royal Square   10
should sweat and blaze, as does my brow;
so that the barefoot streets should grow cold,
so that the whistling wind should shudder

the tall houses, the gardens, the statues

15   at the crossroads, the embankments, the ships

on the convulsing waters! . . .

[*calls out*]

Ella! . . . Ella! . . .

[ELLA *enters, elegantly coiffed but in a dressing gown.*]

TREMENS:

Give me some port and that glass phial,

the one on the right, with the green tag . . .

So, you are going dancing?

ELLA [*uncorks the decanter*]:

Yes.

TREMENS:

20   Will your Klian be there?

ELLA:

He will.

TREMENS:

Is it love?

ELLA [*sits down on the arm of the chair*]:

I don't know . . . It's all so strange . . .

322

It's not at all as it is in songs . . . Last night
I dreamt that I was a new white bridge,
made out of pine, I think, and covered in tears
of resin, thrown lightly over an abyss . . . And so   25
I waited. Alas, there were no timid footsteps –
the bridge yearned to yield sweetly, to crunch
in torment beneath the thunder of blind hooves . . .
I waited – and then, suddenly, I saw:
towards me, towards me, blazing, wailing,   30
whirled forth the form of a Minotaur,
with the broad chest and face of Klian!
Blissfully I surrendered – and awoke . . .

TREMENS:

I understand, Ella . . . Well, this pleases me –
it is my blood which has cried out in you,   35
my greedy blood . . .

ELLA [*preparing the medicine*]:

                           One drop . . . two drops . . . five,
six . . . seven . . . Enough?

TREMENS:

                             Yes. Get dressed,
go . . . it's late . . . Wait – stoke the fire . . .

ELLA:

> Coals, coals, you blushing hearts . . . Fain burn!
>
> [*looks at herself in the mirror*]

40   How is my hair? I'll wear a gold gauze dress.

> I am going . . .
>
> [*On her way out, she stops.*]
>
>   . . . Oh, Klian brought me
>
> his poems the other day; he sings them
>
> so amusingly, flaring his nostrils slightly,
>
> closing his eyes – like this, look – his palm

45   stroking the air as if it were a little

> dog . . .
>
> [*Exits, laughing.*]

TREMENS:

>   My greedy blood . . . And yet her mother
>
> was so trusting and so tender; yes,
>
> tender and cleaving, like pollen, drifting
>
> through the air, onto my chest . . . Off with you,

50   you sunny piece of fluff! . . . Thank you, Death,

> that you took this tenderness away from me:
>
> free am I, free and reckless . . . Henceforth,
>
> my servant Death, shall we oft agree . . . O,
>
> I will send you out into this very night,

55   into those blazing windows above dark mounds

> of snow; into those houses where life

twirls and dances . . . But I must wait . . .

It is not time yet . . . I must wait.

 [*Falls asleep. There is a knock at the door.*]

TREMENS [*shaking off sleep*]:

      Come in! . . .

SERVANT:

There is, my lord, a man out there – a dark,

bedraggled man – he wants to see you . . .   60

TREMENS:

      His name?

SERVANT:

He won't say.

TREMENS:

   Let him in.

 [SERVANT *exits. A* MAN *enters through the open door and stops on the threshold.*]

TREMENS:

    What do you want?

MAN [*slowly grinning*]:

> . . . And still

the same spotted blanket on his shoulders . . .

TREMENS [*looks closer at him*]:
Forgive me . . . my eyes are bleary . . . but,
I do recognize, I recognize . . . Yes,
65   for certain . . . Is it you, – you? Ganus?

GANUS:
You weren't expecting me? My friend, my leader,
my Tremens, you weren't expecting me? . . .

TREMENS:
Four years, Ganus! . . .

GANUS:

> Four years? Not years,

but stony boulders! Rocks, hard labour,
70   loneliness – and then – an indescribable
escape! . . . Tell me, how is my wife, Midia?

TREMENS:
She lives, she lives . . . Yes, I recognize you,
friend – the same Ganus, quick as fire,

the same passion in your speech and movements . . .
So you fled? And . . . what of the others?   75

GANUS:

I escaped – they still languish . . . You know,
I came to you, like the wind – straight away,
I've not yet been home . . . So you say, Midia . . .

TREMENS:

Listen, Ganus, I need to explain to you . . .
It is strange that the main rebel leader . . . No, no,   80
don't interrupt me! In truth, is it not strange
that I am free, when I know that my friends
suffer in black exile? I live just as before:
rumour does not name me; I'm still the same
twisted and secret leader . . . But believe me,   85
I did everything to burn in hell with you –
when they seized you all, I, incorruptible,
wrote a denunciation against Tremens . . .
Two days went by, on the third day I received
an answer. What was it? Well, listen: it was,   90
I remember, a dull and windy evening. I was
too lazy to put on the lights. It was growing
dark. I sat here and shook with fever,
rippling like a reflection in an ice-hole.
Ella had not yet returned from school. Suddenly –   95

327

a knock, and a man enters; his face obscured
in shadow, his voice muffled, as though it too
were tinged with darkness. Ganus, you are
not listening! . . .

GANUS:

My friend, my dear friend,
100   you can tell me this later. I'm agitated,
I cannot follow. I want to forget, forget
all this – the smoke of revolutionary
conversation, the backstreets in the night . . .
Advise me, what shall I do: go to Midia now,
105   or wait? Oh, don't be angry! Don't! . . .
Please, go on . . .

TREMENS:

Understand, Ganus, I must
explain! There are more important things
than earthly love . . .

GANUS:

. . . And so, this stranger . . .
tell me . . .

TREMENS:

. . . was very strange. Quietly

he approached me: 'The King has read your letter   110
and thanks you for it,' he said, taking off
his glove, and a smile, it seemed, slipped across
his hazy face. 'Yes . . .' the messenger
continued, theatrically slapping his glove,
'you are a clever conspirator, while the King   115
punishes only the foolish; from this follows
a conclusion, a challenge: walk free, magnet,
and gather up, magnet, the scattered needles,
the revolutionary souls, and when you gather them,
we'll sweep them up, and start again; so walk free,   120
shine on, attract . . .' Ganus, you are not listening . . .

GANUS:

On the contrary, my friend, on the contrary . . .
What happened next?

TREMENS:

                    Nothing. He left,
calmly bowing . . . For a long time after, I stared
at the door. Since then, I rage in passionate   125
idleness . . . Since then I wait; I stubbornly await
a blunder from the strained powers that be,
so I can make a move . . . Four years I wait.
I dream enormous dreams . . . Listen, the time

130   is near! Listen, you living piece of steel,
        will you be drawn to me again? . . .

GANUS:

                                    I don't know . . .
        I don't think so . . . You see, I . . . But Tremens,
        you haven't told me about my Midia!
        What does she do?

TREMENS:

                        Her? She strays.

GANUS:

135   How dare you, Tremens! I must confess
        I am unused to your blaspheming words –
        and I will not tolerate . . .
        [ELLA has appeared, unnoticed, in the doorway.]

TREMENS:

                            . . . in other times
        you would have laughed . . . My right-hand man –
        hard, clear, and free – has become tender,
140   like an ageing maid . . .

GANUS:

                        Tremens, forgive me,

330

if I misunderstood your joke, but you
do not know, you do not know . . . I have
suffered greatly . . . The wind in the reeds
whispered to me of adultery. I prayed. I bribed
my creeping doubts with forced memories,   145
with the most winged, the most sacred ones,
which lose their colour as they fly into words,
and now, suddenly . . .

ELLA [*approaching*]:

                    Of course he was joking!

TREMENS:

  Eavesdropping, eh?

ELLA:

                  No. I've long known –
you love equivocating little words,   150
riddles, that's all . . .

TREMENS [*to* GANUS]:

                  Do you recognize my daughter?

GANUS:

  What, surely it can't be – Ella? That girl

who always lay spread out with a book, here
on this fur, while we reduced worlds to ashes? . . .

ELLA:

155 And you would blaze louder than the rest,
and smoke so much, sometimes, it seemed there were
not people but ghosts dancing in the grey-blue
waves . . . But how did you return?

GANUS:

          I stunned
two sentries with a log and wandered lost
160 for half a year . . . And now, having finally
arrived, the fugitive dares not enter
his own home . . .

ELLA:

        I go there often.

GANUS:

           How nice . . .

ELLA:

Yes, I am very friendly with your wife.
Many a time in your dark drawing room
165 have we spoken of your bitter fate. In truth,

332

    sometimes it was hard for me: for no one
    knows that my father . . .

GANUS:

               I understand . . .

ELLA:

                                    Often,
    in soundless splendour, she cried, as you know
    Midia cries – silently and without blinking . . .
    In the summer, we strolled in the city outskirts,   170
    where you had strolled with her . . . Recently,
    she told your fortune by looking at the moon
    through a glass of wine . . . I'll tell you more:
    this very evening I'm going to a party
    at her house – there will be dancing, poets . . .   175
       [*points to* TREMENS]
    Look, he has dozed off . . .

GANUS:

               A party –
    but without me . . .

ELLA:

            Without you?

GANUS:

I am

an outlaw: if they catch me, I'm done for . . .

Listen, I'll write a note – you can give it

180 to her, and I'll wait downstairs for an answer . . .

ELLA [*twirling around*]:

I've got it! I've got it! How splendid!

You see, I study at a theatre school,

I have paints and pomades here in seven

different colours . . . I'll smear your face in such

185 a way that God himself, on Judgement Day,

won't recognize you! Well, do you want to?

GANUS:

Yes . . . It's just that . . .

ELLA:

I'll simply say

that you're an actor, an acquaintance of mine,

and haven't taken off your make-up –

190 because it was so good . . . Perfect! It's not

up for discussion! Sit down here, closer

to the light. That's good. You shall be Othello –

the curly-haired, old, dark-skinned Moor.

I'll also give you my father's frock-coat
and black gloves . . .   195

GANUS:

How amusing: Othello
in a frock-coat! . . .

ELLA:

Sit still.

TREMENS [*grimacing, he wakes up*]:

Oh . . . I think
I fell asleep . . . Have you both lost your minds?

ELLA:

He cannot see his wife otherwise.
There will be guests there after all.

TREMENS:

Strange:
I dreamt that the King was being strangled   200
by a colossal negro . . .

ELLA:

I think our chance

335

remarks seeped into your dream, got mixed up
with your thoughts . . .

TREMENS:

Ganus, what do you suppose,
will it be long? . . . will it be long? . . .

GANUS:

What? . . .

ELLA:

205   Don't move your lips, talk of the King can
wait a little . . .

TREMENS:

The King, the King, the King!
Everything is full of him: the people's souls,
the air, and it is said that in the clouds
at sunrise, it is his coat-of-arms that shines,
210   and not the dawn. Meanwhile, no one knows
what he looks like. On coins he wears a mask.
They say, he walks amongst the crowds, sharp-sighted
and unrecognized, throughout the city,
in the market places.

ELLA:
                    I've seen him ride
to the senate, accompanied by horsemen.   215
The carriage gleams all over in blue lacquer.
On the door there is a crown, and in
the window the blind is lowered . . .

TREMENS:
                                    . . . and, I think,
inside there's no one. Our King walks
on foot . . . And the blue lustre and the black steeds   220
are for show. He is a fraud, our King!
He should be . . .

GANUS:
                Stop, Ella, you have
put paint in my eye . . . May I speak . . .

ELLA:
                                Yes,
you may. I will look for a wig . . .

GANUS:
                            Tell me, Tremens,
I don't understand: what do you want?   225
While wandering through the country I have

noticed that in four years of radiant peace –
after wars and revolutions – the country
has grown wonderfully strong. And the King
230   alone achieved all this. What then do you want?
New upheavals? But why? The power of the King
is living and harmonious, it moves me now
like music . . . I too find it strange, but I
have understood that to rebel is criminal.

TREMENS [*rising slowly*]:
235   What did you say? Did I mishear? Ganus,
you . . . repent, regret, and practically
give thanks for your punishment!

GANUS:

                         No.

For the sorrows of my heart, for the tears
of my Midia, I will never forgive the King.
240   But, consider: while we were declaiming
grand words – on the oppressed, on poverty
and the suffering of the people – the King
himself was already acting in our stead . . .

TREMENS [*walks heavily around the room, drumming his fingers on the
    furniture as he passes*]:
Hang on, hang on! Did you really think

that I worked with such determination   245
for the good of an imaginary 'people'?
So that every manure-filled soul, some
drunken goldsmith or another, some gnarled
stable-boy could polish his dainty nails
up to a mirror sheen, and bend his little   250
finger back in affectation, when shaking
off his snot? No, you were mistaken! . . .

ELLA:

Move your head to the right a little . . . I'll pull
the astrakhan fur on for you . . .

                              Papa,
sit down, I beg you . . . You are dizzying me   255
with your movements.

TREMENS:

                    You were mistaken!
Revolts there may have been, Ganus . . . Time and again,
in city squares across the ages, have gathered
low-browed criminality, mediocrity,
and baseness . . . Their words I was repeating,   260
but I meant something more – and I had thought
that through those blunt words you felt my true fire,
and that your fire answered mine. But now,

your flame has tapered, it has turned to passion
265   for a woman . . . I feel great pity for you.

GANUS:

But what is it you want? Ella, don't get
in the way while I'm talking . . .

TREMENS:

                    Did you see,
one windy night, by moonlight, the shadows
of ruins? That is the ultimate beauty –
270   and towards it I lead the world.

ELLA:

                  Don't protest . . .
Sit still! . . . Press your lips together. A little
touch of arrogance . . . There. Some carmine
inside the nostrils – no, don't sneeze! Passion –
in the nostrils. Now yours are like those
275   of Arabian horses. There we go.
Please be quiet. After all, my father
is absolutely right.

TREMENS:

            You say:
the King is a great sorcerer. Agreed.

The sun has swollen the taut granaries,
the wonders of science are accessible to all,   280
labour is lightened by the play of hidden forces,
and the air is clean in the warbling workshops –
with all this I agree. But why do we
always want to grow, to climb uphill
from one to a thousand, when the downward path –   285
from one to zero – is faster and sweeter? Life
itself is the example – it rushes headlong
into ash, it destroys everything in its way:
first it gnaws through the umbilical cord,
then tears up plants and birds into shreds,   290
and our heart beats inside us like a greedy hoof,
till it smashes through our chest . . . And the poet,
who breaks up his thoughts into sounds? Or
the maiden, who prays for the blow of a man's love?
Everything, Ganus, is destruction. And   295
the faster it is, the sweeter, the sweeter . . .

ELLA:

                                        Now
for the frock-coat, the gloves – and you're ready!
Really, Othello, I am pleased with you . . .
    [*declaims*]
'But yet I fear you; for you are fatal then
when your eyes roll so: why should I fear I know not,   300

341

since guiltiness I know not; but yet I feel fear . . .'
Oh, your boots are shabby – well, never mind . . .

GANUS:

Thank you, Desdemona . . .

[*looking at himself in the mirror*]

Well, look at me!

It's been a while, it's been a while . . . Midia . . .

305   a masquerade . . . Lights, perfume . . . quick, quick!
Hurry, Ella!

ELLA:

We're going, we're going . . .

TREMENS:

So,
you've decided to betray me, my friend?

GANUS:

Don't, Tremens! We'll talk some other time . . .
It's hard for me to argue now . . . Perhaps
310   you are right. Farewell, dear friend . . . You
understand . . .

ELLA:

I won't be late . . .

TREMENS:

Go, go.
Klian has long been cursing you, himself
and everything else. Ganus, don't forget . . .

GANUS:

Hurry up, hurry up, Ella . . .
[*They leave together.*]

TREMENS:

So, you
and I are left alone, my serpent chill?   315
They're gone – my fugitive slave and poor
twirling Ella . . . Yes, seized and exhausted
by the simplest passion, Ganus seems to have
forgotten his true calling . . . But somehow
I sense that hidden within him is that spark,   320
that scarlet comma of contamination,
which will spread the wondrous cold and fire
of tormenting illness across my country:
deathly revolts; hollow destruction;
bliss; emptiness; non-existence.   325

CURTAIN

SCENE TWO

A party at MIDIA's *house. The drawing room: to the left the entrance to the salon; to the right [at the back] a lighted niche by a tall window. [*MIDIA *with] several* GUESTS *[including* KLIAN, DANDILIO, *and the* FOREIGNER].

FIRST GUEST:

Morn says – though he himself is not a poet –
'It should be thus: in the flicker of daily life,
unexpectedly, in the chance combination
of light and shadow, you feel within yourself
5   the divine happiness of conception:
it grabs you and is gone; but the muse knows
that in a quiet hour, in the seclusion
of the night, the poem will begin to beat
and fly off the tongue, fiery and babbling . . .'

KLIAN:

10   I have never felt like that . . . I myself
create differently: with persistence, disgust,

344

tying a wet rag around my head . . . Perhaps
that's why I am the genius . . .

   [*Both of them pass on.*]

FOREIGNER:

                       Who is that –
the one that looks like a horse?

SECOND GUEST:

                  The poet Klian.

FOREIGNER:

   Talented?   15

SECOND GUEST:

        Shh . . . He's listening . . .

FOREIGNER:

                     And that one,
the silvery one, with the bright eyes – speaking,
at the doorway, to the mistress of the house?

SECOND GUEST:

You don't know? You sat beside him at dinner –
it is the carefree Dandilio, the grey-haired
lover of antiquity.   20

MIDIA [to DANDILIO]:

But why? It is

a sin: Morn, Morn and only Morn,

and the blood sings out . . .

DANDILIO:

There is no sin on earth.

Loves, sorrows – all are necessary, all

are beautiful . . . One must snatch the hours of fire,

25   the hours of love from life, as a slave grasps

at shells underwater – blindly, hungrily:

there is no time to prise them open, to choose

the sick one, with its precious tumour . . . They

shimmer, suddenly turn up, so grab at them

30   in handfuls, whatever's there, however you can –

and at that very moment when your heart

is bursting, you push off with your heel

convulsively, and, stumbling and panting,

empty out the treasure on the sunlit shore

35   at the feet of the Creator – he'll sort them out,

he knows . . . So let the broken shells be empty,

for the whole sea hums with mother of pearl.

And he who seeks only pearls, setting aside

shell after shell, that man shall come to

the Creator, to the Master, with empty hands –   40
and he will find that he is deaf and dumb
in heaven . . .

FOREIGNER [*approaching*]:
                            I often heard your voice
in my childhood dreams . . .

DANDILIO:
                            Really, I never
can remember who has dreamt me. But
your smile I do remember. I meant to ask you,   45
courteous traveller, where have you come from?

FOREIGNER:
I have come from the Twentieth Century, from
a northern country, called . . .
    [*Whispers.*]

MIDIA:
                            Which one is it?
I don't know that one . . .

DANDILIO:

How can you say that!

50   Don't you remember, from children's fairy tales?

Visions . . . bombs . . . churches . . . golden princes . . .

revolutionaries in raincoats . . . blizzards . . .

MIDIA:

But I thought it didn't exist?

FOREIGNER:

Perhaps. I

entered a dream, but are you sure that I

55   have left that dream? . . . So be it, I'll believe

in your city. Tomorrow I shall call it

a dream . . .

MIDIA:

Our city is beautiful . . .

[*She moves away.*]

FOREIGNER:

I find

in it a ghostly resemblance to the distant

city of my birth – that likeness which exists

60   between truth and high fantasy . . .

SECOND GUEST:

It is,
believe me, the most beautiful of all cities.
[SERVANTS *serve coffee and wine.*]

FOREIGNER [*with a cup of coffee in his hand*]:
I am struck by its spaciousness, by its clean,
extraordinary air: in it music sounds
differently; houses, bridges, and stone arches,
all the architectural outlines in it,   65
are boundless, light, like the passage
from the happiest sigh to sublime silence . . .
I am also struck by the ever-cheerful gait
of passers-by; the absence of cripples;
the melodious sound of footsteps and of hooves;   70
the flight of sledges across white squares . . . And
they say the King alone has done all this . . .

SECOND GUEST:
Yes, the King alone. Gone are the times
of hardship, never to return. Our King –
a masked giant, in a fiery cloak –   75
took the throne by force, and that very year
the last wave of revolts died down.
A conspiracy was uncovered: its members
were swept aside – and, by the way,

80   Midia's husband too, although one shouldn't
        mention it – and sent to distant mines,
        from whence the law will never call them back;
        I say the members, for the main rebel,
        their nameless leader, was never found . . .
85   Since then, the country has been at peace.
        Ugliness, boredom, blood – all have evaporated.
        The pure sciences reach for lofty heights,
        but, recognizing beauty in the past,
        the King has protected poetry, the agitation
90   of bygone ages – horses, and sails, and live
        ancient music – although alongside these,
        there wander through the air transparent,
        electrical birds . . .

    DANDILIO:
                            In bygone days
        flying machines were otherwise constructed:
95   sometimes they would flap upwards,
        to the thunder of the glinting propeller,
        to the explosion of petrol, emitting a smell
        of tea into the empty sky . . . Forgive me,
        but where is our interlocutor? . . .

SECOND GUEST:

I didn't

notice how he disappeared . . .   100

MIDIA [*approaching*]:

And now

the dances will begin . . .

[*Enter* ELLA, *with* GANUS *behind.*]

MIDIA:

And here's Ella! . . .

FIRST GUEST [*to the* SECOND GUEST]:

Who is that blackamoor? What a scarecrow!

SECOND GUEST:

And to think he's wearing a frock-coat! . . .

MIDIA:

You are so luminous . . . so ethereal . . .

How is your father?   105

ELLA:

Still the same: fever.

Here, do you remember, I told you? –

our tragic hero . . . I begged him to keep
his make-up on . . . It is Othello . . .

MIDIA:

                                        Very good!
Klian, come here . . . tell the violinists
110   to begin . . .

    [*The* GUESTS *move through into the salon.*]

MIDIA:

                        Why does Morn not come?
I do not understand . . . Dandilio!

DANDILIO:

But one must love even anticipation.
Anticipation is a flight into the dark.
Then all at once there's light, a fall into
115   the happy light, but then the flight is over . . .
Ah, music! Please, allow me to offer
you my arm.

    [ELLA *and* KLIAN *walk past.*]

ELLA:

                        Is something bothering you?

KLIAN:

Who is your consort? Who is your black-faced
consort?

ELLA:

      A harmless actor, Klian. Why,
are you jealous? 120

KLIAN:

        No. No. No.
I know that you are faithful to me, my bride . . .
O, God! To enter you, oh, to enter,
would be like entering a tight and searing
sheath, to peer into your blood, to break
through your bones, to learn, to grasp, to touch, 125
to press your being in between my palms! . . .
Listen, come to me! It is a long time
until spring, until our wedding day! . . .

ELLA:

Don't, Klian . . . you promised me . . .

KLIAN:

Oh, come to me! Let me break into you! 130
It is not I who beg, but my starved genius,
tormented by you, writhes in the ashes,

353

scrunching its wings, it begs . . . Oh, understand,
it is not I who beg, not I! See –
135 the muse wrings her hands . . . there is a wind
in the Olympian gardens . . . Pegasus's eyes
are filled with blood and dawn . . . Ella, will you come?

ELLA:

Don't ask, don't ask. It scares me, it delights me . . .
You know, I am only a white bridge,
140 I am but a flimsy bridge over the torrent . . .

KLIAN:

Tomorrow then – at ten sharp – your father
goes to bed early. At ten. Yes?
[GUESTS *walk past*.]

FOREIGNER:

Who then
do you think is the happiest in this city?

DANDILIO [*taking snuff*]:

It's me, of course . . . I have deduced happiness,
145 determined it, like a scientific theorem . . .

FIRST GUEST:

I want to make a correction. In our city

354

each and every one will answer: 'It's me,
of course!'

SECOND GUEST:

      No. There is one unhappy man:
that dark conspirator, unknown to us,
the one who wasn't caught. Somewhere he lives,   150
even now, and knows that he is guilty . . .

LADY:

That poor negro there is also unhappy.
He wanted to astonish everyone
with his frightening appearance, but nobody
has taken notice of him. Awkward Othello   155
sits in the corner, drinking gloomily . . .

FIRST GUEST:

. . . and looks out from under his brow.

DANDILIO:

                  And what
does Midia think?

SECOND GUEST:

          Look, our stranger

has disappeared again! It is as though,
160 passing between us, he slipped behind the curtain . . .

MIDIA:

I think, happiest of them all is the King . . .
Ah, Morn!

[MISTER MORN *enters, laughing, with* EDMIN *following.*]

MORN [*as he walks*]:

Splendid, blissful people! . . .

VOICES:

Morn! Morn!

MORN:

Midia! Greetings, Midia,
radiant lady! Give me your hand, Klian,
165 you thunderous madman, you crimson soul!
Ah, Dandilio, you gay dandelion . . .
Music, music, I need heavenly music! . . .

VOICES:

Morn is here, Morn!

MORN:

Splendid, blissful

people! What snow, Midia . . . what snow!
As cold as the kiss of a ghost, as hot as tears   170
on your eyelashes . . . Music! Music! And who
is this? An ambassador from the East?

MIDIA:

An actor, a friend of Ella's.

FIRST GUEST:

                              Before you came,
we were trying to decide who is the happiest
in our city; we thought – the King; but then   175
you entered: first place is yours, I think . . .

MORN:

What is happiness? The flutter of celestial wings.
What is happiness? A snowflake on one's lip . . .
What is happiness? . . .

MIDIA [*quietly*]:

                              Listen, why did you
come so late? The guests will be leaving soon: 180
it looks like my belovèd deliberately
arrived for their departure . . .

MORN [quietly]:

My joy, forgive me:

work . . . I have been very busy . . .

VOICES:

Dancing!

Dancing!

MORN:

Ella, may I have this dance . . .

[The GUESTS move into the salon. Only DANDILIO and GANUS remain.]

DANDILIO:

185   I see Othello is missing Desdemona.

Oh, the demon is in that name . . .

GANUS [glancing in the direction of MORN]:

What a

passionate gentleman . . .

DANDILIO:

What can one do, Ganus . . .

GANUS:

What did you say?

DANDILIO:

> I said, has it been long
> since you left Venice?

GANUS:

> Leave me, I beg you . . .
> [DANDILIO *moves into the salon.* GANUS *is left hunched at a table.*]

ELLA [*enters briskly*]:
> Is there anyone here? 190

GANUS:

> Ella, this is
> hard on me . . .

ELLA:

> What is wrong, my dear?

GANUS:

> There is something I don't understand:
> This suffocating make-up feels like
> it's straining my heart . . .

ELLA:

> My poor Moor . . .

359

GANUS:

195   Before, you said . . . I felt so happy . . .
       You were telling the truth, weren't you?

ELLA:

                                        Come on,

       smile . . . Listen, the violin bows are
       sparkling from the hall!

GANUS:

                            Will it end soon?
       This heavy, mottled dream . . .

ELLA:

                                  Yes, soon, soon . . .
       [GANUS *moves into the salon.*]

ELLA [*alone*]:

200   How strange . . . my heart suddenly sang out:
       I would give my whole life for this man
       to be happy . . . a kind of light breeze
       has passed by, and now I feel capable
       of the most humble feat. My poor Moor!
205   I'm such a fool, why did I bring him with me?
       I never noticed before – only just now,

in feeling jealousy on his behalf,
did I at long last see that some secret
reverberating sound connects Midia
to swift Morn . . . All this is strange . . .   210

DANDILIO [*comes out, looking for someone*]:

                            Did
you see? Did that Foreigner come past here?

ELLA:

I didn't see him . . .

DANDILIO:

                   What a curious fellow!
He slipped away like a shadow . . . We were
just having a conversation with him . . .
   [ELLA *and* DANDILIO *pass on.*]

EDMIN [*leads* MIDIA *to a chair*]:
You do not dance tonight, Midia?   215

MIDIA:

                       While you,
as always, are mysteriously silent –
perhaps you would like to tell me what
Morn does all day?

EDMIN:

What does it matter?

Whether he's a businessman, a scholar,

220   an artist, a warrior, or just an impassioned man –

isn't it all the same to you?

MIDIA:

And what

is it you do yourself? Stop it – stop shrugging

your shoulders! Conversation with you

is such a bore, Edmin . . .

EDMIN:

I know . . .

MIDIA:

225   Tell me, when Morn is here, you guard, alone

beneath the window, and after leave with him.

Friendship is friendship, but this . . .

EDMIN:

I like it this way.

MIDIA:

Is there not a woman – unknown to us –

with whom you would more pleasantly spend

the nights, while Morn is here, than with the spectre   230
of someone else's happiness? . . . How foolish –
you've grown pale . . .

   [MORN *enters, wiping his brow.*]

MORN:

                What is happiness?
Klian ran past me and, like the wind,
took Ella from me . . .

   [*to* EDMIN]

                Friend, brighten up!
Your face is painfully contorted, as though   235
you were about to sneeze . . . Go dance . . .

   [EDMIN *exits.*]

. . . Oh, my Midia, how you do resemble
happiness! No, do not move, do not spoil
your splendour . . . I am cold from happiness.
We are on the crest of a wave of music . . . Wait,   240
don't speak. This very moment is the peak
of two eternities . . .

MIDIA:

              A mere two moons
have rolled by since that vivid day, when
mysterious Edmin brought you to me. That day
you conquered me with the piercing glance   245

363

of your deep eyes. In them, an intense force
sparkles around the pupils with a yellow light . . .
Sometimes it seems to me that, walking
down the street, you could, with the even breath
250   of your eyes alone, inspire in passers-by
whatever you wanted: happiness, wisdom,
the heat of passion . . . I'll put it this way –
but don't laugh: my soul has fixed itself
to your eyes, as when in childhood
255   one's tongue sticks to cloudy metal if,
for a lark, you lick it in the flaring frost . . .
Now tell me, what do you do all day?

MORN:

And your eyes – no, show me – are
slightly slanted, satin-like . . . Oh, my dear . . .
260   May I kiss the rays of your collarbone?

MIDIA:

Wait, be careful – that black tragedian
is watching us . . . soon the guests will leave . . .
Be patient!

MORN [*laughing*]:

        Well, that should not be hard:

A whole night will make me tire of you
yet . . .   265

MIDIA:

            Don't joke like that, I don't like it . . .
[*The music dies down. The* GUESTS *exit the salon.*]

DANDILIO [*to the* FOREIGNER]:
Wherever did you disappear to?

FOREIGNER:
I had woken up. The wind roused me.
It rattled the window frame. I barely
fell back asleep . . .

DANDILIO:

            People here will find
that hard to believe.   270

MORN:

            Ah, Dandilio . . .
I haven't had a chance to talk with you . . .
What new things have you collected? What
rusty screws, what bracelets of pearl?

DANDILIO:

Things
are bad. Recently I found a fiery parrot –
275   huge and sleepy, with a crimson feather
in his tail – I found him in a little shop,
where he sits remembering the tunnel
of a smoking tropical river . . . I would have
bought him but I have a cat – these two
280   divine, mysterious creatures could not live
together . . . Each day I go and admire him:
he is a sacred parrot, he does not speak.

FIRST GUEST [to the SECOND GUEST]:
Time to go home. Take a look at Midia,
I think her smile is a suppressed yawn.

SECOND GUEST:
285   No, wait, they're bringing more wine. Let's drink.

FIRST GUEST:
But it's getting rather dull . . .

MORN [opening a bottle]:

Here! Fly,
you cosmic cork, into the stuccoed heavens!

Burst forth, foam, like chaos, gushing, welling . . .
whoa . . . between the fingers of the Creator.

GUESTS:

To the King! To the King! 290

DANDILIO:

How about you, Morn?
Will you not drink?

MORN:

Certainly not. One gives
one's life to the King, but drink – why
on earth drink?

FOREIGNER:

To this happy kingdom.

KLIAN:

To the Milky Way!

DANDILIO:

This wine will make
the stars flow in our heads . . . 295

367

ELLA:

                              Down in one,

to the fiery parrot!

KLIAN:

                    Ella, to our 'tomorrow'!

MORN:

To the mistress of the house!

GANUS:

                         I want to ask . . .

It is unclear to me . . . Can we not toast
the previous master of the house?

MIDIA [*dropping her glass*]:

                              There.

300   All over my dress.
        [*Pause.*]

FIRST GUEST:

              Put salt on it.

368

DANDILIO:

There is
a saying: with the tears of happiness, any stain
immediately disappears . . .

MIDIA [*to* ELLA, *quietly*]:

Listen, your actor
is drunk, I think . . .
  [*Wipes her dress.*]

MORN:

I read in a rare treatise –
here, Dandilio, you are a man of books –
that, while creating the world, God made a joke   305
at just the wrong moment . . .

DANDILIO:

In that same book,
I remember, it is also said that a guest
is as necessary to a house as air,
but if the breath drawn in is not released –
you will turn blue and die. So, Midia . . .   310

MIDIA:

What! So early?

DANDILIO:

It's time, it's time. My cat

is waiting . . .

MIDIA:

Do come again . . .

FIRST GUEST:

It's also time

for me, lovely Midia.

MIDIA:

That's terrible!

You should stay . . .

ELLA [to GANUS, quietly]:

I beg you, please

315   also leave . . . You can visit her tomorrow

morning . . . She's tired.

GANUS [quietly]:

I . . . don't understand?

ELLA [quietly]:

Where is the joy in a reunion when one

is tired?

GANUS [*quietly*]:

No, I will stay . . .

[*Moves off into semi-darkness by the round table. Meanwhile the* GUESTS *have been saying goodbye.*]

FOREIGNER [*to* MIDIA]:

I won't

forget my stay in your bewitching city:
the closer a fairy tale is to reality,   320
the more magical it is. But I fear something . . .
Trouble is ripening here unseen . . . In
the splendour, in the mirrors, I sense it . . .

KLIAN:

Don't listen to him, Midia! He is only
here by chance. Quite the magician! I happen   325
to know he's just a merchant's errand boy . . .
he carries specimens of foreign goods around . . .
Is that not so? He's slipped away!

MIDIA:

How funny

he is . . .

ELLA:

Farewell, Midia . . .

MIDIA:

Why so cold?

ELLA:

330   Not at all . . . I'm a little tired . . .

EDMIN:

I too

shall go . . . Goodnight.

MIDIA:

Foolish man!

[*She laughs.*]

SECOND GUEST:

Farewell.

If a guest really is like a breath of air,
then I leave here like a short, sad sigh . . .

[*Everyone leaves except* MORN *and* GANUS.]

MIDIA [*stands in the doorway*]:

Till next week.

[*returns to the centre of the drawing room*]

Ah, finally!

MORN:
Shh . . .

We're not alone.   335

    [*Points to* GANUS *sitting inconspicuously.*]

MIDIA [to GANUS]:
I say, you are far kinder

than my other guests, you've stayed . . .

    [*Sits down beside him.*]

Tell me,

where have you acted? Your terrifying make-up

is excellent . . . Have you known Ella long?

A child . . . like wind . . . like a glimmer of water . . .

Klian is in love with her, the one with   340

the Adam's apple and the horse's mane –

a bad poet . . . No, really, it is frightening,

you are truly, truly an Arab . . . Morn, stop

whistling through your teeth . . .

MORN [*at the other end of the room*]:
You have

a nice clock here . . .   345

MIDIA:
Yes, it is very old . . .

In its depths there plays a crystal brook . . .

373

MORN:

It's good . . . It's a little slow, don't you think? . . .

MIDIA:

Yes, I do . . .

[to GANUS]

And you . . . Is your home

far from here?

GANUS:

It's close. Nearby.

MORN [*by the window, yawning*]:

What stars . . .

MIDIA [*nervously*]:

350   It must be slippery out in the street . . .

The snow has been spiralling since morning . . .

I was at the ice-rink today . . . Morn flutters

like a bird on ice . . . why is the chandelier

lit for no reason . . .

[*quietly to* MORN *as she passes by*]

Look – he's drunk . . .

MORN [*softly*]:

355   Yes, he was plied by Ella . . .

[*approaches* GANUS]

It's very late!

Time to go home. It's time, Othello!

Do you hear?

GANUS [*heavily*]:

Well, what can I say . . .

I dare not keep you . . . go . . .

MIDIA:

Morn . . . I'm scared . . .

His voice is thick, as though he's strangling someone! . . .

GANUS [*gets up and approaches*]:

Enough . . . I will reveal my voice . . . enough!   360

I do not have the strength to wait any longer.

Off with my glove!

[*to* MIDIA]

Are you familiar

with these fingers?

MIDIA:

Oh! Morn, you must leave.

GANUS [*passionately*]:

Greetings! Are you not pleased? For it is I –
365   your husband! Risen from the dead!

MORN [*utterly calmly*]:

Risen indeed.

GANUS:

You are still here?

MIDIA:

Don't!

I beg you both! . . .

GANUS:

Damned fop! . . .

MORN:

The hot whistle

of your black glove pleases me. I
answer it with mine . . .

MIDIA:

Ah! . . .

[*She runs to the back of the stage, towards the niche, and opens the
window in jerks.* MORN *and* GANUS *fight with their fists.*]

MORN:
                        The table,
you'll knock over the table! . . . What a windmill! . . .   370
Don't swing your arms around so much! The table . . .
the vase! . . . I knew that would happen! . . . Ha-ha!
Stop tickling! Ha-ha! . . .

MIDIA [*shouts out of the window*]:
                        Edmin! Edmin! Edmin! . . .

MORN:
Ha-ha! The make-up's running! . . . There, tear up
the carpet! . . . Go on! Don't wheeze, don't yelp! . . .   375
Fight more cleanly! Here comes a comma
and a full stop!
    [GANUS *collapses in a corner.*]

MORN:
                Blockhead . . . He's undone my tie.

EDMIN [*rushes in, pistol in hand*]:
What happened?

MORN:
                A mere two blows: the first
is called 'a hook', the second 'a left jab'.

377

380   And, by the way, this gentleman here is —
        Midia's husband . . .

EDMIN:

                        Is he dead?

MORN:

                                Not likely . . .
        Watch, he'll come to now. Ah, welcome
        back! This is my second at your service . . .
            [He notices that MIDIA is lying unconscious at the back of the
            stage, near the window.]
        O, God! My poor love! . . . Edmin . . . wait . . .
385   Yes, call someone . . . Oh, my poor love . . .
        You shouldn't have, you shouldn't have . . . really . . .
        We were just playing . . .
            [Two MAIDS rush in: they and MORN attend to MIDIA at the
            back of the stage.]

GANUS [gets up heavily]:

                        I . . . accept . . . the challenge.
        Horrible . . . give me a handkerchief . . . or something . . .
        How horrible . . .
            [wipes his face]
                        Ten paces apart and the first
390   shot is mine . . . by right: I am the wronged party . . .

                            378

EDMIN [*looks around frantically*]:

    Listen . . . wait . . . you may find this strange . . .
    But I must . . . ask you . . . to decline the duel . . .

GANUS:

    I don't understand? . . .

EDMIN:

                 If you wish, I will take
    his place . . . face your bullet . . . I am ready . . .
    Right now, if you like . . .   395

GANUS:

                 Evidently I am
    losing my mind.

EDMIN [*quietly and briskly*]:

             Well then, I'll break my vow! . . .
    I will reveal it to you . . . duty requires me . . .
    But you must swear to me, on love, disdain,
    or on your hatred, on what you will, that you
    will never speak of this terrible secret . . .   400

GANUS:

    . . . I'm sorry, but what is all this about?

EDMIN:

Here, I'll reveal it to you, he – this man –
he is . . . oh, I can't!

GANUS:

Hurry up!

EDMIN:

Oh, come what may! He is . . .
[*Whispers in his ear.*]

GANUS:

That's a lie!

[EDMIN *whispers.*]

405   No, no . . . It cannot be! O, God . . .
what should I do? . . .

EDMIN:

You must decline!
There is no other way . . . Decline! . . .

MIDIA [*to* MORN *at the back of the stage*]:

My joy,
don't leave . . .

MORN:

> Wait . . . let me just . . .

GANUS [*firmly*]:

> No!

EDMIN:

Why did I break my . . .

MORN [*approaching*]:

> So, have you decided?

GANUS:

Yes, we have decided. But I'm not much   410
of a murderer: we shall fight *à la courte paille*.

MORN:

Excellent . . . A solution has been found. We
shall agree the details tomorrow. Goodnight.
May I add that duels are not to be
discussed with ladies. Midia could not bear it.   415
Keep silent to the end. Let's go, Edmin.
    [*to* MIDIA]
I'm leaving, Midia . . . Be calm . . .

MIDIA:

Wait . . . I'm frightened . . .
What was the outcome?

MORN:

Nothing. We made up.

MIDIA:

Listen, take me away from here! . . .

MORN:

Your eyes
420   are like swallows in autumn, when they cry out:
'Southwards . . .' Let me go . . .

MIDIA:

Wait, wait . . .
You're laughing through tears! . . .

MORN:

Through rainbows, Midia!
I am so happy that my happiness,
as it glimmers, overflows the brim.
425   Adieu – Edmin, let's go. Adieu. All's well . . .
    [MORN and EDMIN leave. Pause.]

GANUS [*slowly approaches* MIDIA]:
   Midia, what is all this? Oh . . . say something –
   my wife, my bliss, my madness – I am waiting . . .
   Tell me all this is a joke, a motley, evil
   masquerade, in which a gentleman in tails
   strikes a painted Moor . . . do smile! For I   430
   am laughing . . . I'm cheery . . .

MIDIA:
                     I don't know what
   to say to you . . .

GANUS:
            Just say one word; I will
   believe anything . . . anything . . . Empty jealousy
   intoxicated me – is that not so? –
   like wine drunk in port after one's been   435
   long tossed at sea. O, say something . . .

MIDIA:
   Listen, I will explain . . . You left – that much
   I remember. God saw how I grieved.
   Your things spoke to me, they smelled of you . . .
   I was unwell . . . But gradually my memory   440
   of you lost its warmth . . . You grew cold

in me – you were still living and yet
already incorporeal. Then you became
transparent, a kind of familiar ghost;
445   and finally, faint and translucent, you left
my heart on tiptoe . . . I thought – forever . . .
I resigned myself. And then my heart
renewed itself and came alight. I wanted
so much to live, to breathe, to whirl about.
450   Oblivion granted me freedom . . . And now,
suddenly, you come back from the dead, now,
suddenly, you burst so violently into a life
that's foreign to you . . . I don't know what to say
to you . . . How do I talk to a ghost who has
455   come back to life? I just don't know . . .

GANUS:

                             The last
time I saw your face was through bars.
You lifted up your veil, to dab your nose –
with a crumpled handkerchief – like this,
like this . . .

MIDIA:

                    Who is to blame? Why did you leave?
460   Why did you need to fight – against happiness,
against fire and truth, against the King? . . .

GANUS:

    Ha-ha . . . The King . . . O, God . . . The King! . . .

    This is madness . . . madness! . . .

MIDIA:

                           You frighten me –

    don't laugh like that . . .

GANUS:

                     It's nothing. It has passed . . .

    Three nights I have not slept . . . I'm rather tired.   465

    All autumn-long I wandered lost. Understand,

    Midia, that I fled: I could not stand

    my punishment . . . I came to know the sleepless

    sound of night pursuits. I starved.

    I too cannot tell you . . .   470

MIDIA:

                   . . . And all this

    just to paint your face, and afterwards . . .

GANUS:

    But I wanted to please you!

MIDIA:

                      . . . and afterwards

to be beaten and to roll around
like a drunken fool in the corner,
475   and to forgive the wrongdoer everything,
and to turn the insult into a joke,
to humiliate yourself in front of me . . .
Disgusting! Take this pillow, smother me!
For I love another! . . . Smother me! . . . No,
480   all he can do is cry . . . Enough . . . I'm tired . . .
Go . . .

GANUS:

          Forgive me, Midia . . . I didn't know . . .
It is as though for four years I eavesdropped
at a door, entered it — and found no one.
I'll leave. Just let me see you . . . Once a week,
485   no more . . . I will live at Tremens's. Only
don't go away . . .

MIDIA:

             Let go of my knees!
Leave . . . do not torture me . . . Enough —
I will go mad! . . .

GANUS:

          Farewell . . . Don't be angry . . .
forgive me — for I did not know. Give me

386

your hand – no, just to say goodbye. I must   490
look funny – I've smudged my make-up . . . Well . . .
I'm leaving . . . Lie down . . . It's getting light . . .

   [*Leaves.*]

MIDIA:

                                       Fool!

   CURTAIN

Act Two

TREMENS's room. TREMENS is in the same pose as in Act One, scene one. GANUS sits at the table, laying out playing cards.

TREMENS:

The bliss of emptiness . . . Non-existence . . .
So shall I keep repeating to you, until
with trembling hands you squeeze together
your exploding head; until I deafen your soul
with the thunders of my devastating dream! . . .   5
I am tormented by idleness, and yet I know
that my stifled will is like the water, which,
falling drop after drop upon the head
of a condemned man, gives birth to madness,
gnawing his skull and eating through his reason;   10
like water, which, seeping drop after drop
through stone, into the fiery bowels of the earth,
provokes the eruption of a volcano –
the madness of the earth . . . Non-existence . . .

15 Though I have fallen in love with twilight,
I must live on and suffer the stings of life,
that I may give the people the joy of eternal
death – yet my steadfast soul does not cry out,
crucified though it be on the bone cross
20 of the human skeleton, on the black thunderous
Golgotha of existence . . . You are pale, Ganus . . .
Stop laying out those cards, stop ruffling your
wild hair and glancing at the face of the clock . . .
What's there to fear?

GANUS:

                                Be quiet, I beg you! It's quarter to . . .
25 This is unbearable! The clock-hands move
like hunchbacks; like a widow and an orphan
behind a catafalque . . .

TREMENS:

                    Ella! My medicine!

GANUS:

Tremens . . . No, don't let her come in!
O, God!

    [ELLA *enters lazily, dragging her shawl behind her.*]

390

ELLA:

It's cold in here . . . I'm not sure
that clock is right . . .   30
   [*Looks at the wall-clock.*]

TREMENS:

What's it to you?

ELLA:

Nothing.
Strange: the fire is lit, but it's cold . . .

TREMENS:

My cold,
Ella, it's my cold! I feel the chill of life,
but wait – soon I will let loose such fire . . .

GANUS:

This is unbearable! Ella, you're jangling
the glass bottles . . . for God's sake, don't . . .   35
What was I about to say? Oh, yes:
the other day you promised to give me
an envelope and a stamp . . .

TREMENS:

. . . With a masked man . . .

ELLA:

I'll fetch them. It's cold here . . . Maybe I am

40   imagining it. I keep yawning all day . . .

     [*Leaves.*]

GANUS:

What did you say?

TREMENS:

              I said that the stamp

depicts our noble . . .

GANUS:

              Tremens, Tremens, O,

if you only knew! Not that. Listen, I

deliberately asked Ella . . . You must send

45   her away, somewhere, for an hour . . . They are

coming now: we decided on ten o'clock,

you checked the cartel yourself . . . I beg you,

give her an errand . . .

TREMENS:

              On the contrary, Ganus.

Let her learn. Let her see fear and courage.

50   Death is a spectacle worthy of the gods.

GANUS:

You are a monster, Tremens! How can I,
under the gaze of her child-like eyes . . . O
Tremens, I beg you! . . .

TREMENS:

Enough. It's part of my plan.
Today I shall unleash my monstrous carnival.
Your opponent – now what's his name? I have   55
forgotten . . .

GANUS:

Tremens! My friend! Six minutes remain!
I implore you! They're coming now . . . It's Ella
I pity!

TREMENS:

. . . your opponent is just some flitting,
flashy buffoon; but if he should draw death
from the fist by its little white ear, I would be   60
content: one less soul on this earth . . . Oh, how
I long to sleep . . .

GANUS:

Five, five minutes left! . . .

TREMENS:

Yes: this is the hour I go to bed . . .

[ELLA *returns.*]

ELLA:

Here, take them. I could barely find them . . .
65   My face drifts up out of the semi-darkness
to meet me, like a murky jellyfish, and
the mirror is like black water . . . And my hair
is tired and dishevelled . . . And I – a bride.
I – a bride . . . Ganus, are you happy for me? . . .

GANUS:

70   I don't know . . . Yes, of course I'm happy . . .

ELLA:

After all, he's a poet, he's a genius,
unlike you . . .

GANUS:

Yes, Ella . . . Well, well . . .
soon the clock will strike . . . strike through my soul . . .
Oh, what does it matter! . . .

ELLA:

                        Can I ask you
  something? You have told me nothing, Ganus –   75
  what happened there when we left? Ganus!
  Well, then – he's silent . . . Are you really angry
  with me? Truly, I did not know that our
  little masquerade would not come off . . .
  How can I help? Perhaps there are some words –   80
  they flower in the shadows of high songs, –
  I'll find them. What a foolish, sulking man,
  he bites his lips, and doesn't want to know me . . .
  I will be understanding . . . Look at me . . .
  It is sinful to be silent with me. What else   85
  is there for me to say?

GANUS:

                    What, Ella, what
  do you want from me? You want to talk?
  Oh, let's, let's talk! About anything you want!
  About unfaithful women, about poets,
  about spirits, about the blind gut and its   90
  missing glasses, about fashion, about the planets –
  whisper, roar with laughter, chatter over
  one another, chatter ceaselessly! Well,
  what then? I'm having fun! . . . O, God! . . .

ELLA:

Don't! . . .

95   You're hurting me . . . You cannot understand.
      Don't. Ah! It's striking ten . . .

GANUS:

Ella — look —

I'll tell you . . . I must ask you to . . . Listen . . .

ELLA:

What card is that? Even?

GANUS:

Yes, it's even —

what difference does it make . . . Listen . . .

ELLA:

An eight.

100   I've thought of a number. Klian will be waiting
      at ten. When I go — it will all be over. The card
      says — to stay . . .

GANUS:

No — go! Please, go!

It is meant to be! Believe me! I know —

love does not wait! . . .

ELLA:

                    Listless languor
and a slight chill . . . Is that really love?   105
In any case, I shall do as you tell me . . .

GANUS:

Go, quickly, quickly! – before he wakes up . . .

ELLA:

No, but why? He will allow me to go . . .
Father, wake up. I'm leaving.

TREMENS:

                  Oh . . . the pain . . .
Where are you going so late? No, stay,   110
I need you.

ELLA [to GANUS]:

          Shall I stay?

GANUS [quietly]:

               No, no, no . . .
I beg you, I beg you! . . .

ELLA:

> You . . . You . . . are

pitiful.

[*She goes out, throwing on a fur wrap.*]

TREMENS:

> Ella! Wait! Damn her . . .

GANUS:

She's gone, gone . . . The door downstairs crashed

115 like glassy thunder . . . I feel relieved now . . .

[*Pause.*]

It's after ten . . . I don't understand . . .

TREMENS:

To be late is duelling etiquette. Or maybe

he's lost his nerve.

GANUS:

> There is another rule

as well: not to insult someone else's

120 opponent . . .

TREMENS:

           And I will tell you this: the soul
must fear death as a maiden fears love. Ganus,
what do you feel?

GANUS:

            The fire and cold of revenge,
and I stare steadily into the cat-like eyes
of steely fear: the animal tamer knows
that he need only turn away – the beast   125
will spring. But, fear apart, there is another
feeling, gloomily watching over me . . .

TREMENS [*yawns*]:
Damned drowsiness . . .

GANUS:

              This feeling is the worst
of all . . . Here, Tremens, a business letter –
send it by post; here, a letter to my wife –   130
give it to her yourself . . . Oh, how it sticks
in the throat, oh, how it sticks! . . . Stay calm . . .

TREMENS:

                       So.

Did you look at the stamp? I can always feel

that taut neck under my fingers . . . You must
135   help me, Ganus, if death spares you . . . Help me . . .
We'll find some savage mercenaries . . . We'll
penetrate the gloomy palace . . .

GANUS:

                      Don't
distract me with your mad drowsy muttering.
For me, Tremens, this is very hard . . .

TREMENS:

                              Sweet sleep . . .
140   Everlasting sleep . . . My lashes stick together.
Wake me . . .

GANUS:

               He sleeps. He sleeps . . . fiery and blind!
Shall I reveal it to you, shall I? Oh, how
late they are! The anticipation will kill me . . .
O, God! Shall I reveal it? It's all so simple:
145   not a meeting, not a duel, but a trap . . .
one short gunshot . . . Tremens himself will do it,
not I, and he will say that I have placed
higher than honour the cold duty of a rebel,
and he'll give thanks to me . . . Away, away,
150   trembling temptation! There is but one reply,

but one reply to you, – the disdainful one –
it is ignoble. Ah, here – they come . . . Oh,
that carefree laugh behind the door . . . Tremens!
Wake up! It's time!

TREMENS:

What! Oh! They've come?
Who is that laughing there? A familiar lilt? . . .   155
    [MORN *and* EDMIN *enter.*]

EDMIN:

Allow me to introduce Mister Morn.

TREMENS:

Delighted to be at your service. Have we met?

MORN [*laughs*]:
I don't recall.

TREMENS:

In my half-sleep it seemed . . .
But it doesn't matter . . . Where is the arbiter?
That sprightly old man – Ella's godfather –   160
what's his name . . . oh, my memory!

EDMIN:

                                        Dandilio
will be here shortly. He doesn't know anything.
It's better that way.

TREMENS:

                        Yes, fate is blind. That's
an old joke. Sleep overcomes me. Forgive me,
165   I am unwell.
            [*Two groups: to the right, by the fire,* TREMENS *and* GANUS; *to
            the left, on the darker side of the room,* MORN *and* EDMIN.]

GANUS:

                    Waiting . . . more waiting . . .
I'm getting weak, I cannot bear this . . .

TREMENS:

                                            Oh,
Ganus, poor Ganus! You are the mirror
of suffering; oh, to breathe some warmth
into you to cloud the glass! Look, for instance:
170   a kind of warm shadow swathes your opponent.
He gazes at my paintings, whistles quietly . . .
I cannot see, but it seems his face is calm . . .

MORN [*to* EDMIN]:

    Look: a green meadow, and there, beyond it,

    a forest of firs in black oils, a pair

    of clouds pierced by slanting golden light . . .   175

    the time is nearly evening . . . and in the air,

    perhaps, a church bell . . . the midges swarm . . .

    Ah, to go there, to go into that picture,

    into the reverie of its green, airy colours . . .

EDMIN:

    Your calm is a pledge of immortality.   180

    You are magnificent.

MORN:

                  You know, it amuses me:

    I have been here before. It amuses me,

    I keep wanting to laugh . . . My unhappy

    opponent dares not look me in the eye.

    I repeat that you were wrong to tell him . . .   185

EDMIN:

    But I wanted to save half the world! . . .

TREMENS [*from his chair*]:

    Which is the picture you like? I can't see –

    is it the birches over a backwater?

MORN:

                              No, –

evening, a green meadow . . . Who painted it?

TREMENS:

190   He is dead. Only his cold bones remain.
        Something is crucified on them – rags, a soul . . .
        Oh, I really don't know why I keep
        these paintings. Leave them, you mustn't
        look at them!

GANUS:

                          Ah! A knock at the door! No,

195   it's someone with a tray. Tremens, Tremens,
        do not laugh at me! . . .

TREMENS [to the SERVANT]:

                              Put it here.

Here, drink this, Ganus.

GANUS:

                          I don't want it.

TREMENS:

        As you wish. My dear sirs, I pray do not
        refuse.

MORN:

Thank you. But tell us, Tremens, when
was it that you stopped painting?   200

TREMENS:

When I became
a widower.

MORN:

And are you now not tempted
to put your thumb through the palette once more?

TREMENS:

Listen, we've gathered to decide on death, –
a question of high importance; this is no place
for small talk. Let us talk of death. You laugh?   205
So much the better; but let us talk of death.
What is the ecstasy of death? It is a pain,
like lightning. The soul is like a tooth, God
wrenches out the soul – crunch! – and it is over . . .
What comes next? Unthinkable nausea and then –   210
the void, spirals of madness – and the feeling of being
a swirling spermatozoid – and then darkness,
darkness – the velvety abyss of the grave,
and in that abyss . . .

EDMIN:

Enough! This is worse

215 than talking about a bad painting! Here.

Finally.

[*The* SERVANT *shows in* DANDILIO.]

DANDILIO:

Good evening! Ooph, how hot it is

in here! It's been a while, Tremens, since

we've seen each other – you live like a hermit.

I was astounded by your invitation:

220 but the wise man, they say, invites the moth.

For Ella – here – a box of glossy sugar plums –

she loves them. Greetings, Morn! Edmin,

you must be sleeping badly. You are as pale

as a lily of the valley . . . Ah – can it really

225 be Ganus? We once were well acquainted. It

is a secret, is it not, that you have returned

to us? When last night you and I . . . how did

I know? Well, by the brand, by the blue number –

here – above your wrist: you wrung your hands

230 and the number was revealed. I noticed it,

and, as I recall, I said that in Desdemona . . .

TREMENS:

Here, have some wine, biscuits. Soon Ella
will be back . . . You see, I live quietly,
but happily. Pour some for me. By the way,
there's been a disagreement here: these   235
gentlemen here want to decide which
of them shall pay for a dinner . . . in honour
of some fashionable dancer. If you could
just . . .

DANDILIO:

　　　　Of course! I'll pay with pleasure!

TREMENS:

　　　　　　　　　　　　No, no,
not that . . . clasp the handkerchief and let out   240
two ends – one with a knot.

MORN:

　　　　　　　　　　Which can't be seen,
of course. Really, he's a child – one must explain
everything! Do you recall, you carefree dandelion,
how one night I planted you atop a street lamp:
the light shone through your grey tufts,   245
and you were trying to pull a shaggy top hat
over the moon and smacked your lips so happily . . .

407

DANDILIO:

And after that, the top hat smelled of milk.
You prankster, I forgive you!

GANUS:

Hurry . . . We asked you . . .
250   This must be resolved . . .

DANDILIO:

Come, come, my friend –
patience . . . Here is my handkerchief. Not
a handkerchief but a multi-coloured flag.
Forgive me. I'll turn my back to you . . . Ready!

TREMENS:

He who pulls out the knot shall pay. Ganus,
255   pull.

GANUS:

No knot!

MORN:

You are lucky, as always . . .

GANUS:

I can't . . . what have I done! I shouldn't have . . .

TREMENS:

    He clutches his head, mutters – but it's not you –
    he's the one who's lost.

DANDILIO:

                    Forgive me, what's this . . .
    I have made a mistake . . . There is no knot,
    I didn't tie one, look – what a miracle!   260

EDMIN:

    Fate, fate, fate decided thus! Listen
    to fate. That's the outcome! I beseech
    you – beseech you – to be reconciled!
    All is well!

DANDILIO [*taking snuff*]:

           And I shall pay for the dinner . . .

TREMENS:

    The art connoisseur looks worried . . . Enough   265
    jesting with fate: give me that handkerchief!

DANDILIO:

    What do you mean – give it to you? I need it –
    I sneeze, – it's covered in tobacco, it's damp;
    and what is more – I have a cold.

TREMENS:

We'll make it
270   simpler, then! Here, with cards . . .

GANUS [mumbling]:

I can't.

TREMENS:
Quick, which suit?

MORN:

Well, I love the colour
red – life, and roses, and sunrises . . .

TREMENS:

Now
I shall show the card! Ganus, stop!
What a fool he is – he's gone and fainted!

DANDILIO:
275   Hold him – oh, he's heavy! Hold him, Tremens, –
my bones are made of glass. Ah, there –
he's come to.

GANUS:

God, forgive me.

DANDILIO:

Let's go, let's go . . .

lie down.

[*He leads* GANUS *to the bedroom.*]

MORN:

He could not bear the repetition
of his good fortune. So. The eight of clubs.
Very good.   280

[to EDMIN]

You've grown pale, friend? Why?
To set in contrast still more sharply
the black silhouette of my fate? Sometimes
despair is the finest of all artists . . . I am
ready. Where is the pistol?

TREMENS:

Not here, though,
please. I don't like mess in my house.   285

MORN:

Yes,
you are right. Sleep soundly, worthy Tremens.
My house is taller. The shot will resound
more sonorously in it, and tomorrow

will come a dawn in which I have no part.

290 Let's go, Edmin. I shall spend the night
at Caesar's.

[MORN and EDMIN exit, the former supporting the latter.]

TREMENS [alone]:

Thank you . . . My chill has been
replaced by a flowing warmth . . . How pleasing is
that grin anticipating death and the mortal
glimmer in his eyes! He keeps his spirits up,

295 he plays . . . I have no interest in the actor
himself, yet – strange – it still seems to me
that this is not the first time I have heard
his voice: as when one remembers the tune
but not the words; perhaps there are none:

300 only a movement of thought – and the tune
itself melts away . . . I am content with today's
motley scenes, with these images of the unknown.
Yes! I am pleased – and feel in my veins
a living languor, a warmth, a thaw . . . Now!

305 Climb out of my sleeve, thou five of diamonds!
I don't know how it happened, but, inspired
by a momentary pity, I substituted
the card I'd grabbed – the raspberry rhombuses –
with another, the one I showed. One – two!

310 The eight of clubs! – if you please! – and death

412

peered out of its funereal clover at Morn!
While the fools were talking of roses – a slip
of the palm, a sleight of hand – so swiftly
is fate made. But never shall my Ganus
know that I cheated, that it was to him,   315
fortunate man, that death fell . . .

    [DANDILIO *returns from the bedroom.*]

DANDILIO:

                      They've left?
But they forgot to bid me farewell . . . This
snuff box is an antique . . . For three centuries
tobacco wasn't taken – and now it's fashionable
again. Would you like some?   320

TREMENS:

                What's wrong with Ganus?
A fit?

DANDILIO:

      It's nothing. He's pressed to the bed, muttering
something and flinging out his hands, as though
to catch, by their coat-tails, invisible passers-by.

TREMENS:

Leave him, – it's good for him. He'll learn.

413

DANDILIO:

                                        Yes,

325   all grain is grist for the mill of the soul, you're right . . .

TREMENS:

        I meant something else. Ah, the steps

        of my infatuated Ella! I know,

        I know where she has been . . .

            [ELLA *enters.*]

ELLA:

                        Dandilio!

DANDILIO:

        What is it, my dear, what, my lightness? . . .

ELLA:

                                        Only

330   splinters remain . . . splinters! He . . . Klian . . .

        O, God . . . Don't touch me! Leave me . . . I am sticky . . .

        I am drenched in cold pain. Lies! Lies!

        Surely this cannot be what they call bliss.

        It's death, not bliss! My soul has been brushed

335   by the coffin lid . . . pinched . . . it hurts . . .

TREMENS:

That is my blood. Let her cry.

DANDILIO:

There . . .

there . . . Let me brush away that lock . . .
You have pearls and roses on your cheeks,
a shimmer, your hair is dewy from the snow . . .
You're being silly. All is well. While playing,   340
a child scratches itself – and cries. Life,
its skirts flying up and rustling, will run
through all the rooms, like a young mother,
fall down upon her knees before the child,
and, laughing, will kiss the scratch away . . .   345

CURTAIN

Act Three

SCENE ONE

A huge study. A starry night can be seen through the tall windows, but the stage is in darkness. Two figures [MORN and EDMIN] enter cautiously.

MORN:

And so, it's over. I'll spend the night at Caesar's! . . .
And so, it's over, dear friend . . . For the last time,
like two regicides, have we stolen after midnight
by the secret passages, into my palace . . . Light
a candle. The wax will drip – stand it straighter.   5
One more . . . there. Better than a sober lamp!
Now listen. I foresaw the possibility
of death. Here, in this table, in its oak
and malachite depths, sleep my papers –
contracts, plans, the drafts of laws . . . and   10
dried flowers . . . I hand the keys to you.
I also hand over this will, in which it states
that in a fit of sweet and blinding visions,

I decided to yield to death. Let my crown,
15   – like a taut ball kicked aside, – be caught,
and clasped in the arms of my young nephew;
let the grey-haired owls – the senators, in whose
charge he is – noiselessly govern my country,
whilst on the throne sits but a little boy,
20   dangling his legs . . . But the people must not
know. Let my carriage, with its blue lacquer
and coat-of-arms gleaming, rush as before
along the square and over the bridge. I will
become a ghost. And when my heir grows up,
25   I want him to reveal how it was I died:
he will begin the fairy tale with a fairy tale.
My mantle, embroidered with flames, may fit
him perfectly . . . You, Edmin, my confidant,
my subtlest counsellor, soften the edges of power
30   with your light subtlety, encircle its movements
with your serenity . . . You understand?

EDMIN:
    I'll do it all . . .

MORN:
                    One thing more: today,
in a meditative hour, I wrote a childish,

418

but to me necessary, edict — that anyone
who is successful in escaping exile   35
will be pardoned for his courage . . .

EDMIN:

                                        I'll do it all.
And if you would only hint, with one
movement of your eyelids, that I should
accompany you into unknown eternity . . .

MORN:

. . . Light these candles too. Let the mirrors   40
be filled with visions, with winds . . . I shall return
shortly. I am going to the chamber where
for four years now my fiery crown has burned
and breathed in its velvet nest; let it squeeze
my head with its diamond pain, let it roll   45
off my head when I fall backwards . . .

EDMIN:

                                        My sovereign,
my precious friend . . .

MORN:

                        . . . Not a shot, no, not
a shot! A musical explosion! As though

for a moment a door opens to the heavens . . .
50   While here – how the strings will prolong
the sound! What a fairy tale shall I leave
to the people! . . . You know, in the dark I hit
my knee upon the chair. It hurts.

    [*Leaves.*]

EDMIN [*alone*]:

O, I am like wax! . . . The chronicles will not
55   forget this weakness of mine . . . I am to blame . . .
Why do I not rush to save him? . . . Rise up,
rise up, my soul! No, heavy drowsiness . . .
I could with prayers, persuasions – I know
that such exist – stop him . . . why not, then?
60   As a man in his dreams cannot move his arm –
so I have not the strength even to contemplate
what is about to happen . . . This is – retribution! . . .
When once, in childhood, I was forbidden to go
to the apiary, I for a moment held
65   in my mind the thought of my mother's death, and how,
unsupervised, I would eat the clear honey, –
though I loved my mother to tears, with trembling
heart . . . This is – retribution. Now, once more
I'm stuck to the sweet honeycombs. One thing
70   alone I see, one thing burns in the twilight:
come morning I will bear news of his infidelity!

420

Like some criminal, befogged by wine, I'll enter,
I'll speak, Midia will cry . . . and not hearing
my own words, and trembling, and with tender,
hypocritical consolation, touching her   75
imperceptibly, I will lie to her, so as
to take the place of someone else. Yes,
lie, tell her – about what? – the supposed
unfaithfulness of him, before whom we two –
are dust! If he had lived I would have kept   80
silent till the end . . . But now my god will leave . . .
I'll be alone, weak and greedy . . . Death is better!
O, if only he would order me to die!
Burn, weak-willed wax . . . Breathe, mirrors,
with a funereal flame . . .   85

   [*He lights the candles. There are many of them.* MORN *re-enters.*]

MORN:
                              Here's the crown.
My crown. Droplets of waterfalls on spikes . . .
Edmin, it's time. Tomorrow you shall call
the senate together . . . announce . . . secretly . . .
Farewell then . . . it's time . . . Before my eyes
pillars of fire surge past . . . Yes, listen –   90
one last thing . . . go to Midia, tell her
that Morn is the King . . . no, not the King,
not that. You'll say: Morn is dead . . . wait . . .

no . . . say: he's left . . . no, I don't know!
It's better you make something up, − but
it shouldn't be about the King . . . And say it
very quietly, and very softly, as is your way.
Why are you crying like that? Don't . . . Get up
off your knees, get up . . . your shoulder blades
are shaking like a woman's . . . Don't cry, dear friend . . .
Go . . . into the other room: when you hear
the gunshot − come back in . . . Enough, I die
merrily . . . Farewell . . . Go . . . wait! Do you
remember how once we stole in darkness
from the palace, and a sentry fired at me,
and shot through my collar? . . . How we laughed
then . . . Edmin? He's gone . . . I am alone,
and all around are flaming candles, mirrors,
and a frosty night . . . Brightness and terror . . .
I am alone with my conscience. So, here's
the pistol . . . an antique . . . six rounds . . . I need
but one . . . Hey, who is there above the rooftops?
You, God? Forgive me, then, what people
will not forgive! What's better − standing or sitting?
Sitting is better. Quick. Just don't think! . . .
Snap − the cartridge, in! The muzzle to the chest.
Below the rib. Here's the heart. Like so.
Now the safety catch . . . goosebumps on my chest.
The muzzle's cold, like the lacquer tube

95
100
105
110
115

applied by a doctor: he breathes in, he listens . . .   120
and his bald pate and the tube rise up
in rhythm with my chest . . .

                  No, wait!

That is not how people shoot themselves . . .
This needs to be thought through . . . One. Two.
Three. Four. Five. Six. Six steps from the chair   125
to the window. The snow shines. How starry
is the sky! God, give me strength,
give me strength, I beg you – give me strength . . .
There sleeps my city, all in hoar-frost,
all in a blue shroud. O, my dear! . . . Farewell,   130
forgive me . . . I ruled for four years . . . created
an age of happiness, an age of harmony . . . God,
give me strength . . . Playfully, lightly I ruled;
I appeared in a black mask in the ringing hall,
before my cold, decrepit senators . . . masterfully   135
I revived them – and left again, laughing . . .
laughing . . . And sometimes, in patched-up clothes,
I sat in a tavern and grunted with the ruddy
drunken coachmen; a dog would wag its tail
under the table, and a girl would tug me   140
by the sleeve, though I looked like a pauper . . .
Four years passed, and now, in the radiant noon
of my life, I must abandon my kingdom, must
jump from the throne to death – O, God, – all

145   because I kissed a shallow woman and struck
      a foolish adversary! I could have had him . . .
      O conscience, conscience – the cold angel
      at the back of thought: thought turns – there's
      no one there; but behind, it rises up again.

150   Enough! I must, must die! O, if only
      it could not be so, not so, but in sight
      of the world, in the hot storm of battle,
      to the thunder of hooves, atop a sweaty steed,
      so as to greet death with an immortal cry

155   and gallop headlong through the sky into
      heaven's yard, where the splash of water
      can be heard, and a seraph scrubs the horse
      of St George! Yes, death would be rapture then! . . .
      But here I am – alone . . . only candle flame –

160   a thousand-eyed spy – watches from under
      the suspicious mirrors . . . But I must die!
      There is no glory – there is eternity
      and man . . . What's this crown for? It digs
      into my temples, damned thing! Off with it!

165   Like so . . . like so . . . roll across the dark carpet,
      like a wheel of fire . . . Now quickly! Don't think!
      Plunge reason in icy water! One movement:
      press the curved trigger . . . One movement . . .
      How many times have I pressed door handles,

170   the buttons of doorbells . . . And now . . . And now . . .

424

I don't know how! My finger on the trigger
is weaker than a worm . . . What's a kingdom to me?
What's valour? To live, only to live . . . O, God!
Edmin!

   [*approaches the door; calls out like a child*]

      Edmin!

   [EDMIN *enters.* MORN *stands with his back to him.*]

         I can't . . .

   [*Pause.*]

               Why do you
stand there, why do you look at me? Or,   175
perhaps, you think that I'm a . . . Listen, here,
I'll explain . . . Edmin, you understand . . . I love her . . .
I love Midia! My kingdom and my soul
I am prepared to yield, if only not
to part from her! My friend, listen, do not   180
blame me . . . do not blame me . . .

EDMIN:

                   My sovereign, I'm happy . . .
You are my hero . . . I'm not even worthy . . .

MORN:

                      Really?
Really? . . . Well then . . . I'm pleased . . . Earthly love
is higher, stronger, than heavenly valour . . . Though you,

425

185   Edmin, don't love . . . you cannot understand
      that a man is capable of burning worlds
      for a woman . . . So then – it is decided.
      I'll flee from here . . . there is no other way.
      For in truth – I ruled without a care.
190   Such carelessness is power. That has gone.
      Oh, how can I rule, when the Devil himself
      has melted the crown on my poor head?
      I'll disappear . . . You understand, I'll disappear,
      I'll quietly live out the rest of my strange life
195   to the secret tune of my royal memories.
      Midia will be with me . . . Why do you keep silent?
      Am I not right? Midia will die without me . . .
      You know that.

EDMIN:

                 My sovereign, I ask but
      one thing: an agonizing request, a crime
200   against my native land . . . though it be!
      I beseech you: take me with you . . .

MORN:

      O, how you love me, how you love, dear friend! . . .
      I have not the power to refuse you . . . I am
      a criminal myself. Listen, do you remember

how I came to power? I came out in a mask   205
and mantle on the golden balcony, – it was
windy, it smelled, for some reason, of the sea,
and the mantle kept slipping off, and from behind
you righted it . . . But, why do I . . . Quickly,
time is running on . . . there is this will here . . .   210
How to change it? . . . What shall we do? How
to act? In it, I write that . . . Burn it! Burn it!
Thankfully the candles are lit. Quick! Meanwhile,
I'll compose a different one . . . But how? My mind
is empty. I move my quill as if on water . . .   215
Edmin, I don't know. Advise me – we must hurry,
to finish by sunrise . . . What's wrong?

EDMIN:

                                        Footsteps . . . They're
coming here . . . Along the gallery . . .

MORN:

                              Quick!
Put out the lights! We'll have to go through
the window – oh, hurry! I can't meet with anyone . . .   220
Come what may . . . What shall I take? Yes,
the pistol . . . put them out . . . put them out . . . the
    papers . . .

the diamonds . . . right. Fling it open! Hurry . . .
My trenchcoat has caught – wait. Ready! Jump! . . .

[*They leave. Darkness on stage. An* OLD MAN *in livery, stooping,
comes in with a candle in his hand.*]

OLD MAN:

225 Looks like somebody's been messing about in here . . .
A burning smell. Table's out of place . . . Hark you now –
Look where they've thrown the crown. Ptfu . . . Ptfu . . .
Shine . . .
I'll rub you . . . And there – that casement's wide open.
That won't do . . . Let's have a listen at the door.

[*Sleepily he crosses the stage and listens.*]

230 The rascal's asleep . . . the master sleeps. For
it's gone four, I dare say . . . O, Lord Jesus!
Oh, how my bones ache, how they ache! Cook
shoved some ointment at me, – says, try it,
rub some on . . . Try arguing . . . That's all I need . . .

235 Old age isn't some ugly mug daubed on
a fence, you can't just paint over it . . .

[*And, muttering, he exits.*]

CURTAIN

SCENE TWO

The same stage set as in the previous scene: the King's study. Only now
the carpet is torn in places and one of the mirrors is broken. Four of the
REBELS, *seated. Early morning. In the window the sun is visible, and there*
is a bright thaw.

FIRST REBEL:

    The firing at the western gate still opens
    wide its swift embraces, so as to catch –
    now a soul, now a melody, now the ringing
    of glass . . . smoke rises from the houses still,
    from the hunched ruins of the senate, the museum   5
    of coins, the museum of banners, the museum
    of old statues . . . We are tired . . . All night long –
    work, tumult . . . It must be past seven already . . .
    What a morning! The senate blazed, like a torch . . .
    We're tired, confused . . . Where's Tremens rushing us?   10

SECOND REBEL:

    The draughty skeleton has clothed itself in flesh
    and fire. It's come to life. It rubs its hands.
    The mob gleefully tears open the cellars, marvels

at the fires . . . I don't know, don't know, brothers,
15   what he's planning . . .

THIRD REBEL:

Not so, not so, did we
once think to make our homeland happy . . . I regret
the sleepless nights of exile . . .

FIRST REBEL:

He is mad!
He ordered that the flying machines be burned
so as to entertain the drunkards! But some
20   nameless heroes came along, and grabbed
the controls just in time . . .

FOURTH REBEL:

This order here,
that I am copying out, is terrifying
in its tigerish playfulness . . .

SECOND REBEL:

Quiet . . .
Here comes his son-in-law . . .
    [KLIAN *enters hurriedly.*]

KLIAN:

Splendid news!
In the suburbs the merry crowd's blown up   25
a school; satchels and rulers are scattered across
the square; about three hundred little mites
perished. Tremens is very pleased.

THIRD REBEL:

He's . . .
pleased! Brothers, brothers, do you hear?
He's pleased! . . .   30

KLIAN:

Well, then, I'll inform the leader
that my news did not much please you . . .
Everything, I shall report everything!

SECOND REBEL:

We say
that Tremens is wiser than us: he knows his goal.
As it says in your last ode, he is a genius.

KLIAN:

Yes. He is worthy of entering the thunders   35
of my melodies. Nonetheless . . . the sun . . .
dazzles my eyes.

[*Looks out of the window.*]

Ah – there's that traitor,

Ganus! There, between the soldiers, standing

at the barriers: they're laughing. They have

40 let him through. There he goes across

the melting snow.

FIRST REBEL [*watching*]:

How pale he is!

Our former friend is unrecognizable!

Everything about him – his gaze, his pursed lips –

reminds one of the saints in stained glass . . .

45 They say his wife has fled . . .

SECOND REBEL:

Was there a lover?

FIRST REBEL:

I don't think so.

FOURTH REBEL:

Rumour has it that one day

he came to his wife, and on the table there was

a note, that come what may she had decided

to go, alone, back to her family . . . Klian,

50 what's so funny about that?

432

KLIAN:

I shall report
everything! Here you are, spinning rumours,
like old women, whilst Tremens thinks that
you are working . . . There are fires out there,
they need to be fanned, whilst you . . . I'll report
everything, everything . . .   55

   [GANUS *stops in the doorway*.]

Ah! Noble Ganus . . .
Most welcome Ganus . . . We were waiting for you . . .
We're glad to see you . . . Please . . .

FIRST REBEL:

Our Ganus . . .

SECOND REBEL:

Greetings, Ganus . . .

THIRD REBEL:

Do you not recognize us?
Your friends? Four years . . . together . . . in exile . . .

GANUS:

Away, you hirelings of a liar! . . . Where's Tremens?   60
He summoned me.

KLIAN:

He's interrogating.

He'll be here soon . . .

GANUS:

Well, I don't need him.

He invited me himself, and if . . . he's not here . . .

KLIAN:

Wait, I'll call him . . .

[*Goes towards the door.*]

FIRST REBEL:

And we will go too . . .

65   Is that not so, brothers? Why stay here . . .

SECOND REBEL:

Yes,

so much to do . . .

THIRD REBEL:

Klian, we're coming with you!

[quietly]

Brothers, I'm scared . . .

FOURTH REBEL:

I'll finish copying later . . .
I'll go . . .

THIRD REBEL:

Brother, brother, what are we doing . . .
[KLIAN *and the* REBELS *leave.* GANUS *is alone.*]

GANUS [*looks around in all directions*]:
. . . A hero lived here . . .
[*Pause.*]

TREMENS [*enters*]:

Thank you for coming,
my Ganus! I know that you've been clouded   70
by the sorrows of life. You've scarcely noticed
that for a month – a month today exactly –
I have ruled over an intoxicated country.
I called for you, so you could tell me directly,
could explain . . . but first let a fortunate man   75
talk of his happiness! You know yourself –
better than anyone, Ganus – that I waited
for my day, in a delirium, in a chill . . .
My day has come – unexpectedly, like love!
Rumour spread like a flame that the country   80
had no king . . . When and how he disappeared,

who strangled him, on what night, and how long
a dead man ruled the land, nobody now knows.
But the people do not forgive deceit:
85   the burial vaults, the senate, were filled
with angry trampling. How splendidly,
how austerely, the old men died, and how
he screamed – O, sweeter than an ardent violin –
the little boy, their ward. The people took revenge
90   for the deception, – I seized the opportunity
to blaze up, and realized that I had waited so long
in vain: there was no king at all – only
a legend, potent and magical! Awakening,
the mob stormed in here, and nothing but echoes
95   resounded through the dead palace! . . .

GANUS:

                          You called
for me.

TREMENS:

      You are right, let's turn to business:
in you, Ganus, I divined a kindred fire;
to you alone I entrusted my thoughts.
But you were tormented by a woman;

436

now she is gone; I'm going to ask you,   100
Ganus, for the last time: will you help me?

GANUS:

You summoned me in vain . . .

TREMENS:

                              Think it over,
don't rush, I will give you a little time . . .
    [*Hurriedly* KLIAN *enters.*]

KLIAN:

My leader, those people, the ones who recently
were singing in the streets, are being tortured . . .   105
There is no one to interrogate them . . .
Your assistants – how can I put it – are feeling
nauseous . . .

TREMENS:

                    All right, I'm coming, I'm coming . . . You,
my Klian, are a fine fellow! . . . I've long known . . .
By the way, one of these days I will   110
surprise you: I'll order that you be hanged.

KLIAN:

Tremens . . . My leader . . .

TREMENS:

As for you, Ganus,

think it over, I ask you, think it over . . .

[TREMENS *and* KLIAN *leave.*]

GANUS [*alone*]:

A single thought torments me: here lived a hero . . .

115   these mirrors here are sacred: they looked on him . . .

He sat here, in this mighty chair. His footsteps

linger in the palace, like the step of a hexameter

dwindling in one's memory . . . Where did he die?

Where did his shot ring out? Who heard it?

120   Perhaps it was out there, outside the city,

in a mournful oak forest, in the snows of night . . .

and his pale friend buried the hot corpse

in a drift of snow . . . Sin, inconceivable sin,

how can I expiate you? All of my blood

125   is grateful for the death of my rival and yet

all of my soul curses the death of the King . . .

We are duplicitous, we're blind – and it is hard

to live, trusting only in life: earthly life

is a murky translation from the divine original;

130   the general thought is clear but the primordial

music is missing in its words . . . What are passions?

Mistakes in the translation. What is love?

A rhyme lost in transmission to our discordant

438

language . . . It's time for me to take up the original! . . .
My dictionary? One simple little book with a cross   135
on its cover . . . I'll seek out the stony arches, there,
where the respite of prayer and the full breath
of the soul will teach me the pronunciation
of life . . .

       There in the doorway, Ella has stopped,
and does not see me, deep in thought,   140
fingering the fringes of her sluggish shawl . . . What
can I say to her? She needs warmth . . . Dear one . . .
She doesn't see me . . .

ELLA [*aside*]:

       How amusing! . . . I opened
and read someone else's letter . . . Handwriting
like the wind, and the smell of the south . . . I   145
resealed it, just as father once showed me
in jest . . . Morn and Midia are together!
How can I give it to him? He thinks that she
is living in that old-fashioned backwater
that she comes from . . . How to give it to him? . . .   150

GANUS [*approaching*]:
You're up early. Me too . . . We seldom meet
now, Ella: another festivity coincided
with your wedding . . .

ELLA:

Morning — an azure
miracle — and not a morning . . . it trickles . . . whispers . . .
155   Has Klian gone?

GANUS:

He's gone . . . Tell me, Ella,
are you happy?

ELLA:

What is happiness? The flutter
of wings, or perhaps a snowflake on one's lip —
that is happiness . . . Who said that? I don't recall . . .
No, Ganus, I was wrong, you know . . . But
160   how bright it is today, it's practically spring!
Everything trickles . . .

GANUS:

Ella, Ella, did you ever
think that the daughter of a powerless rebel
would live in a palace?

ELLA:

Oh, Ganus, I miss
our little old rooms, our peace, the fireplace,
165   the paintings . . . Listen: lately I've come to realize

that my father is mad! We have fallen out
with one another; now we're not speaking . . .
I believed in it at first . . . What for! Rebellion
for the sake of rebellion is both boring
and horrifying – like night-time embraces   170
without love . . .

GANUS:

                    Yes, Ella, you have truly
understood . . .

ELLA:

                    The other day all the squares
gazed at the sky . . . Laughter, screams, howls
of fury . . . Saving themselves from the flames,
the flyers soared up from all directions, came   175
together like crystal swallows, and quietly
the shimmering flock slipped away. One
fell behind and froze for a moment above
the tower, as though he had left his nest there,
and then unwillingly caught up his sorrowful   180
companions, – and all of them melted away
into a crystal dust in the sky . . . I realized,
when they had disappeared, when in my eyes
swam blinding circles – from the sun –

441

185   I suddenly realized . . . that I love you . . .
     [*Pause.* ELLA *looks out of the window.*]

GANUS:

                               I have
remembered! . . . Ella, Ella . . . How frightening! . . .

ELLA:

    No, no, no – keep silent, dear. I look
    at you, I look into the palace garden,
    I look into myself, and now I know
190   that all is one: my love and the raw sun,
    your pale face and the bright trickling icicles
    beneath the roof, the amber spot upon
    the porous sugary snow mound, the raw sun
    and my love, my love . . .

GANUS:

                        I've remembered:
195   it was ten o'clock, and you left, and I
    could have stopped you . . . Yet another blind,
    momentary sin . . .

ELLA:

                I don't need anything
from you . . . Ganus, I will never tell you again.

442

And if I told you now, it was only because
the snow today is so translucent . . . Really,   200
all is well . . . Days follow days . . . And then
I will become a mother . . . other thoughts
unwillingly will occupy me. But now,
you are mine, like the sun! Days will flow
after days . . . What do you think – perhaps   205
one day . . . when your sorrow . . .

GANUS:

                                   Don't ask me, Ella!
I don't want to even think of love!
I answer like a woman . . . Forgive me . . . But I
burn with something other, I'm filled with something
other . . . I dream only of the austere wings,   210
the straight brows of angels. For a while
I will go to them – away from life, away
from fires, away from greedy dreams . . . I know
a monastery entangled by cool wisteria.
There I will live; through iridescent glass   215
I'll look on God, listen as the bellows
of the organ breathe the world's soul
up to the triumphant heights, and think
about vain feats, about a hero who prays
in the murk of sleeping myrtles, amidst   220
the fire-flies of Gethsemane . . .

443

ELLA:

Oh, Ganus . . .

I forgot . . . here, a letter came yesterday . . .
addressed to my father, with a note saying
it's for you . . .

GANUS:

A letter? For me? Show me . . .

225   Ah! I knew it! Don't . . .

ELLA:

So, can I

tear it up?

GANUS:

Of course.

ELLA:

Give it to me . . .

GANUS:

Wait . . .

I don't know . . . that smell . . . that handwriting,
which flies headlong into my memory,
into my soul . . . Wait! I won't let it in.

ELLA:

Well, read it . . .   230

GANUS:

             And let it in? Read it? So that
the old pain can unfurl itself once more?
Once you asked me, should you go . . . Now
I ask you, shall I read it? Shall I?

ELLA:

                 I answer: no.

GANUS:

You're right! There! To shreds . . . And put this heap
of dried falling stars here . . . under the table . . .   235
in the basket woven with a coat-of-arms . . .
My hands smell of perfume . . . There . . . It's over.

ELLA:

Oh, how bright it is today! . . . The spring
shines through . . . Chirruping. The snow is melting.
There are droplets on the black branches . . .   240
Let's go, let's go, for a walk, Ganus? Do you
want to?

445

GANUS:

Yes, Ella, yes! I am free,
free! Let's go.

ELLA:

You wait here . . . I'll go
get dressed . . . I won't be long . . .
    [*Leaves.*]

GANUS [*alone, looking out of the window*]:

Yes, truly,

245   it is wonderful; a beautiful day! A pigeon
flew by there . . . Brightness, dampness . . . wonderful!
A workman forgot his spade . . . Somehow she lives
out there, at her sister's, in that distant place . . .
Does she know of his death? . . . Begone, you

250   cunning devil! Because of you, I destroyed
my homeland . . . Enough! I hate this woman . . .
Come back to me, O music of repentance!
Prayers, prayers . . . I am free, I am free . . .
    [*Slowly* TREMENS *and the four* REBELS *return, with* KLIAN
    behind them.]

FIRST REBEL:

Be more careful, Tremens, don't be angry,
255   understand, you must be more careful!

446

It's a dangerous path . . . You yourself have
heard: under torture they sang of the King . . .
ever more finely, ever more blissfully . . .
The King is a dream . . . The King has not died
in their souls, merely grown quiet . . . the dream   260
folded its wings – a moment – and now extends them . . .

KLIAN:

My leader, it's gone eight; the city is awake,
it stirs . . . The people call you to the square . . .

TREMENS:

Coming, coming . . .
    [to the FIRST REBEL]
                        So what are you saying?

FIRST REBEL:

I'm saying that a winged legend flies,   265
turning in the sun! Mothers whisper
the fairy tale to their children . . . Beggars
speak of the King over home-brewed beer . . .
How can you outlaw the wind itself?
You are too angry, too merciless.   270
It's a dangerous path! Be more careful,
we ask, there's nothing stronger than a dream! . . .

TREMENS:

>I'll break its neck! You dare to teach me? I'll break it!
>Or, perhaps, the dream is dear to you?

SECOND REBEL:

275 You have misunderstood us, Tremens,
>we wanted to warn you . . .

KLIAN:

>   The King is nothing but
>a straw scarecrow . . .

TREMENS:

>   Enough! Leave me, you
>woeful cowards! Ganus, well then, have you . . .
>decided?

GANUS:

>   Tremens, truly, do not torment me . . .
280 You know yourself. I want only prayer,
>only prayer . . .

TREMENS:

>   Leave, and quickly!
>I have suffered you too long . . . Everything

has its limit . . . Help him, Klian – he can't
open the door, he's pulling at it . . .

KLIAN:

Here,

let me – towards yourself . . .   285

GANUS:

. . . But perhaps

she's calling for me! Oh!
    [*Throws himself at a table.*]

KLIAN:

Wait . . . Calm down . . .

Save yourself, Tremens, he's . . .

GANUS:

Let go! Just don't

touch me, do you understand? There's no need
to touch me . . . Where's the basket? Move away!
The basket! . . .   290

TREMENS:

He's mad . . .

GANUS:

Here . . . in pieces . . .
in my palms . . . silver . . . Oh, that impetuous
handwriting!

[*reads*]

Here . . . here . . . 'my fan . . . send me . . .
He's worn me out' . . . Who's he? Who's he? The pieces
are all jumbled up . . . 'Forgive me' . . . That's not it.
295   That's not it either . . . Some address . . . strange . . .
in the south . . .

KLIAN:

Shall I call the guard?

GANUS:

Tremens! . . .
Listen . . . Tremens! It must be I see things
differently from everyone else . . . Take a look . . .
After the words 'and I'm unhappy' . . . That name . . .
300   See it? That name there . . . Can you make it out?

TREMENS:

'Mark is with me' – no, not Mark . . . 'Morn',
is it? Morn . . . That sounds familiar . . . Ah,
I've remembered! How glorious! That's fate

for you! So that buffoon tricked you?
Where are you going? Wait . . .   305

GANUS:

                              Morn lives,
God is dead. That's all . . . I go to kill Morn.

TREMENS:

Wait . . . No, no, don't pull away . . .
I've had enough . . . You hear? I talked to you
of chasms, of giants – and you . . . how dare you
bring in here the spirit of masquerade,   310
the babble of life, the squeak of mousy passion?
Wait . . . I am tired of you putting your . . . anguish –
your heart, that ace of hearts pierced by an arrow, –
above my, my thunderous worlds!
Enough of your living in this anguish!   315
I am jealous! No, lift up your face!
Look, look into my eyes, as into a grave.
So, you wish to assuage your fate? Stop
pulling away! Listen, do you remember
a certain happy evening? The eight of clubs?   320
Know, then, that it was I – cursed Tremens –
that your fate . . .

ELLA [in the doorway]:

Father, leave him be!

TREMENS:

. . . your fate . . . I pity . . . Leave. Hey, somebody!
He's grown faint – take him under the elbows!

GANUS:

325   Be off, you ravens! The corpse of Morn – is mine!
[Leaves.]

TREMENS:

Close the door behind him, Klian. Tightly.
There's a draught.

SECOND REBEL [quietly]:

I said there was a lover . . .

FIRST REBEL:

Quiet, I'm feeling frightened . . .

THIRD REBEL:

How Tremens frowns.

SECOND REBEL:

Unhappy Ganus . . .

452

FOURTH REBEL:

> He's happier than us . . .

KLIAN [*loudly*]:

> My leader! I shall dare to repeat myself.   330
> The people are gathered in the square. They wait
> for you.

TREMENS:

> I know . . . Hey, follow me, you sheep!
> Why have you gone so quiet? Look lively!
> I will give such a speech, that tomorrow
> nothing but ashes will remain of the city.   335
> No, Klian, you aren't to come with us:
> your neck hints too much of the gallows.
>
>> [TREMENS *and the* REBELS *leave.* ELLA *and* KLIAN *remain on stage.*]

KLIAN:

> Did you hear that? Your father is a splendid
> joker. I like it. It's funny.
>> [*Pause.*]
>
>> Ella, you have
> a white hat on – are you going somewhere?   340

ELLA:

Nowhere. I've changed my mind . . .

KLIAN:

My wife
is beautiful. I don't find time to tell you that
you are beautiful. Only from time to time,
in my poems . . .

ELLA:

I don't understand them.

[*Screams are heard offstage.*]

KLIAN:

345   Hark! The howl of the crowd . . . That welcoming peal!

CURTAIN

Act Four

A drawing room in a southern villa. A glass door onto a terrace, leading out to a fantastical garden. In the middle of the stage is a table set with three places. A foul spring morning. MIDIA *stands with her back to the audience, looking out of the window. Somewhere a servant strikes a gong. The noise dies down.* MIDIA *doesn't move.* EDMIN *enters from the left with the newspapers.*

EDMIN:

Again there is no sun . . . How did you sleep?

MIDIA:

On my back, and on my side, and even
in the foetal position . . .

EDMIN:

                              Are we taking
coffee in the drawing room?

MIDIA:

Yes,

5   as you can see. The dining room is gloomy.

EDMIN:

The news is even more terrible than before . . .
These are not newspapers, but shrouds
drenched with death, with the dankness of the grave . . .

MIDIA:

They must have got wet in the postman's bag.
10   It has rained since morning, the gravel is dark.
And the palm trees have drooped.

EDMIN:

Here, listen:
the suburbs are ablaze . . . the crowds have looted
the museums . . . they light bonfires in the squares . . .
And drink, and dance . . . Execution follows
15   execution . . . And into the drunken city
has come the plague . . .

MIDIA:

What do you think, will
the rain stop soon? It's so dull . . .

EDMIN:

> Meanwhile,
> their savage leader . . . You knew his daughter . . .

MIDIA:

> Yes,
> I think so . . . I don't remember . . . What's death
> to me, chaos, blood, when I'm so bored   20
> that I don't know what to do with myself!
> Oh, Edmin, he has given up shaving,
> he walks around in his dressing gown,
> he's gloomy, and abrupt, and stubborn . . .
> It's as though we've crossed from a fairy tale   25
> to the most banal reality . . . He is becoming
> duller, has started hunching his shoulders,
> ever since we came to live here, in this swamp . . .
> The palm trees, you know, always remind me
> of the hallways of rich merchants . . . Edmin,   30
> leave the newspapers . . . It's nonsense . . . You are
> always so reserved with me, as though
> I were a whore or a queen . . .

EDMIN:

> Not at all . . .
> I only . . . You do not know, Midia, what

35 you are doing! . . . O, God, what is there
for us to talk about?

MIDIA:

I loved his laughter:
he laughs no longer . . . While once it seemed
to me that this tall, happy, quick-witted man
must be some kind of artist, a wondrous
40 genius, concealing his visions for the sake
of my jealous love, – and in not knowing
there lay for me a blissful thrill . . . Now I
have understood that he is dull and empty,
that my dream does not live in him,
45 that his light has gone out, he has fallen
out of love with me . . .

EDMIN:

You mustn't bewail
things so . . . Who could fall out of love with you?
You are so . . . well, enough – come on, smile!
Your smile is the movement of an angel . . .
50 I beg you! . . . Today, even your fingers are
motionless . . . They too do not smile . . . Ah, there! . . .

MIDIA:

Has it been long?

EDMIN:

Has what been long, Midia?

MIDIA:

Well. That's interesting . . . I've never seen you
like this. No, in fact, I did once ask you
what the point was of your standing guard   55
in the street . . .

EDMIN:

I remember, remember
only the curtain in your tormenting window!
You swam past in the embraces of another . . .
In the snowstorm I cried . . .

MIDIA:

How funny you are . . .
All dishevelled . . . Let me smooth your hair!   60
There. Now do my fingers laugh? Leave me . . .
oh, leave me . . . don't . . .

EDMIN:

My happiness . . . allow me to . . .
just your lips . . . just touch . . . like touching fluff,
the wingbeat of a butterfly . . . allow me . . . happiness . . .

MIDIA:

65   But no ... wait ... we're by the window ... the
gardener ...

. . . .

MIDIA:

My little one ... don't breathe like that ... Wait,
show me your eyes. Like that, closer ... closer ...
My soul would do nothing but bask and swim
70   in their soft darkness ... Wait ... more quietly ...
later ... There now! My hair comb's slipped ...

EDMIN:

                                     My life,
my love ...

MIDIA:

                You are so little ... So, so
little ... You are a silly little boy ...
What, did you not think I could kiss that way?
75   Wait, you will have time yet, for you and I
will leave for some enormous, noisy city
and will dine on the rooftop ... You know,
below us, in the dark, will be the whole city,
all in lights; coolness, night ... The rosy
80   reflection of a glass on the tablecloth ... And

a frenzied fiddler, now all hunched up, now
raising his fiddle to the heavens! Will you
take me away? Will you? Ah . . . shuffling . . .
let me go . . . it's him . . . move away . . .

[MISTER MORN *enters, in a dark robe, dishevelled.*]

MORN:

Night? Day? I do not notice the shift.   85
Morning is a continuation of sleeplessness.
My temples ache. As though someone has pressed,
screwed into my head a cast-iron cube.
Today I shall take coffee without milk . . .
   [*Pause.*]
Again, the newspapers are scattered all over   90
the place! Why . . . you are cheerless, Edmin! . . .
How astonishing: I need only enter
and immediately there are long faces –
like shadows in the evening sun . . . Strange . . .

MIDIA:

It is a foul spring . . .   95

MORN:

                              I am to blame.

MIDIA:

. . . And the news is dreadful . . .

MORN:

And I am to blame

for that too, is that not so?

MIDIA:

The city burns.

Everything has gone mad. I don't know

how it will end . . . Yet they say the King's

100   not dead, but is walled up underground

by the rebels . . .

MORN:

Eh, Midia, that will do!

You know, I will forbid the newspapers

to be brought. I have no peace from these

conjectures; rumours, news of bloodshed

105   and idle gossip. I've had enough! Trust me,

Midia, you need not try to be clever

in front of me . . . Be bored, anguished, change

your hairstyle, your dresses, lengthen your eyes

with a blue line, look in the mirror – but don't

110   try to be clever . . . What's wrong with you, Edmin?

EDMIN [*rises from the table*]:

   I can't . . .

MORN:

          What's wrong with him? What's wrong with him?
Where are you going? It's damp on the terrace . . .

MIDIA:

   Leave him. I shall tell you everything. Listen,
   I too can take no more. I am in love
   with him. I am leaving with him. You will   115
   get used to it. Really, you don't need me.
   We would torment each other. Life calls . . .
   I need happiness . . .

MORN:

              I understand – where
   is the sugar bowl? . . . Ah, here it is.
   Under the napkin.   120

MIDIA:

          So then, you do not wish
   to listen? . . .

MORN:

No, on the contrary –
I am listening . . . grasping, comprehending,
what more can I do? Do you wish to leave
today?

MIDIA:

Yes.

MORN:

I think it's about time
125   you started packing.

MIDIA:

Yes. Don't hurry me.

MORN:

According to the rules of separation,
you must still throw over your shoulder the phrase:
'I curse the day . . . '

MIDIA:

You never loved . . . You never
loved! . . . Yes, I have the right to curse
130   that faithless day, when your laugh entered
my quiet house . . . Why did you . . .

464

MORN:

By the way,
tell me, Midia, did you write to your husband
from here?

MIDIA:

I . . . I thought – it was not worth
reporting . . . Yes, I wrote to my husband.

MORN:

What exactly? Look me in the eyes.   135

MIDIA:

Nothing,
really . . . That I ask forgiveness, that you are
here with me, that I won't go back to him . . .
that it rains here . . .

MORN:

And you sent your address?

MIDIA:

Yes, I think . . . Asked him to send my fan . . .
I forgot it there, at home . . .   140

MORN:

And when

did you send it?

MIDIA:

About two weeks ago.

MORN:

Wonderful . . .

MIDIA:

I'll go . . . I need to . . . my things . . .
[*Leaves to the right.* MORN *is alone. Through the glass door, on
the terrace, the motionless back of* EDMIN *can be seen.*]

MORN:

Wonderful . . . Ganus, having received the letter,
will remind me of my debt. He'll force his way
145   out of the haze of the maddened city, out
of the mangled fairy tale, here, to the grey
south, into my hollow, humdrum existence.
Not long to wait. He must be on his way.
We shall meet once more, and, handing me
150   the pistol, he, clenched and pale, will demand
that I should kill myself, and I shall, perhaps,
be ready: death ripens in solitude . . .

                                        I am
amazed . . . Life has forsaken me so abruptly.
But I mustn't think of my homeland, –
or I'll end up rushing around a dungeon   155
with padded mattresses instead of walls and
with the number of madness above the door . . .
I don't believe it . . . How else to live? Edmin!
Come here! . . . Edmin, do you hear? Your hand,
give me your hand . . . My faithful friend, thank you.   160

EDMIN:

What can I say? Not blood but a cold shame
flows through my veins. I feel that you must now
look into my eyes as one looks at those
dirty pictures, that for a tuppence you can
gawp at through a peep-hole . . . My heart is full   165
of shame . . .

MORN:

                        No, it's nothing . . . I am only astonished . . .
Death is an astonishment. In life, too,
we are sometimes astonished: the ocean, the colour
of a cloud, the twist of fate . . . It is
as though I am standing on my head. I see   170
everything the way, they say, that babies see it:
the candle flame, tip pointing downwards . . .

EDMIN:

My sovereign, what can I say to you? You
betrayed a kingdom for a woman, I
175 betrayed a friendship for a woman – the very
same one . . . Forgive me. I am only human,
my sovereign . . .

MORN:

And I, I am Mister Morn –
that is all; an empty space, an unstressed
syllable in a poem without rhyme.
180 Oh, no one would have been unfaithful
to the King . . . But – to Mister Morn . . .
You should go. I have understood – this
is retribution. I'm not angry. But leave.
It is hard for me to talk with you. Only
185 a moment, and it is as though one has
shaken the coloured glass inside a tube,
glanced through it – and life has changed . . .
Farewell. Be happy.

EDMIN:

I will come back to you,
if you but call . . .

MORN:

I will meet you only
in heaven. No earlier. There, in the shade   190
of an olive tree, I'll introduce you to Brutus.
Go . . .

[EDMIN *leaves.*]

MORN [*alone*]:

Well. It's over.

[*Pause. A* SERVANT *enters.*]

MORN:

The table needs
to be cleared. Hurry up . . . Is the carriage
ordered?

SERVANT:

Yes, sir.

MORN:

Tomorrow morning,
have the barber come from the town –   195
the moustached, silent one. That is all.

[*The* SERVANT *leaves. Pause.* MORN *looks out of the window.*]

MORN:

The sky

is murky. The flowers tremble in the garden . . .
The artificial grotto blackens: the rain
stretches out in strings against the black . . .
200   Only one thing is left now: to await
Ganus. My soul is almost ready. How
the wet greenery shines . . . The rain quivers
as though in senile drowsiness . . . The house
meanwhile has awoken . . . The servants bustle . . .
205   The trunks clatter . . . And here she is . . .

[Enter MIDIA *with an open suitcase.*]

MORN:

Midia,

are you happy?

MIDIA:

Yes. Move. I need
to pack these . . .

MORN:

A familiar suitcase:
I carried it once at dawn. The snow crunched.
And the three of us were hurrying.

MIDIA:

    These things go in it – books, portraits . . .   210

MORN:

    That's fine . . . Midia, are you happy?

MIDIA:

    There's a train at midday exactly: I shall
    fly away to a marvellous foreign city . . .
    I wish I had some paper – this might break . . .
    And whose is this? Yours? Mine? I don't   215
    recall, I don't recall . . .

MORN:

                     Only don't cry,
    I beg you . . .

MIDIA:

             Yes, yes . . . you are right.
    It has passed . . . I won't . . . I didn't know
    that you would let me go so easily,
    so willingly . . . I jerked the door open . . .   220
    I thought you held the handle tightly on
    the other side . . . I jerked it open with all
    my might, – you were not holding it, the door
    opened easily, and I fell back . . . You

225   understand, I am falling . . . In my eyes
there is rippled darkness, and I think
I will perish – I cannot find a foothold! . . .

MORN:

Edmin is with you. He is happiness . . .

MIDIA:

                         I don't
know anything! . . . Only it's strange: we loved –
230   and it has all gone somewhere. We loved . . .

MORN:

These two engravings here are yours, aren't they?
And this porcelain dog?

MIDIA:

               . . . It's strange . . .

MORN:

                        No, Midia.
In harmony there is nothing strange. And life
is a vast harmony. I've understood this.
235   But, you see – the moulded whimsy of a frieze
on a portico keeps us from recognizing,
sometimes, the symmetry of the whole . . .

472

You will leave; we'll forget one another;
but now and then the name of a street,
or a street organ weeping in the twilight,   240
will remind us in a more vivid and more
truthful way than thought could resurrect
or words convey, of that main thing
which was between us, the main thing which
we do not know . . . And in that hour, the soul   245
will miraculously sense the charm
of past trifles, and we will understand
that in eternity all is eternal –
the genius's thought and the neighbour's
joke, the bewitched suffering of Tristan   250
and the most fleeting love . . . Let us part
without bitterness, Midia: some day, perhaps,
you will discover the unspoken reason
for my deep sorrow, my cold anguish . . .

MIDIA:

I dreamt, at the beginning, that beneath   255
the laughter you were hiding a secret . . . So,
there is a secret?

MORN:

                    Shall I reveal it to you?
Will you believe it?

473

MIDIA:

> I shall.

MORN:

>   So listen then:
> when we saw one another in the city,
260 I was – how shall I say? – an enchanter,
> a hypnotist . . . I read thoughts . . . I
> predicted fate, twirling my crystal;
> beneath my fingers the oak table rocked
> like the deck of a ship, and the dead sighed,
265 spoke through my larynx, and the kings
> of bygone ages inhabited me . . .
> Now I have lost my gift . . .

MIDIA:

>   And that is all?

MORN:

> That is all. Are you taking these music scores
> with you? Let me squeeze them in – no,
270 they don't fit. And this book? Hurry, Midia,
> there is less than an hour till the train . . .

MIDIA:

Well . . .
I am ready . . .

MORN:

Here they come with your trunk.
One more. Coffins . . .
    [*Pause.*]

Well then, farewell, Midia,
be happy . . .

MIDIA:

I keep thinking I have forgotten
something . . . Tell me – were you joking about
the spinning tables?

275

MORN:

I don't remember . . . I don't
remember . . . it doesn't matter . . . Farewell. Go.
He is waiting for you. Don't cry.
    [*They both go out onto the terrace.*]

MIDIA:

Forgive me . . .
We loved – and it has all gone, somewhere . . .
We loved – and now our love is frozen,

280

and now it lies, one wing spread out, raising
its little feet – a dead sparrow on the damp
gravel . . . But we loved . . . we flew . . .

MORN:

Look,

the sun is coming out . . . Watch your step –
285   it's slippery here, be careful . . . Farewell . . .
farewell . . . Remember . . . Remember only
the shimmer on the tree trunk, the rain, the sun . . .
only that . . .

[Pause. MORN is on the terrace alone. We see him slowly turn
his face from left to right, as he follows with his gaze those
departing. Then he returns to the drawing room.]

MORN:

Well. It is over . . .

[He wipes his head with a handkerchief.]

The flying rain has settled in my hair.

[Pause.]

290   I fell in love with her at the very moment,
when, at a street corner, her hat flashed past,
the wet wing of a carriage – and disappeared
into an avenue of cypresses . . . Now I'm
alone. The end. And so, having deceived

destiny, thrown my crown to the Devil
for his sport, and yielded my belovèd   295
to a friend . . .
   [*Pause.*]
                    How quietly she went down
those steps, putting the same foot forward
every time – like a child . . . Be still,
my heart! A hot, hot shriek, a howl,   300
rises, grows in my chest . . . No! No!
There is a way: to stare at the mirror,
to hold back the sobs that turn my face
into a toad's . . . Oh! I cannot . . .
In an empty house and eye to eye   305
with the cold angel of my sleepless conscience . . .
How do I live? What do I do? My God . . .
   [*Cries.*]
Well . . . well . . . I feel better. That was Morn
crying; the King is absolutely calm.
I feel better . . . Those tears removed the speck   310
caught in my eye – the point of pain. I will
not wait for Ganus, after all . . . My soul
is growing, my soul gains in strength – preparing
for death is like preparing for a holiday . . .
But let the preparations go on in secret.   315
Soon it will be day – I will not wait

for Ganus after all – day will break,
and lightly I will kill myself. One cannot
summon death with a strained thought; death
320 shall come itself, and I will pull the trigger
as if by accident . . . Yes, I feel better –
perhaps it is the sun, shining through
the slanted rain . . . or tenderness – younger
sister of death – that mute, radiant tenderness
325 that rises up when a woman leaves forever . . .
She's forgotten to push in these drawers . . .

  [*walks around, tidying things*]

. . . The books have fallen over on their sides,
as thoughts do, when sadness pulls one out
and carries it off: the one about God . . .
330 The piano is open on a barcarole:
she loved elegant sounds . . . The little table,
like a meadow mowed: here there was
a portrait of her family, of someone else,
cards, some kind of jewellery box . . .
335 She took everything . . . And, as in the song –
I have been left with only these roses here:
their crumpled edges slightly touched with
tender mildew, and in the tall vase the water
smells of rot, of death, as it does
340 under ancient bridges. I am stirred, roses,
by your honeyed decay . . . You need fresh water.

478

[*Goes out by the door on the right. The stage is empty for some time. Then — quick, pale, in tattered clothes — * GANUS *enters from the terrace.*]

GANUS:

Morn . . . Morn . . . where's Morn? By a stony path,
through bushes . . . some kind of garden . . . and now —
I'm in his drawing room . . . This is a dream,
but before I wake up . . . It's quiet here . . .   345
Can he have left? What should I do? Wait?
Lord, Lord, Lord, allow me to meet
with him alone! . . . I will take aim and fire . . .
And it will be over! . . . Who is that? . . . Oh,
only the reflection of a ragged fellow . . .   350
I am afraid of mirrors . . . What shall I do
next? My hand trembles, — it was unwise
to drink wine there, in that tavern,
beneath the hill . . . And there's a din in my ears.
But, perhaps? Yes, definitely! The rustle   355
of footsteps . . . Now quick . . . Where should I . . .

    [*And he hides to the left, behind the corner of a cupboard,
    having pulled out his pistol.* MORN *returns. He fusses over the
    flowers on the table, with his back to* GANUS. GANUS, *stepping
    forward, aims with a trembling hand.*]

MORN:

    Oh, you poor things . . . breathe, flame up . . .

    You resemble love. You were made

    for similes; it is not for nothing that from

360   the first days of the universe there has flowed

    through your petals the blood of Apollo . . . An ant . . .

    Funny: he runs, like a man amidst a fire . . .

      [GANUS *takes aim*.]

    CURTAIN

Act Five

SCENE ONE

Old DANDILIO'*s room. A cage with a parrot, books, porcelain. Through the windows — a sunny summer's day.* KLIAN *charges around the room. In the distance gunshots can be heard.*

KLIAN:

It seems to be getting quieter . . . All the same,
I'm doomed! The lead will strike into my brain
like a stone into glistening mud — an instant —
and my thoughts will splatter out! If only
it were possible to juicily belch up the life   5
one's lived, chew it anew and gulp it down,
and then once more to roll it with a fat,
ox-like tongue, to squeeze from its eternal
dregs the former sweetness of crisp grass,
drunk with the morning dew and the bitterness   10
of lilac leaves! O, God, if only one could
always feel deathly terror! That, God,
would be bliss! Every terror signifies

481

'I am', and there's no higher bliss! Terror —
15 but not the stillness of the grave! The groans
of suffering — but not the silence of the corpse!
This is wisdom, there can be no other!
I am prepared, having strummed my lyre,
to break it, to give up my melodious gift,
20 to become a leper, to weaken, to grow deaf, —
if only to remember some little thing, be it
the rustle of nails scratching a sore, — to me
that is sweeter than the songs of the otherworld!
I'm frightened, death nears . . . My taut heart
25 lurches heavily, like a sack in a cart, clattering
downhill, towards a cliff, towards an abyss!
It can't be stopped! Death!

[DANDILIO *enters from a door on the right.*]

DANDILIO:

                            Hush, hush, hush . . .
Ella has only just fallen asleep in there;
the poor thing lost a lot of blood; the child
30 is dead and the mother has lost her second
soul — the dearer one. But she seems better . . .
Only, you know, I am no doctor — I used
what books I had, but still . . .

KLIAN:

Dandilio!
My dear Dandilio! My wonderful, my radiant
Dandilio! . . . I cannot, I cannot . . .   35
for they will catch me here! I am doomed!

DANDILIO:

I must confess, I was not expecting such
guests; you could have warned me yesterday:
I would have decorated the parrot's cage –
he's very gloomy for some reason. Tell me,   40
Klian – I was busy with Ella, I didn't fully
understand – how was it that you escaped
with her?

KLIAN:

I am doomed! How awful . . .
What a night! They forced their way . . . Ella
kept asking where the child was . . . The crowds   45
broke into the palace . . . We were overcome:
for five terrifying days we fought against
the hurricane that was the people's dream;
last night all fell to ruins: they hunted us
through the palace – myself and Tremens,   50
others too . . . I ran, with Ella in my arms,
from hall to hall, through inner galleries,

and back again, and up and down, and heard
the howls, the shots, and once or twice Tremens's
55   cold laugh . . . How Ella moaned, how she moaned!
Suddenly – a scrap of curtain, a chink behind it, –
I tugged: a passage! You understand – a secret
passage . . .

DANDILIO:

                Of course I understand . . . It was,
I should think, needed by the King,
60   so he could fly away unnoticed – and,
then, after his winged adventures, return
to his labours . . .

KLIAN:

                        . . . and so I stumbled
in the sepulchral darkness, and walked and walked . . .
Suddenly – a wall: I pushed – and found myself
65   miraculously in an empty alley!
Only a gunshot sounded from time to time
and tore the air at its seam . . . I remembered
you live nearby – and so . . . we came to you . . .
But what shall we do next? To stay with you
70   would be madness! They will find me! Indeed,
the whole city knows you were once friendly
with mad Tremens, and christened his daughter! . . .

484

DANDILIO:

She is weak: she won't survive another
such excursion. But where is Tremens?

KLIAN:

He fights . . .

I don't know where . . . He himself advised me,   75
the day before, that I bring my sick Ella
to you . . . but it is dangerous here, I
am doomed! Understand, – I don't know how,
I don't know how to die, and it's too late –
I won't learn now, there is no time! They're   80
coming for me now! . . .

DANDILIO:

Flee alone.

You still have time. I'll give you a false
beard and glasses and you'll be on your way.

KLIAN:

You think so?

DANDILIO:

Or if you want, I have the masks
that people used to wear on Shrovetide   85
in bygone days . . .

KLIAN:

                                    . . . Yes, you may mock!
You know yourself that I will never abandon
my weak Ella . . . That's where the horror lies –
not in death, no, – but in the fact that some
90   sort of whimpering feeling has inhabited
my blood, a mixture of untold jealousy
and shunned desire, and such tenderness
that all sunsets are but puddles of paint
beside it – such is my tenderness!
95   No one knew! I am a coward, a viper,
a flatterer, but here, in this . . .

DANDILIO:

                                    Enough, friend . . .
Calm down . . .

KLIAN:

                        Love has squeezed my heart
in its palms . . . holds it . . . won't let it go . . .
If I pull it – it contracts . . . But death
100   is near . . . yet how can I tear myself
from my own heart? I'm not a lizard, I can't
grow it back . . .

DANDILIO:

        You're rambling, calm down:
it's safe here . . . The street is sunny and deserted . . .
Where is death to be seen? On the spines
of my sleepy books there is a smile.   105
And my blessèd parrot is calm as a vision.

KLIAN:

That bird dazzles my eyes . . . Please understand,
they will descend upon us now — there is
no way out! . . .

DANDILIO:

        I sense no danger:
a blind rumour blown in from the south,   110
that the King is alive, has intoxicated
souls with an unheard-of joy; the city is so
tired of executions that, having finished
with Tremens, the chief madman, they will
hardly start searching for his accomplices.   115

KLIAN:

You think so? Yes, it's true, the sun is shining . . .
And the gunshots have died down . . . Shall I open
the window, shall I look out? Eh?

487

DANDILIO:

Moreover,

I have this little thing . . . shall I show you?
120   Here, in this soft case . . . My talisman . . .
Here, look . . .

KLIAN:

The crown!

DANDILIO:

Wait, you'll drop it . . .

KLIAN:

Do you hear? . . . O, God . . . Someone . . . On the stairs . . .
Ah!

DANDILIO:

I said you'd drop it!
[Enter TREMENS.]

TREMENS:

Golden thunder!

I'm touched! But in vain were you preparing
125   to crown me. Congratulate me, Klian: half
a kingdom is promised for my bald pate! . . .
[to DANDILIO]

Tell me, blithe old man, when and how
did you come by that piece of lustre?

DANDILIO:

One
of those who searched the palace sold it to me
for a gold coin.   130

TREMENS:

Well, well . . . Give it here. It fits.
But I confess, right now, I would prefer
a night cap. Where is Ella?

DANDILIO:

Nearby. She's sleeping.

TREMENS:

Ah . . . good. Klian, why are you whining?

KLIAN:

I can't . . . Tremens, Tremens, why did I follow
you? You are death, you are the abyss!   135
We will both perish.

TREMENS:

You're absolutely right.

KLIAN:

My friend, my leader . . . You are the wisest of all.
Save me – and Ella . . . Teach me – what should
I do? . . . My Tremens, what should I do?

TREMENS:

140   What should you do? Sleep. I shiver once more;
once more that naked concubine – fever –
clings to my stomach with her cold thighs,
strokes, strokes my back with her icy palms . . .
Give me something to throw over my shoulders,
145   old man. That's it. Yes, my dear Klian,
I am convinced that our friends were right
when they warned us that . . . By the way,
I executed all four of them –
they tried to betray me . . . All I needed!
150   I am going to sleep. Let the soldiers
find me themselves.

KLIAN [cries out]:

Ah! . . .

DANDILIO:

Don't shout . . .
don't. There. I knew that would happen.
[ELLA enters from the right.]

490

TREMENS:

My daughter, Ella, do not fear: all is well!
Klian here is singing his latest poems . . .

ELLA:

Father, are you wounded? There's blood.   155

TREMENS:

                              No.

ELLA:

Your hand is once more, once more cold . . .
and your nails, they look as though you've eaten
wild strawberries . . . I will stay here, Dandilio . . .
I will lie down, give me a pillow . . . Really,
I feel better . . . All night they fired . . . My child   160
cried . . . But where is your cat, Dandilio? . . .

DANDILIO:

Some prankster struck it with a stone bottle . . .
Otherwise I would not have bought the parrot . . .

ELLA:

Yes, the fiery one . . . Yes, I do
recall . . . We drank to its health . . . Ah!   165
    [laughs]

'And yet I fear you . . . For you are fatal then . . . '
– where is that from? Where's it from? No,
I have forgotten.

KLIAN:

Enough . . . Ella . . . my love . . .
close your eyes . . .

ELLA:

. . . You are as pale as a fresh
170   pine-board . . . and droplets of resin . . . I don't
like it . . . Go away . . .

KLIAN:

Forgive me . . . I won't, I just . . .
I wanted to fix your pillow . . . There . . .
   [*He sinks down at her bedside.*]

TREMENS:

What was I saying? Yes, they search badly;
there, around the senate, around the palace,
175   the people crowd about, cleaning the royal
chambers, airing the carpets, and sweeping up
my cigarette butts and Ella's hair pins . . .
Very amusing! And what an amusing rumour,
that apparently a burglar – somewhere in the south,

492

you see – climbed into the house and whacked   180
the owner on the head – who, in turn,
if you please, turned out to be that very ruler
who abandoned his city half a year ago . . .
I know, I know, these are all fantasies. But
with just such a fantasy they swept me aside.   185
There, Ella sleeps. It's also time for me . . .
The chill strokes, creeps up my back . . . But
it's a shame, Dandilio, that the imaginary
thief did not destroy the made-up king! . . .
You laugh? Do I joke well?   190

DANDILIO:

                            Yes, poor Ganus!

He was unlucky . . .

TREMENS:

                    What do you mean – Ganus?

DANDILIO:

Well, he received the letter . . . Ella told me . . .
How well the poor girl sleeps . . . Klian,
cover her feet with something . . .

TREMENS:

                                    Listen, listen,

195 Dandilio, perhaps amongst your antique toys,
your dusty knick-knacks, your magic books,
you have half a dozen good warm shirts?
Lend them to me . . .

DANDILIO:

I would have given them
to you sooner, but they would have been
200 too small for you . . . What is it you want to say?

TREMENS:

Once, Dandilio, we were friends, we argued
about art . . . Then I became a widower . . .
Then the revolt – the first one – enthralled me,
and we met less frequently . . . I am not inclined
205 to idle sentimentality, but in the name
of that distant friendship, I ask you,
tell me clearly, what do you know of the King! . . .

DANDILIO:

What, have you not understood? It was all
so simple. Once, four years ago, having
210 come to your house, I lingered in the hall
amongst the coat-hangers, in the rough darkness,
and two people entered; I heard their quick
whispers: 'My sovereign, it is dangerous, he is

494

an unrestrained rebel . . . ' The other laughed
in response and whispered: 'You wait downstairs,   215
I won't be long.' And again quiet laughter . . .
I hid. After a minute, he left and, slapping
his glove, ran down the stairs – your carefree guest . . .

TREMENS:

I recall . . . of course . . . How did I not connect . . .

DANDILIO:

You were immersed in dusky thoughts. I kept   220
silent. We saw each other rarely: I don't like
cold and gloomy people. But I remembered . . .
Four years passed – I still remembered; and then,
when I met Morn at those recent parties,
I recognized the laughter of the King . . . Then,   225
when on the day of the duel you substituted . . .

TREMENS:

Wait, wait, you noticed that too?

DANDILIO:

                    Yes,
my eyes have grown used to chance details
in diligently tracing the trails of little beetles
and the scratches on the surface of antique   230

495

furniture, of peeling paint, the specks of dust
on nameless canvases.

TREMENS:

                    And you kept silent!

DANDILIO:

Of the two hearts, dearer to me was his
whose passion was keener. There is a third heart:
235   look – with what sorrow and tenderness,
not characteristic of him, does Klian
gaze on dreaming Ella, as though his fear
has gone to sleep with her . . .

TREMENS:

                              O, it amuses me
that, secretly from me, my very thought
240   and will had been at work, that after all,
I myself, with my own hand, sent death,
albeit an illusive one, to the King!
And secretly, I was not mistaken in Ganus:
he was the blind weapon of a blind man . . .
245   I don't complain! With a cold curiosity
I examine those cunning patterns – causes
and consequences – upon the bright blade
placed against my chest . . . I am happy

that, even for a moment, I taught people
the sweet anarchy of destruction . . . No,   250
my lesson will not pass without a trace!
That is to say, there is no thought, no
momentary weakness, which does not
reveal itself in a future action: the King
will clearly deceive again . . .   255

KLIAN:

                              You've woken up?
Sleep, Ella, sleep. It's frightening to think,
Ella . . .

TREMENS:

            O, it amuses me! If I had known
all this, I would have shouted to the people:
'Your king is a weak and shallow man. There is
no fairy tale, there's only Morn!'   260

DANDILIO:

                              Don't,
Tremens, be quiet . . .

ELLA:

                  Morn and . . . the King?
Is that what you said, father? The King in a blue

497

carriage, – no, not that . . . I danced with Morn –
no . . . wait . . . Morn . . .

DANDILIO:

Enough, he was joking . . .

TREMENS:

265   Klian, keep quiet, don't sob! . . . Listen, Ella . . .

DANDILIO:

Ella, can you hear us?

TREMENS:

Is her heart beating?

DANDILIO:

Yes. It will pass soon.

TREMENS:

Her eyes are open . . .
She can see. Ella! A pillar of salt . . . I didn't
know such fainting fits were possible . . .

KLIAN:

Voices!

270   In the street . . . It's them!

TREMENS:

Yes. We were expecting them . . .

Let's have a look . . .

[*Opens the window.* VOICES *can be heard from the street below.*]

FIRST VOICE:

. . . the house.

SECOND VOICE:

Right! He can't get out.

Do we have all the exits?

FIRST VOICE:

All of them . . .

TREMENS:

May as well close it . . .

[*Closes the window.*]

KLIAN [*rushing around*]:

Save me . . . quickly . . .

Dandilio . . . anywhere . . . I want to live . . . quick . . .

if only there was time . . . Ah!   275

[*Rushes out of the room through the door on the right.*]

TREMENS:

Could this be the end?

DANDILIO:

Yes, it seems so.

TREMENS:

I'll go out to them,
so Ella doesn't see. What do you feed
this orange bird?

DANDILIO:

He likes little ants' eggs,
raisins . . . Nice, isn't he? You know, try
280   the attic, and then the roof . . .

TREMENS:

No, I'll go.
I'm tired . . .

    [He goes towards the door, opens it, but the CAPTAIN and four
    of his SOLDIERS push him back into the room.]

CAPTAIN:

Stop! Get back!

TREMENS:

Yes, yes —

I am Tremens; but let's talk in the street . . .

CAPTAIN:

Get back. There.

[to a SOLDIER]

Search both of them.

[to DANDILIO]

Your name?

DANDILIO:

There, you've spilled my tobacco, oh dear!

Who looks for a man's name in his snuff box?   285

May I offer you some?

CAPTAIN:

Are you the master here?

DANDILIO:

Indeed.

CAPTAIN:

And who is this?

DANDILIO:

A sick girl.

CAPTAIN:

You shouldn't have concealed a criminal here . . .

TREMENS [*with a yawn*]:

I ran in here by chance.

CAPTAIN:

Are you Tremens, the rebel?

TREMENS:

290   I want to sleep. Hurry . . .

CAPTAIN:

By the order issued
by the senate today, the nineteenth of June,
you are here and now to be . . . Hey! There is
someone else in there.
    [*to the* SOLDIERS]
                    Hold them.
I'll take a look . . .
    [*Leaves by the door on the right.* TREMENS *and* DANDILIO
    talk amongst themselves, surrounded by mute, almost lifeless
    SOLDIERS.]

TREMENS:

> How he dawdles . . .

I want to sleep.   295

DANDILIO:

> Yes, we shall soon sleep well . . .

TREMENS:

We? Please, they will not touch you.

Do you fear death?

DANDILIO:

> I love all this: shadows,

light, the specks of dust in a ray of sunshine;

these pools of light on the floor; and large books

that smell of time. Death is curious, I don't   300

dispute . . .

TREMENS:

> Ella's like a doll . . . What's wrong with her?

DANDILIO:

Yes, this won't do.

> [to a SOLDIER]

> Listen to me, my brother,

take this sick girl here to the bedroom, and after
we'll send for the doctor. What, are you deaf?

TREMENS:

305   Leave him. It's not necessary. They'll dispatch me,
somewhere to the side, – she won't even see.
Dandilio, you spoke of the sun . . . It's strange,
it seems to me we are alike, but in what way
I cannot comprehend . . . Let's settle it now.
310   Do you accept death?

DANDILIO:

                  Yes. Matter must decay
for matter to be resurrected – and from that,
the Trinity is clear to me. In what way?
Space is God, and matter is Jesus, and time
is the Holy Ghost. Hence my conclusion:
315   a world made up of these three, – our world –
is divine . . .

TREMENS:

              Yes, continue.

DANDILIO:

                  Do you hear

what trampling there is in my rooms? Those
are boots!

TREMENS:

    All the same, our world . . .

DANDILIO:

         . . . is divine;
and therefore all is happiness; and so we must
all sing as we work: to live in this world   320
means to work for the master in three forms:
space, matter, and time. But the work ends
and we depart to the eternal feast, having
given our memory to time, our image
to space, and our love to matter.   325

TREMENS:

       You see –
fundamentally I agree. But I don't need
the slavery of happiness. I rebel,
rebel against the master! Do you hear!
I call on all to drop their work! Head off
to the eternal feast: there in blissful   330
abysses we will rest.

DANDILIO:

They've caught him. A cry.

TREMENS:

I had forgotten Klian . . .

[KLIAN bursts in from the right.]

KLIAN:

Ah! A trap!

They're here too!

[Flings himself back into the room on the right.]

ELLA [raising herself up]:

Morn . . . Morn . . . Morn . . .

It is as though I heard a voice in my sleep:

335   Morn is the King . . .

[Becomes still again.]

VOICE OF CAPTAIN [in the room to the right, the door of which remains open]:

Enough of this rushing

around the rooms!

VOICE OF KLIAN:

I beg you . . .

VOICE OF CAPTAIN:

Your name!

VOICE OF KLIAN:

I beg you . . . I am young . . . I am so young!
I am great, I am a genius! They don't
kill geniuses! . . .

VOICE OF CAPTAIN

Answer the question!

VOICE OF KLIAN:

My name is Klian . . . But I will serve the King . . .   340
I swear . . . I know where the crown is . . . I'll give it
back . . . I swear . . .

VOICE OF CAPTAIN:

Stop grabbing at my calves,
I'll shoot a hole in my boot.

VOICE OF KLIAN:

Have merc— . . . !
[*A gunshot.* TREMENS *and* DANDILIO, *surrounded by
motionless* SOLDIERS, *continue their conversation.*]

TREMENS:

Space is God, you say. Excellent. That is

345 the explanation for wings, those wings with which

we populate heaven . . .

VOICE OF KLIAN:

       Ah! . . . There is no end,

no end . . .

VOICE OF CAPTAIN:

    He's full of life, the wretch.

DANDILIO:

           Yes.

We are stirred by swift flights, by wheels, sails,

and − in childhood − by games and, in our youth,

350 by dances.

 [. . .]*

* Lines missing in the original Russian text, including 'curtain' to
mark the end of the scene.

SCENE TWO

[MORN *and* EDMIN *with the* FOREIGNER *and other* GUESTS.]

[MORN]:
   [. . .]*
   Those killed by a bullet to the heart ought not
   to be beaten by gossip's petty pellets . . .
   This evening will be blue, like three hundred
   July days, condensed and thickened into darkness,
   creaking now with the urgent longing of toads   5
   on ponds, now with the convulsion of oily leaves . . .
   Had I not been King, I would have been a poet
   with a lyre hot in this night, saturated
   in blueness, in this vivid night, which quivers
   along its length under a swarm of stars,   10
   like the sensitive back of black Pegasus . . .
   But we shall not – shall we? – talk of death,
   – but with a bright conversation about
   the kingdom, about power, and about
   my happiness, you shall refresh my soul,   15

* Lines missing in the original Russian text.

509

chase from the light the long, soft butterflies –
and gulp of wine will follow gulp, so that
the words of the soul may sound more sweetly
and sincerely . . . I'm happy.

LADY:

Sovereign, will there

20   be dancing? . . .

MORN:

Dancing? There is no room to, Ella.

LADY:

My name is not Ella . . .

MORN:

I am mistaken . . .
so . . . I've remembered . . . I was saying there is
no room to dance here. But in the palace,
perhaps I will host a ball – an enormous one,

25   by candlelight, yes, by candlelight,
to the magnificent hum of an organ . . .

LADY:

The King . . . the King is laughing at me.

MORN:

I am happy! . . . And if I'm pale, it is from happiness! . . .
The bandage . . . it is too tight . . . Edmin, tell . . .
no, do it yourself . . . fix it . . . like that . . .   30
good . . .

GREY-HAIRED GUEST:

                    Perhaps the King is tired? Perhaps
the guests should . . .

MORN:

                              Oh, how alike he is! . . .
Look, Edmin – how alike! . . . No, I am not tired.
Have you been away from the city long?

GREY-HAIRED GUEST:

My sovereign, I was driven out by a storm: 35
the mob, having shied away from you,
accidentally pushed into me, almost crushing
my soul. I fled. Since then I have thought
and wandered. Now I will return, blessing
my sorrowful exile for the sweetness of return . . .   40
But in wine there are bees' wings; and in joy,
for me, there is a grief translucent: my old
house, where since childhood I have lived,
my house is burned . . .

EDMIN:

But the nation has been saved!

GREY-HAIRED GUEST:

45   How can I explain? A nation is a bodiless divinity,
whilst our favourite corner of our homeland –
that is the visible image of the bodiless.
We only know God by his parted beard;
we recognize our nation by the traits
50   of our dear home. No one can take God
or our homeland from us. But it's still sad
to lose the warm little image. My house
has perished. I weep.

MORN:

I swear, I will build
that very same house in the very same spot
55   for you. And not an architect, but your love
will check the blueprints; your memories, not carpenters,
will aid me; not painters, but the alert eyes
of your childhood: in childhood we see the souls
of colours . . .

GREY-HAIRED GUEST:

Sovereign, I thank you: I know
60   that you are a magician, I'm happy that

you've understood me, but I do not need
a home . . .

MORN:

I made a vow . . . What's in a vow?
The babble of pride. And when you look, death
is always there. What's in a vow? Even
the star deceives the stargazer, by sometimes   65
not returning at the expected time.
Wait . . . Tell me . . . did you know that old man –
Dandilio?

GREY-HAIRED GUEST:

Dandilio? No, sovereign, I don't recall . . .

SECOND VISITOR [*quietly*]:

Look at the King, he's displeased with something . . .

THIRD VISITOR [*quietly*]:

As though a shadow – the shadow of a bird –   70
flew across his bright, pale face . . . Who's that?
    [*There is movement to the left, by the door.*]

VOICE:

Excuse me . . . What is your name? You cannot
come in here!

FOREIGNER:

I am a Foreigner . . .

VOICE:

Wait!

FOREIGNER:

No . . . I shall come in . . . I'm just . . . I'm nothing.
75   I'm simply asleep . . .

VOICE:

He's drunk, don't let him in! . . .

MORN:

Ah, a new guest! Come in, come in, quickly!
I am so happy that I'd welcome with a smile
even an angel mournfully dragging himself
beneath the funereal hump of his folded wings;
80   or a beggar with some brilliant trick;
or an executioner with his tidy frock-coat
tightly fastened . . . Well then, my dear guest,
approach!

FOREIGNER:

They say you are the King?

EDMIN:

How dare you! . . .

MORN:

Leave him. He's foreign. Yes, I am the King . . .

FOREIGNER:

So, then . . . I'm pleased: I dreamt you up well . . .   85

MORN:

Keep silent, Edmin – it's amusing. Have you
come from afar, my nebulous guest?

FOREIGNER:

From
commonplace reality, from the dull real world . . .
I am asleep . . . All this is a dream . . . the dream
of a drunken poet . . . A recurring dream . . .   90
I dreamt of you once: some ball . . . some city . . .
frosty and merry . . . Only you had a different
name . . .

MORN:

Morn?

FOREIGNER:

Morn. That's it . . .
An elaborate dream . . . But you know,

95   I was glad to wake up ... I remember something
wasn't right there. But what I don't recall ...

MORN:

Does everyone in your country speak so ...
dreamily?

FOREIGNER:

        Oh, no! In our country all is not well,
not well ... When I wake up, I will tell them
100   what a magnificent king I dreamt of ...

MORN:

Curious fellow!

FOREIGNER:

        But what makes me uneasy?
I don't know ... Just like last time ... I'm frightened ...
My bedroom must be stuffy. Something fills me
with fear ... an illusion ... I'll try to wake up ...

MORN:

105   Wait! ... Where did my ghost slip off to? ... Wait,
come back ...

VOICE [from the left]:

        Hold him!

SECOND VOICE:

I can't see him . . .

THIRD VOICE:

Night . . .

EDMIN:

My sovereign, how can you bear to listen to that?

MORN:

Past kings had fools: they spoke the truth darkly,
cunningly – and the kings loved their fools . . .
While I have this spurious somnambulist . . .   110
Why have you grown quiet, dear guests?
Drink to my happiness! And you, Edmin.
Eh, brighten up! All drink! The heart of Bacchus
is like cut glass: in it is blood and sunshine . . .

GUESTS:

Long live the King!   115

MORN:

The King . . . the King . . .
Heavenly thunder rumbles in that earthly word.
So! We've drunk! Now I will hearten my subjects:
I intend to return tomorrow!

EDMIN:

Sovereign . . .

517

GUESTS:

Long live the King!

EDMIN:

. . . I beg you . . . the doctors . . .

MORN:

120   Enough! I said – tomorrow! Go back, back –
in a flying coffin! Yes, in a steel coffin,
on fabricated wings! And what is more:
you said 'fairy tale' . . . It makes me laugh . . .
and God laughs with me! The stupefied mob
125   does not know that the knight's body is dark
and sweaty, locked in its fairy tale armour . . .

VOICE [quietly]:

What is it that the King is saying? . . .

MORN:

. . . they do not know that the poor Eastern bride
is barely alive beneath her tasselled weight,
130   but across the sea the wandering troubadours
will sing of a fairy tale love, will tell lies
to the ages, their fingers barely touching
the sheep sinews – and dirt becomes a dream!
     [Drinks.]

VOICE:

What is the King saying?

SECOND VOICE:

He's inebriated! . . .

THIRD VOICE:

His eyes shine with madness! . . .   135

MORN:

Edmin, pour me

some more . . .

LADY [*to the gentleman*]:

Let's go. I am frightened . . .

[. . .]*

[KING]:

A dream once interrupted cannot be resumed,
and the kingdom which sailed before me in a dream
is suddenly revealed as merely standing
on the earth. Reality has suddenly intruded.   140
That, which is flesh and blood, once seemed to glide
like translucent ether; now, suddenly,
stomping like a rough giant, it has entered
into my solid but fragile dream. I see

* Lines missing in the original Russian text.

145 around me the ruins of towers which soared up
to the clouds. Yes, a dream is always
an illusion, all is a lie, a lie.

EDMIN:

She lied
to me too, my sovereign.

KING:

Who lied, Edmin?
[*suddenly remembers*]
Oh, you talk of her? . . . No, my kingdom
150 was an illusion . . . The dream was a lie.
[. . .]*

[MORN]:†

Edmin, give it to me! . . . What else should I do?
Fall to my knees? Would you like that? Ah, Edmin,
I must die! I am guilty, not before Ganus,
but before God, before you, before myself,
155 before my people! I was a bad king:
unseen, without courtiers, I ruled by deception . . .
All my power lay in my mysteriousness . . .

---

* Lines missing in the original Russian text.
† 'KING' changes back to ' MORN' in the Russian (Azbuka) edition
of the play.

The wisdom of my laws? The creativity
and joy of power? The love of the people?
Yes. But empty and deceiving, like the pale jester　　　160
in his moon-like smock, was the soul of the ruler!
I appeared now in a mask upon the throne,
now in the drawing room of a vain lover . . .
Deception! And my flight was the lie, the trick –
do you hear? – of a coward! And this glory　　　165
is but the kiss of a blind man . . . Am I
really a king? A king who killed a girl?
No, no, enough, I will fall – to death –
to fiery death! I am but a torch,
thrown into a well, flaming, whirling, flying,　　　170
flying downwards to meet its reflection,
that grows in the darkness like the dawn . . .
I beg you! I beg you! Give me my black pistol!
You do not speak?

   [*Pause.*]

                  Well then, don't . . . There are
other deaths in this world: precipices　　　175
and maelstroms, poisons and blades, and the knot.
No! You can no more stop a sinner killing
himself, than a genius from being born!

   [*Pause.*]

But then, I am demeaning myself in vain
by these requests . . . A complicated game　　　180

521

with such a simple denouement is boring.

[*Pause.*]

Edmin, I am your king. Give it to me.

You understand?

[EDMIN, *without looking, extends the pistol to him.*]

MORN:

Thank you. I will go out
onto the terrace. Only the stars will see me.

185   I am happy and lucid; I could not speak
more truthfully . . . Edmin, I'll lightly kiss
your light brow . . . Silence, silence . . . Your
silence is sweeter than any known songs.
So. Thank you.

[*walks towards the glass door*]

The blue night takes me away!

[*He goes out onto the terrace. His figure, illuminated by the
night rays, can be seen through the glass door.*]

EDMIN:

190   . . . .
. . . .
. . . No one must see how
my King presents to the heavens,
the death of Mister Morn.

CURTAIN